Management Accounting
A Cases Approach

PEARSON

At Pearson, we take learning personally. Our courses and resources are available as books, online and via multi-lingual packages, helping people learn whatever, wherever and however they choose.

We work with leading authors to develop the strongest learning experiences, bringing cutting-edge thinking and best learning practice to a global market. We craft our print and digital resources to do more to help learners not only understand their content, but to see it in action and apply what they learn, whether studying or at work.

Pearson is the world's leading learning company. Our portfolio includes Penguin, Dorling Kindersley, the Financial Times and our educational business, Pearson International. We are also a leading provider of electronic learning programmes and of test development, processing and scoring services to educational institutions, corporations and professional bodies around the world.

Every day our work helps learning flourish, and wherever learning flourishes, so do people.

To learn more please visit us at: www.pearson.com/uk

Management Accounting
A Cases Approach

Jan Bergstrand

Stockholm School of Economics, Stockholm, Sweden
Norwegian School of Economics, Bergen, Norway

PEARSON

Harlow, England • London • New York • Boston • San Francisco • Toronto • Sydney
Auckland • Singapore • Hong Kong • Tokyo • Seoul • Taipei • New Delhi
Cape Town • São Paulo • Mexico City • Madrid • Amsterdam • Munich • Paris • Milan

Pearson Education Limited
Edinburgh Gate
Harlow
Essex CM20 2JE
England

and Associated Companies throughout the world

Visit us on the World Wide Web at:
www.pearsoned.co.uk

First published 2012

ISBN: 978-0-273-75705-4

British Library Cataloguing-in-Publication Data
A catalogue record for this book is available from the British Library

Library of Congress Cataloging-in-Publication Data
Bergstrand, Jan, 1943-
  Management accounting : a cases approach / Jan Bergstrand. -- 1st ed.
      p. cm.
  Includes index.
  ISBN 978-0-273-75705-4 (pbk.)
  1. Managerial accounting. I. Title.

  HF5657.4.B46 2012
  658.15′11--dc23

                                                2011033611

10 9 8 7 6 5 4 3 2 1
15 14 13 12 11

Typeset in 10.5/13pt Minion by 35
Printed by Ashford Colour Press Ltd., Gosport

Brief contents

Contents

(An errata document will be available to view online, at www.pearsoned.co.uk/bergstrand)

Preface

■ The author's vision

This is a book of cases in management accounting and control. There are some 40 cases and there are solutions or comments for every case, depending on the situation. There is also a little bit of theory, normally included in the solutions to the first one or two cases in each chapter. There is only as much theory as is needed to solve the cases.

This book can be used as a collection of cases for those courses in management accounting with a dedicated textbook. There are plenty of textbooks available on the market and most of them will be suitable. However, I believe this book can stand alone too, without a textbook, if an experienced teacher wished to use it in this way. The teacher would provide the necessary theory for each case – only as much as is needed. Taught this way the subject may well be more stimulating for students, as there won't be any need for dull theoretical lectures! After all, if a student can solve all my cases, they will have mastered the subject!

The cases are organized into eight chapters. In seven of them (Chapters 1–7) the cases deal mainly with one type of problem at a time, with the main subject highlighted by each chapter. In Chapter 8 the problems are all combined.

Generally, the cases are ordered in such a way that a thoughtful reader should be able to read the book from the beginning to the end without any deviations. But occasionally a case crops up that requires the reader to have information that is covered in a later chapter. In these cases I mention at the start what might be needed. Some readers may have already covered the topics in earlier studies, in which case they can proceed undisturbed. However, others may choose to skip a case and to go back to it after reading later chapters.

Most of the cases are on management accounting and can be solved using well-known methods from the likes of budgeting, product costing or corporate investment theory, while a small number assume knowledge of several of these fields. But in Chapter 8 there is a change in approach. While the cases in this chapter may still be solved primarily by one type of method, they normally require an overview of several parts of the management control system. Sometimes they are downright contradictory, showing that certain methods can be in conflict with one another.

■ Planning a course

In order to plan a course, you will need to know something about the cases. To that end, here are some short descriptions, organized by chapters.

Chapter 1: Budgeting and planning

Modern Drinks is a very simple case, introducing the basic ideas of fixed and variable costs and showing how to make a simple budget, draw a break-even diagram and find the break-even volume. These ideas are followed up in *Farmer's Monthly*, but here I also introduce the problem of cash planning when starting a small business.

Svenberg Furniture deals mainly with fixed and variable costs, profit planning and shows how a liquidity crisis could easily arise when there is a growing volume. *Quality Printing* deals with the budget of a small company, presented in Excel, and offers an initial discussion on how to build the budget.

Grondal Industrial Rolls is an example of variance analysis, emphasizing managerial accountability when certain things go wrong.

Forest Wheels is an example of the balanced scorecard, and *Worldwide Group* discusses why you might want to give up the budget altogether and to replace it with rolling forecasts.

Three budgetary processes describes alternative ways to organize the budget process in a very large company.

Chapter 2: Product costing

In *Sporting Goods* I show the basic approach to full costing and how various allocation models can lead to very different outcomes. These discussions are continued in *Little Shop of Pants*, a case that emphasizes the inability of full costing to indicate what products to select in a production program.

In the *Electronic Parts Co.* and *Western Dialysis Clinic* cases, I show the change from full costing to activity-based costing. But to solve *Western Dialysis Clinic* the student will also need to know how to deal with capital costs, which are described in Chapter 5.

Metropolitan Transfer and *Road Connections at Barken Lake* discuss how to allocate savings from pooling resources. In both cases, two parties work together to increase the efficiency of production and need to find a formula to share the profits. To solve the *Road Connections* case students will again need to know a little bit of theory on capital costs.

Seaside Breweries contrasts direct costing, full costing and ABC costing and discusses the properties of each of these methods for a number of different purposes.

Chapter 3: Internal transfer pricing

Premium Motors gives a first introduction to transfer pricing in a very well-known situation, describing a car seller with a repair shop and a spare parts dealer.

In *Cardboard coating* I establish the ideas of direct cost and opportunity cost as a starting point for internal transfer pricing. In *Super Pricing* things get a little more difficult, because the opportunity costs emanate from a different product from the one I am primarily dealing with.

Finally, in *Magnetic resonance imaging*, I discuss alternative methods of pricing central services. This case is actually very close to product costing and you will need to know how to deal with capital costs to solve it.

Chapter 4: Corporate investment projects

In *Hillary Motors* and *Modernizing the Distribution Co.*, I introduce the basic ideas around discounting and net present value and explain how to deal with taxes in a corporate investment case. The same ideas are pursued further in the case on the *Dalecarlia Showboat.*

In the *Paper Pulp Co.* case, we introduce an Excel model for capital budgeting in inflation and point out that quick calculations without taxes might actually indicate lower profitability than proper calculations including taxes and a correct discount rate.

After this, the cases become more difficult. *Buying growing forest* takes a very different approach to capital budgeting and emphasizes that logical thinking is vastly superior to complicated calculations. In *Interest rate sensitivity* I emphasize the great importance of differences in interest rates when dealing with long periods of time.

The Beautiful Bridge highlights how growth and inflation interrelate in long-lasting projects. Right in the middle of capital budgeting, students will need to remember ABC costing in order to deal with complaining economists when prices are set. In *Regulating WACC* we turn to the serious issue of regulating the mono-poly profits of electric utilities.

Parabella Kitchenware is so rich in information that you will need to select those things that you actually need. After selecting the important items, the outcome can be found quite easily! Finally, *The Superior Power Co.* deals with real and nominal payments over a long period of time and can only be solved when you clearly separate discounting from inflation.

Chapter 5: Capital costs

This chapter deals with issues around the determination of indirect costs. Those costs can be estimated as a sum of depreciation and interest or as some kind of annuity. In both cases you can apply a nominal or a real analysis, adjusting your interest rate to the character of the other items.

The basic analysis is provided in *The Glamorous Drilling Co.* After that, there are two cases illustrating the privatization of telephone and heating companies. In *Deregulating telephones*, students are asked to find a way to regulate the price of access to existing networks owned by the former monopoly. In *Warm and cosy* the privatization of heating services leads to conflicts around pricing and a debate on the ethics of privatization when customers have already paid municipal fees for a period of time.

Chapter 6: Inventory management

There are only two cases on inventory management. The first, *The Garage at Korsheden*, provides the basic introduction to the formula of the economic order quantity. There is also a small problem of capital budgeting when the garage owner considers expanding his fuel tank in order to save money on order costs.

In the *Beare Market* case, Lillie Beare comes home from university with some fairly unrealistic opinions on how to lower the costs of the little wilderness shop owned by her father and uncle. What's new here is her idea to organize shortages and to deliver animal feed with a delay, mainly to save on holding costs.

Chapter 7: Profit measurement

The company behind the *Northern Trucks* case is an excellent firm and I really admire them for their achievements in the trucking business. This case deals with designing their system of profit measurement in one of their sales departments.

The *Shareholder value* case describes the fairly modern approach to increasing shareholder value by getting rid of unnecessary cash. It shows very clearly that you can improve profitability and actually raise the prices of shares simply by adjusting the capital structure. In fact, companies often show this kind of thinking in their comments on their annual reports.

Chapter 8: Control system cases

Working through *Broad-gauge Transport* will bring the different approaches and problems together in one case. Here you will find present values, annuities, full costing, internal transfer pricing, questionable instructions from the controller's department and profit measurements that go completely awry.

Changing cars is very different. This case is about intuitive decision making and comparing the outcome to regular analyses of net present values.

I shall never forget the *Southern Electronics* case. As a consultant I solved it very quickly and easily, but still they scolded me for reaching the same conclusions that their own chief accountant had already arrived at. The problem was that the CEO could not believe that two parts of the international group's management control system could give completely contradictory indications. Low profit will give a high bonus and vice versa. The case deals with present values, profit measurement and the value of a loan.

To solve *The Water treatment plant*, you will need to consider setting different internal transfer prices for different buyers. You will need to know about cost accounting and capital budgeting.

In *The food ship*, a shipping company is selling an overpriced time charter contract to a food importer. There is an old letter confusing cash payments with costs and double counting profits. It takes an effort to sort it out. Also you will need to calculate weighted cost of capital in an unusual situation. But the whole case stays mainly inside capital budgeting and related areas on the cost of capital.

The Broadcasting Co. is a fairly broad case on management control. You will need to calculate the cost of capital when there are several business areas. You will also need to select a tool for profit measurement and to find a method of internal transfer pricing. You will practically design a whole control system.

Finally, *Rail connections* is not a very difficult or complicated case. But you will need to question the choice of discount rate for the municipal transport organization since it is quite clear that they cannot follow their own instructions. If they do the calculations at the low discount rate they suggest, then they will run out of money completely. You will need to suggest a change.

■ About the writing process

There are 43 cases in this edition. Most of them are the products of many years of teaching and consulting in the field. Some of the cases are really old; one or two are even updated versions of cases inherited from my own teacher, Paulsson Frenckner, long ago. But most of the cases are new and the vast majority are my own.

Typically, the cases are highly fictionalized and simplified versions of my real-life experiences working with individuals, companies, institutions and on major infrastructure projects. And, for the most part they are anonymized. No real names are used, either of companies or of individuals. I am thankful to all the individuals I have worked with as a consultant over the years; they have made my life more interesting and every case I have worked on has been something of a learning experience.

As a book on management accounting and control, this one is not very thick, but it is quite intense. It will take some time for an interested reader to take it all in. But once you know it all, you will know an awful lot about my subject. I wish you good luck!

Overlooking the Barken Lake in February 2011
Jan Bergstrand

Acknowledgements

We are grateful to the following for permission to reproduce copyright material:

Figures

Figure 1.9 adapted from 'The Balanced Scorecard – Measures that Drive Performance', *Harvard Business Review*, Jan/Feb, 71–79 (Kaplan, R.S. and Norton, D.P. 1992), © 1992 by the Harvard Business School Publishing Corporation, and from 'Using the balanced scorecard as a strategic management system', *Harvard Business Review*, Jan/Feb, 75–85 (Kaplan, R.S. and Norton, D.P. 1996), © 1996 by the Harvard Business School Publishing Corporation; all rights reserved.

Text

Case Study 2.3 from *Ekonomisk analys och styrning (Accounting for Management Control)*, Studentlitteratur (Bergstrand, J. 2009); Case Study 2.4 adapted from Applying ABC to Healthcare, *Management Accounting*, February, pp. 22–33 (West, T.D. and West, D.A. 1997), Copyright 1997 by IMA, Montvale, N.J., www.imanet.org, used with permission.

In some instances we have been unable to trace the owners of copyright material, and we would appreciate any information that would enable us to do so.

Chapter 1

Budgeting and planning

1.1 Modern Drinks, Inc.

This little case is provided mainly to introduce some basic ideas of management accounting. To solve it we will need to know about fixed and variable costs. There will also be a short introduction to the break-even diagram, break-even volume and to safety margins. After that, we shall be ready to take on the tough tasks we will meet later in the book!

Two young students – Lisa and Kalle – received permission to arrange a sales tent to sell modern, tasty, sugar-free soft drinks at the horse races on a lovely summer's night.

Lisa and Kalle decided to buy the drinks from a big supplier charging €1 per bottle. They felt that they would be able to sell them between the races at €2.50. After all, that amount is less than an average bet on a horse, so everybody ought to be able to afford them.

Unfortunately, they had to rent the tent and the site from the horse-racing society and they had to pay €270 for just one night. But the manager of the horse-racing society told them that the likely volume in those tents was around 300 drinks, which would give them a good profit.

Would you advise Lisa and Kalle to start the business?

Solution: Modern Drinks, Inc.

The income is assumed to be €2.50 per bottle. It is variable and directly proportional to the volume.

There are two kinds of costs. First, there are **variable costs** amounting to €1 per bottle. Since there are no volume discounts, variable costs are directly proportional to the volume, just like the income.

Secondly, there are costs for the site and the tent. Those costs are independent of the sales volume. Therefore they are called **fixed costs**. This expression is sometimes misunderstood, because the costs are not really fixed in the normal sense of the word. The fixed costs can easily be changed if the horse-racing society decides to raise or lower the fee for the site. But the fixed costs are independent of the production volume and that is the main point.

Now, let us investigate the **profit equation** of the case. It looks like this:

$$2.50 \times X - 1 \times X - 270 = \text{Profit}$$

In the equation, X represents the sales volume, and we assume that the variable cost per unit is constant. Also, we have to assume that surplus drinks can be returned to the supplier at no charge or saved for the next racing night.

First we would like to know the **break-even volume**, i.e. the volume needed not to make a loss. We set profit equal to zero and find:

$$2.50 \times X - 1.00 \times X - 270 = 0$$
$$1.50X = 270$$
$$X = 180$$

Thus, Kalle and Lisa would have to sell 180 drinks to break even. If their forecasts are correct, that should not be too difficult. But actually, they will have to work for 4 hours each during the races and one of them will have to spend two additional hours picking up the drinks and arranging the tent. All told, that will be 10 working hours.

Being students, they feel that they need at least €8 per hour, which means €80 for the entire night. Let us put the required profit into the equation:

$$2.50 \times X - 1.00 \times X - 270 = 80$$
$$1.50X - 270 = 80$$
$$X = 233$$

Now, we can see that they need to sell more than 233 drinks to make a decent business.

If the likely volume is really 300 drinks as the manager said, there is a **safety margin** corresponding to $300 - 180 = 120$ drinks compared to the break-even volume. In relation to the estimated volume, the margin is:

$$(300 - 180)/300 = 0.40$$

That is, the safety margin is 40 percent of the estimated volume.

To illustrate the situation let us create a **break-even diagram** showing income and total costs as a function of the volume (see Figure 1.1).

From the break-even diagram we can see that the profit at 300 drinks looks quite good. We can find the details through the profit equation:

$$2.50 \times 300 - 1 \times 300 - 270 = 180$$

Clearly, if the manager is trustworthy, it should be possible to make a decent business. If Kalle and Lisa have estimated the working hours correctly, the project appears to hold some promise.

Let us wish them good luck!

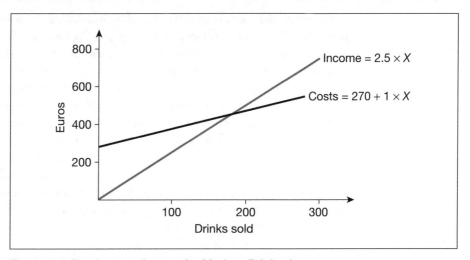

Figure 1.1 Break-even diagram for Modern Drinks, Inc.

■ Learning outcomes

Although this is not a real case, but rather an introduction to some of the ideas in costing theory, you should now understand the following ideas:

- ■ variable costs and fixed costs
- ■ break-even volume
- ■ safety margins.

1.2 *Farmer's Monthly*

Now, this case is already very serious business. Too many young entrepreneurs start their activities with faulty budgeting, or perhaps no budgets at all. Discovering that you need another €100 000 might help if there is still some time to spare. A budget might alert you to the problems in time and help you to talk to your banker when and if needed!

During the financial crisis Johan decides to take voluntary redundancy from his position as a printer at a large printing company. As compensation he receives €24 000 plus the possibility of buying out some old printing equipment in order to start a small printing shop of his own.

The old printing press will cost €60 000 and Johan thinks that it will work quite well for 4 years more. After that period of time the press will probably not be very valuable. To be on the safe side, Johan decides not to include it in his planning.

To finance the project Johan could spend the €24 000 that he received from his old employer. In addition, he will borrow the remaining €36 000 from the local savings bank. The bank will charge 5 percent interest to be paid quarterly. The loan will have to be repaid through quarterly installments every quarter for 3 years.

The bank manager explains to Johan that, in addition to the loan for the printing press, he will also need some working capital. The bank is willing to offer him an open account where he can borrow short loans as needed. The bank will charge 6 percent per year for the contract plus 0.5 percent per month for whatever amount is used during the month. After a discussion Johan and the bank manager agree that Johan will need a loan contract for €30 000 as a starting point.

The large printing company promised Johan that he could take over the contracts on two small journals, *Farmer's Monthly* and *Growing Forest*. Each is printed once a month, and the combined circulation is around 100 000 copies per month.

The journals are issued through the local farmer association. They will pay €0.285 per copy. Johan expects to pay €0.15 per copy for paper and printing ink. Since he is unknown among the suppliers, he will have to pay cash for the supplies before the printing can take place.

Johan has found some premises costing €1300 per month to be paid monthly in advance and he has also found a small car that will cost him €800 per month to be paid at the end of each month. He will have to employ an assistant printer earning €2000 per month and he thinks it is fair to take home the same amount for himself. In both cases he will have to add 40 percent to the amounts for employment taxes and personnel insurances.

Finally, there will be costs for maintenance of the press and the car, office supplies, cleaning, utilities and so on. These will add up to €2100 per month.

After producing the journals, Johan will invoice the customer after the end of each month. The payment terms are 30 days. The buyer is assumed to be a trustworthy customer who always pays according to agreements.

Finally, to simplify our discussion, let us assume that there is no value added tax to be charged or paid.

Now, let us investigate the pros and cons of the *Farmer's Monthly* project.

Solution: *Farmer's Monthly*

To find out if the project is a good one, we need to study the profitability of the project. If it is profitable we will also need to know if the financing can be managed. After all, many little businesses that are profitable run into financing difficulties. But let us start with profitability.

■ Profitability of the printing company

First we need to find the likely monthly income and costs according to the description of the case. Clearly, income will depend on the volume, which will be around 100 000 copies a month. Since the price is €0.285 per copy, the monthly income will be:

$$0.285 \times X$$

In the equation, X signifies the monthly production volume.

Variable costs to be paid monthly

There are several kinds of monthly costs. First, there are some costs that vary according to production volume, just like the income. These are paper and printing ink and they vary according to the volume. They are called variable costs and they will be:

$$0.15 \times X$$

where X is still the production volume. The costs that depend on the volume are called variable costs.

Fixed costs to be paid to suppliers and employees

However, most of the costs do not depend on the monthly volume. First, we have some costs that have to be paid every month. Since the amount will be independent of the volume, they are called fixed costs:

	€
Premises	1 300
Car lease	800
Salaries for Johan and his assistant	4 000
Employment taxes	1 600
Maintenance, supplies and utilities, etc.	2 100
Fixed costs so far	**9 800**

Fixed costs to be paid to the bank

In addition, there are costs to be paid to the bank, as follows:

- contract for working capital
- monthly interest on working capital credit
- interest on the main loan.

If the first estimate of Johan and the bank manager is correct they will sign a contract for €30 000. The cost of the contract is 6 percent × 30 000 = €1800 per year. Actual interest on €30 000 will be 0.5 percent × 30 000 per month. Therefore the monthly costs will be:

$$6\% \times 30\,000/12 + 0.5\% \times 30\,000 = €300$$

During the first quarter, interest on the main loan will be:

$$5\% \times 36\,000/4 = €450$$

But since all other payments are calculated on a monthly basis, let us divide by three to find a monthly amount to be set aside for the interest costs:

$$450/3 = €150$$

Now we have covered all payments except the quarterly installments on the main loan. These payments, however, are not costs, but just payments to pay back a loan. They will reduce our cash and reduce our debts by the same amount.

Fixed costs that do not need to be paid right now

There are some costs that are not payments, but they are just as important as regular payments. In this case there is depreciation on the printing press. According to our information, the press cost €60 000 and it can be used for 4 years. Thus it will have to be depreciated every month by:

$$60\ 000/48 = €1250$$

These costs would have to be recovered every month to make sure that Johan can afford the printing press. If he manages to cover them he could consider buying a new press when the old one wears out. If not, he had better reconsider the whole business when that day comes.

Adding all fixed costs together

So far, we have found the following fixed costs:

	€
Premises	1 300
Car lease	800
Salaries for Johan and his assistant	4 000
Employment taxes	1 600
Maintenance, supplies and utilities etc	2 100
Working capital	300
Interest on the regular loan	150
Depreciation	1 250
Total fixed costs	**11 500**

Comparing income to costs

At this stage we have found monthly income, which is variable and we have found monthly costs. Some of the costs are variable and the others are fixed. Adding them together we can write the following **profit equation**:

$$0.285 \times X - 0.15 \times X - 11\ 500 = \text{Monthly profit}$$

From the profit equation we can find the monthly volume that is needed to break even by setting the profit equal to zero:

$$0.285 \times X - 0.15 \times X - 11\ 500 = 0$$
$$0.135X = 11\ 500$$
$$X = 85\ 185$$

Now we have found that the break-even volume is somewhat more than 85 000 copies. Since the volume is expected to exceed this number, there will very likely be a monthly profit.

But before we calculate the monthly profit we need to define the new number, 0.135, that appeared in the above calculation. According to this, for each additional copy produced and sold, the profits will increase by €0.135. We say that the **contribution** per copy is €0.135.

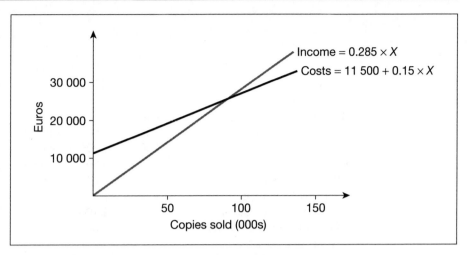

Figure 1.2 Break-even diagram for *Farmer's Monthly*

Now, if the actual volume turns out to be 100 000 copies, as expected, what profit will Johan make? Let us apply the actual volume to the profit equation:

$$0.135 \times 100\ 000 - 11\ 500 = \text{Profit}$$
$$13\ 500 - 11\ 500 = €2000 \tag{1.1}$$

The profit situation can be described in a **break-even diagram** according to Figure 1.2.

Of course, as outsiders we can never know how things are going to turn out, but we can see that the business appears to be profitable if income and costs follow the description in the case. Next, we could do some sensitivity analysis to find out how the break-even and profit would change if the volume gets bigger or smaller or if any of the other parameters change. But right now, these analyses will have to wait, because we have to study the cash situation of the project.

■ Developing a cash budget

Unfortunately, many small companies have difficulties in planning their cash budgets. Inexperienced owners perhaps do not really know what to expect or haven't taken the time needed to make a cash budget.

In the case of Johan's printing company, we may suspect that there will be some quite large payments in the beginning when activities are getting started. Therefore, we have to follow the developments of the cash situation until we can see that it stabilizes (as it should do because monthly income is bigger than monthly costs).

Now, let us assume that Johan starts by buying the printing press, paper and printing ink in the month immediately before printing activities start. Assuming that the original estimate of interest on the working capital credit is correct, **a preliminary cash budget** for the printing company could look like this:

	Month				
	0	*1*	*2*	*3*	*4*
	€	€	€	€	€
Starting cash	60 000	−16 500	−41 600	−66 700	66 750
Monthly income				28 500	28 500
Buying printing press	−60 000				
Paper and printing ink	−15 000	−15 000	−15 000	−15 000	−15 000
Paying rent	−1 300	−1 300	−1 300	−1 300	−1 300
Paying car lease		−800	−800	−800	−800
Paying salaries and employment taxes		−5 600	−5 600	−5 600	−5 600
Paying other fixed costs		−2 100	−2 100	−2 100	−2 100
Paying working capital credit		−300	−300	−300	−300
Paying back bank loan				−3 000	
Paying interest on bank loan				−450	
Monthly cash flow	−76 300	−25 100	−25 100	−50	+3400
Ending cash	−16 500	−41 600	−66 700	−66 750	−63 350

The starting cash in month 0 equals the money that Johan received from his former employer plus the regular bank loan. In the following months the starting cash is equal to the ending cash of the previous month.

Monthly income will be a difficult item. If the work is done in the first month, invoices can be sent at the beginning of the second month and the first payment will be received at the beginning of the third month! From then on, these payments will be constant.

The monthly cost of paper, printing ink and rent will be €15 000 plus €1300 and the payments start in month 0, i.e. before the printing activities have started. After that, the rent is the same every month.

Most of the other fixed costs will only need to be paid when the actual printing has started. These payments will then remain unchanged until volumes or prices change.

Paying back capital and interest on the bank loan will only be required once every 3 months.

From the preliminary cash budget we can see that the ending cash will be negative for every month we have studied. These negative amounts will have to be covered by the working capital credit. But then, looking at the final line of the cash budget we can see that the working capital credit will have to be much higher than the original estimate. Therefore, monthly dues to the bank will rise and fixed costs will rise compared with the original plan.

Revising the cash budget

Since the ending cash in our first cash budget goes as low as − €66 750 and we would like some safety margin, we could perhaps negotiate a contract for €70 000 instead of €30 000. In such a case the yearly contract interest will be 6 percent ×

7000 = €4200. That will be €350 per month and the cost of monthly credit will be the same. To make things easy, we will calculate as if Johan needed the full amount all the time, although there will be a few months in the beginning before he needs all the credit.

Including these changes, the revised cash budget will look as follows:

	Month				
	0	1	2	3	4
	€	€	€	€	€
Starting cash	60 000	−16 500	−42 000	−67 500	66 750
Monthly income				28 500	28 500
Buying printing press	−60 000				
Paper and printing ink	−15 000	−15 000	−15 000	−15 000	−15 000
Paying rent	−1 300	−1 300	−1 300	−1 300	−1 300
Paying car lease		−800	−800	−800	−800
Paying salaries and employment taxes		−5 600	−5 600	−5 600	−5 600
Paying other fixed costs		−2 100	−2 100	−2 100	−2 100
Paying working capital credit		−700	−700	−700	−700
Paying back bank loan				−3 000	
Paying interest on bank loan				−450	
Monthly cash flow	−76 300	−25 500	−25 500	−450	+3000
Ending cash	−16 500	−42 000	−67 500	−67 950	−64 950

In each month the negative ending cash can now be covered by the working capital allowance.

■ Revising the income budget

After finding out about the large working capital credit, it might be wise to revise the income budget.

Fixed costs will rise to €11 900 and monthly profit will again be found from the profit equation:

$$0.135 \times 100\ 000 - 11\ 900 = €1600$$

Comparing this outcome with the profit according to equation (1.1), we can see that quite a big part of the preliminary profit was lost when we revised our needs for a working capital credit.

The monthly break-even volume will also rise:

$$0.135 \times X - 11\ 900 = 0$$

$$X = 88\ 148$$

Thus the break-even volume will rise to somewhat more than 88 000 copies.

■ Learning outcomes

After studying this case you should know:

- the difference between fixed and variable costs; variable costs depend on the volume of production, whereas fixed costs are independent of the volume;
- the profit equation, where you can find the likely profit at various volumes (please test your knowledge by trying to find profits at higher or lower volumes than were mentioned in the case – higher volumes will yield a bigger profit; smaller volumes will yield smaller profits, or even losses);
- the break-even volume, which shows the volume necessary for the business to be profitable;
- the preliminary cash budget, which shows periodic (usually monthly) cash positions in order to negotiate a working capital credit and to revise the fixed credit costs;
- the final cash budget, showing the amount of money that needs to be covered by the working capital credit.

1.3 Svenberg Furniture

To prove – if you did not already know it – that cash and profitability are two very different issues.

The Svenberg Furniture Co is located in southern Sweden. They produce wooden office furniture of premium quality. The founder, Mr Svenberg, is still the boss of the company although he owns only a minority of the shares. Today there are only a small number of employees.

The main product, an office desk, is sold to retailers on yearly contracts, generally signed a long time in advance. Deliveries are distributed fairly evenly over a year. This year (year 0) the price is SEK 5000 and the budget for year 1 is based upon an unchanged price.

The process of production is quite difficult to master. To achieve the highest quality, the timber has to be dried very slowly and carefully. Drying, shaping and storing of pieces therefore takes a full year in the production department. The price of timber is equivalent to SEK 2000 for each unit. The direct costs (mainly labour) in the production department are SEK 500 per unit.

Pieces are sent to the finishing department. Externally bought parts (SEK 500 per unit) are added. Wages in the finishing department are SEK 500 per unit. When the desks are finished they are handed over to the sales department to be stored until delivery. Delivery will normally take place roughly 1 month after pieces reach the finishing department.

Timber is normally paid for 60 days after it was received, whereas external parts have to be paid for on delivery. Customers are allowed 30 days of credit but terms can occasionally be extended to make the selling easier. Since the cash position of the company is good, credit terms have been quite easy at times.

For a few years, volume has been falling gradually and profitability has been low. This year 2400 units are scheduled to be produced. Technical capacity would allow quite a large increase in volume, but more workers would have to be hired.

In spite of the bad years lately, dividends have remained steady at 8 percent of the book value of shares. The board felt that dividends were not using cash that was needed for production and free reserves were available.

In order to improve profitability Mr Svenberg has visited a possible new customer, a large international furniture chain. They are willing buy all of his production, deliveries starting in January year 2, if he can supply 3600 units a year priced at SEK 4800. If he accepts the offer, Mr Svenberg would have to cancel all other contracts from year 2 onwards.

Mr Svenberg knows that he is making losses at the present price of SEK 5000 a unit. Therefore he is reluctant to accept the chain's offer. But he would like some help to find out.

There is already an income budget for year 1 (old volume) and a balance sheet budget to the end of year 0. When solving the case we shall need them as starting points.

Analyze the situation and produce those budgets that are needed to make a decision.

Income budget, year 1

Income: Sales 2400 units × SEK 5000		12 000 000
Costs		
Timber	4 800 000	
Parts	1 200 000	
Wages in production	2 400 000	
Fixed production costs[1]	1 900 000	
Other fixed costs[2]	1 500 000	
Interest costs	400 000	12 200 000
Net loss		200 000

[1] Including 400 000 depreciation on machinery.
[2] Including 200 000 depreciation on buildings.

Balance sheet budget at the end of year 0

Cash	1 000 000	Share capital	3 200 000
Buildings and machinery	1 800 000	Accumulated profits	2 100 000
Inventories[1]	5 300 000	Liabilities	800 000
Accounts receivables	1 000 000	Bank loans[2]	3 200 000
Loss	200 000		
	9 300 000		9 300 000

[1] Evaluated at cost of materials only.
[2] The amount already exceeds the book value of fixed assets. Therefore increases might be difficult to negotiate.

	SEK 000	SEK 000
Sales	3 600 × 4.8	17 280
Timber	7 200	
Parts	1 800	
Wages	3 600	
Fixed PO	1 900	
Fixed admin	1 500	
Interest	400	16 400
		+ 800

Figure 1.3 Income budget, year 2, for Svenberg Furniture

Solution: Svenberg Furniture

■ A profit budget

When investigating the proposal it would be a good thing to make a profit budget for the new situation to see if it is viable at all in spite of the lower price. Assuming that all fixed costs are truly fixed we let them remain unchanged. Also assuming that variable costs are proportional to volume we shall allow them to increase by 50 percent.

At the start of the solution we shall treat the interest costs as fixed costs although we know that they might change if total borrowing changes because of the considerable changes in prices and volumes.

Under those assumptions the income budget for year 2 will be as shown in Figure 1.3.

Timber, parts and wages have increased by 50 percent compared with the original budget. All fixed costs and interest costs have remained unchanged.

We can see that the budgeted profit increases because of the larger volume although prices are down by 5 percent.

■ Cash budgeting

We are happy that the income budget turned out so well. But we have to investigate what is going to happen to the cash situation. In fact, we know that the company has quite a lot of cash and that cash has not been a problem in recent years. But still, the expansion is quite a big one and so we had better investigate carefully what might happen. Timber for the new large volumes will have to be bought in year 1. Therefore, although we produced a new income budget for year 2, we shall have to create a cash budget for year 1.

	Jan	Feb	Mar	April	May	Jun
	SEK 000	*SEK 000*	*SEK 000*	*SEK 000*	*SEK 000*	*SEK 000*
Sales	1 000	1 000	1 000	1 000	1 000	1 000
Suppliers	500	500	700	700	700	700
Wages (production)	150	150	150	150	150	150
Wages (finishing)	100	100	100	100	100	100
Interest	33	33	33	33	33	33
Fixed costs	233	233	233	233	233	233
	−16	−16	−216	−216	−216	−216
Accumulated	−16	−32	−248	−464	−680	−896

Figure 1.4 Cash planning, year 1, new contract for Svenberg Furniture

A cash budget for year 1 can be found in Figure 1.4.

As can be seen, sales income will remain at the original level all through the year. Payments to suppliers, however, will increase after some time. Svenberg needs to buy large new volumes of timber in January, but suppliers of timber are not paid until 60 days after delivery.

Therefore, payments to suppliers in January and February will have to cover the following items:

	SEK 000
Old monthly volume of timber	400
Old volume of parts	100
Total payment	500

From March there will be an increase in the payments for timber, but there will not be any changes in the volume of parts until they are ready for final assembly in December or perhaps at the beginning of year 2. Therefore payments to suppliers from March onward will look like this:

	SEK 000
New monthly volume of timber	600
Old volume of parts	100
Total payment	700

Wages in production will increase immediately at the beginning of the year, but wages in the finishing department will not increase until final assembly increases at a much later point in time.

Interest and all other fixed costs are assumed to be unchanged for the moment. We just need to notice that there is depreciation included in the fixed costs in the original case. This item lowers the value of buildings, machinery and equipment but it does not need to be paid out. Therefore payments of fixed costs are calculated in the following way:

	Original amount SEK 000	Depreciation SEK 000	Net payment SEK 000
Production overheads	1 900	400	1 500
Other fixed overheads	1 500	200	1 300
Totals	3 400	600	2 800
Monthly average	283	50	233

Now we can see clearly that the new contracts will quickly strain the cash situation of the company beyond what can be managed. In fact, since there has to be a full yearly volume of timber in store all the time, inventories will increase by 50 percent just like other volumes. That means that the cash requirements will increase by SEK 2.5 million.

As a comparison it might be interesting to take a look at the old cash budget: You will find it in Figure 1.5.

If the volume stays low, the cash situation will improve every month even though the company will make a loss. This is because inventories remain low and, disregarding depreciation, the company is actually consuming its fixed assets. Such a situation is by no means unusual.

■ Conclusion

The Svenberg Furniture case highlights the importance of regular budgets in order to have advance knowledge of the consequences of alternative managerial decisions. With a large and secure contract, Mr Svenberg might very well succeed in negotiating an additional bank loan if he starts negotiating at the planning stage.

	Jan SEK 000	Feb SEK 000	Mar SEK 000	April SEK 000	May SEK 000	Jun SEK 000
Sales	1 000	1 000	1 000	1 000	1 000	1 000
Suppliers	500	500	500	500	500	500
Wages	200	200	200	200	200	200
Interest	33	33	33	33	33	33
Fixed costs	233	233	233	233	233	233
	+34	+34	+34	+34	+34	+34
Accumulated	34	68	102	136	170	204

Figure 1.5 Cash budget, year 1, old contract for Svenberg Furniture

But if he does not discover the cash problem until he is well under way, it might be too late for negotiations.

1.4 Quality Printing

Here is the reason the owner of a small company thinks he needs a budget, and then there is his budget. First, let us meet him in person.

The owner, Mr Edwin Tower

Mr Edwin Tower operates a small printing company. In fact, it is not that small, as it is bigger than most of the local competitors. But by management standards it is considered a small company.

Edwin is a hard-working man and if you want to see him for any reason you will usually find him at work in his printing shop. When I asked him about this, he told me that it is not so bad, because he takes at least 2 days off every year, Christmas Day in winter and a beautiful Sunday in the middle of the summer.

Edwin Tower on budgeting

A few years ago I asked Edwin for his opinion on budgeting. You can see his reply in Figure 1.6. It does not really matter when you ask Edwin about such things, he will always point out that paper prices are very high right now. This is probably because he feels helpless. There is nothing he can do except pay them and look happy about it.

After he has produced a complete budget, he uses it as a starting point for his selling efforts. Knowing that some 50 percent of company costs are fixed (independent of volume) he also knows that the final profit will improve very much if sales rise.

When I asked Edwin if he needs any other budgets he replied as in Figure 1.7. The cash budget has already been mentioned in the Svenberg Furniture case and here it is again. It's no surprise, as it is highly relevant.

'Do you really need a budget?'

Edwin Tower at Quality Printing:

'Yes, definitely! I run my company as I like, but I always make a budget to see how much I have to sell to break even.'

'I worry most about the profit budget. It is especially important right now, since paper prices are so high.'

Figure 1.6

'Do you need any other budgets?'

Edwin Tower:

'Yes, actually I need several of them. Since we are about to buy new printing equipment, we need a cash budget. We need to plan our cash carefully to avoid borrowing too much.'

'Unfortunately, incoming cash doesn't follow the sales very well. Customers never pay in the same month as we do the work. Some of them pay several months later – if they pay at all!'

Figure 1.7

But on further questioning, Edwin revealed that he does not care much about accounting theory (Figure 1.8). In theory, the investment budget is a document describing what investments to make and when to make them. But the calculation Edwin mentions is a piece of capital budgeting analysis to find the profitability of a project. We shall come back to that kind of analysis in a later section.

■ The basic budget of the Quality Printing Co

Table 1.1 shows the company budget summary. From this budget we can see that the total sales in a year are expected to be €16 055 000. Edwin looks forward to a net profit of €1 362 000. (As it turned out, Edwin never managed to reach his

'Will the bank ask for a budgeted balance sheet?'

Edwin Tower:

'Sometimes they do, but it is difficult to get it right! It should cover the whole period up to New Year's Eve, and that is a long time. Occasionally I try. Right now I don't have one.'

'Now and then I even develop an investment budget. I want to know the profitability of new machinery. The payback time should be less than 3 years!'

(In fact, this is capital budgeting.)

Figure 1.8

Table 1.1 Quality Printing budget: summary

	Jan €000	Feb €000	March €000	April €000	. . .	Dec €000	Total €000
Sales	950	981	1 632	1 571	. . .	1 037	16 055
Cost of materials	457	472	785	756	. . .	499	7 724
Gross profit	493	509	847	815	. . .	538	8 331
Wages and salaries	310	310	310	310	. . .	310	3 850
Other costs	240	242	225	227	. . .	210	2 679
Profit before depreciation	−57	−43	312	278	. . .	18	1 802
Depreciation	20	20	20	20	. . .	25	260
Profit from operations	−77	−63	292	258	. . .	−7	1 542
Financial items	−15	−15	−15	−15	. . .	−15	−180
Net profit	−92	−78	277	243	. . .	−22	1 362

budgeted profit. Every year, there were extraordinary items that caused profits to fall short.)

Unfortunately most years start with a very bleak winter. Volumes are too low. That, says Edwin, is because of the lousy Christmas selling season. Most of Edwin's sales are to other companies and these buyers are at Christmas time busy doing other things rather than ordering printed products.

Building the budget

Typically, when building his budget, Edwin will do most of the work between Christmas and the end of the year to make sure that has access to the full outcome of the previous year. He starts by forecasting sales, which is easy, because he will take last year's monthly outcomes and make them grow by some percentage points, depending on his feelings about general business conditions.

After budgeting sales he will find out what part of the sales was spent last year on paper, photography, composing and so on. He brings last year's actual outcome into this year's budget unless he knows that some item is changing. If he knows about a change, he will adjust that particular number accordingly.

After going through all the items classified as materials, Edwin produced the cost of materials budget (Table 1.2).

You might feel that some of those items are not really materials but purchased services. I agree and, of course, we are theoretically right. But Edwin treats it all in the same way and does not really care how we would classify things. All the items cause payments to outsiders.

You can see how three lines from the budget of materials enter the summary budget. These are:

- sales
- total cost of materials
- gross profit.

Table 1.2 Quality Printing budget: cost of materials

		Jan €000	Feb €000	March €000	April €000	... ...	Dec €000	Total €000
Sales		950	981	1 632	1 571	...	1 037	16 055
Paper	23.0%	219	226	375	361	...	239	3 693
Photography	3.4%	32	33	56	53	...	35	546
Composing	5.0%	48	49	82	79	...	52	803
Copying	2.5%	24	25	41	39	...	26	401
Binding	3.5%	33	34	57	55	...	36	562
Printing	3.0%	29	29	49	47	...	31	482
Consultants	2.6%	25	25	42	41	...	27	417
Stamping	0.6%	6	6	10	9	...	6	96
Transport	1.0%	10	10	16	16	...	10	161
Message services	1.0%	10	10	16	16	...	10	161
Other materials	1.0%	10	10	16	16	...	10	161
Other cost of production	1.5%	14	15	24	24	...	16	241
Total cost of materials	48.1%	457	472	785	756	...	499	7 724
Gross profit		493	509	847	815	...	538	8 331

The next big part of Edwin's budget deals with salaries and wages. In fact, most of it is quite well known in advance. In Table 1.3 you will find the budget for the cost of labor.

The labor budget is easy to build because Edwin knows what employees there are and what salaries they earn. Edwin includes likely salary rises in the budget but he does not show them explicitly. The labor budget includes likely salaries and wages as if they were applicable from the very start of the year.

The next part of the budget covers other costs, such as costs of leasing equipment, service costs for machinery, book-keeping and so on (Table 1.4). Edwin will look at last year's outcome and normally increase most amounts a little bit to be sure that all costs will be included.

Service costs diminish considerably in March because an old service contract expires and Edwin does not feel that he needs to renew it.

After including materials, labor and other costs, Edwin finally makes some rough estimates of depreciation and interest costs. He applies straight-line depreciation for machinery, normally dividing the original buying price by 60 to allocate

Table 1.3 Quality Printing budget: cost of labor

	Jan €000	Feb €000	March €000	April €000	... ...	Dec €000	Total €000
Wages	195	195	195	195	...	195	2 340
Wages during vacations	0	0	0	0	...	0	92
Management	30	30	30	30	...	30	360
Employment taxes	70	70	70	70	...	70	878
Other	15	15	15	15	...	15	180
Total cost of labor	310	310	310	310	...	310	3 850

Table 1.4 Quality Printing budget: other costs

	Jan €000	Feb €000	March €000	April €000	. . . . . .	Dec €000	Total €000
Housing	63	63	63	63	. . .	63	756
Leasing machinery	65	65	65	65	. . .	50	720
Leasing cars	3	3	3	3	. . .	3	36
Electricity and water	10	10	10	10	. . .	10	120
Office	2	2	2	2	. . .	2	24
Service	32	32	12	12	. . .	12	184
Computers	2	4	2	4	. . .	2	32
Book-keeping	15	15	15	15	. . .	15	180
Car service	9	9	9	9	. . .	9	108
Distribution	4	4	4	4	. . .	4	50
Entertaining	5	5	10	10	. . .	10	109
Advertising	10	10	10	10	. . .	10	120
Other costs	20	20	20	20	. . .	20	240
Total other costs	240	242	225	227	. . .	210	2 679

depreciation over a full 5 years. These items are brought straight into the summary budget.

Finally, Edwin makes a cash budget, which is a tricky thing in the printing business. After all, as he stated in our first discussion: 'Customers never pay in the same month as we do the work. Some of them pay several months later . . . if they pay at all!'

Edwin has a rule of thumb, saying that nobody pays in the month when the work is done. Some 60 percent pay 1 month later, 30 percent pay 2 months later and 10 percent pay 3 months later. Including these points, Edwin built the cash budget shown in Table 1.5.

For material, the cash budget differs from the original budget of material. First, there is a 1-month delay in all payments, because Edwin pays all suppliers 1 month after delivery. Secondly, he adds value added tax (VAT) to all items because those taxes will be included in the invoices from suppliers. Thirdly, if you check the numbers very carefully, you will find some more very small differences, which occur because Edwin does not work very efficiently in Excel. Sometimes he just writes a number instead of a formula.

In the wages line you can see that wages are expected to rise from €170 000 per month in the beginning of the year to €195 000 per month towards the end of the year. Somewhere among the months that are not shown he plans to pay additional wages to make up for the low amounts in the beginning.

Finally, there are some details around rents and payable VAT that we will not investigate in detail.

As you can see, Edwin expects to have negative cash at the beginning of April. In reality, this means that he will have to talk to his banker in order to organize new credit in time. This is a very important point because the banker will not be impressed if he discovers the problem too late. But if he shows up in January, telling his

Table 1.5 Quality Printing budget: cash budget

	Jan €000	Feb €000	March €000	April €000	. . . . . .	Dec €000	Total €000
Turnover, net	950	981	1 632	1 571	. . .	1 037	16 055
Turnover, including VAT	1 220	1 260	2 096	2 018	. . .	1 332	20 621
Starting cash	400	299	137	−2	. . .	1 169	
Loans	0	0	0	0	. . .	0	0
Receipts from customers	600	732	756	1 258	. . .	1 156	12 173
	360	300	366	378	. . .	636	5 869
	130	120	100	122	. . .	212	1 874
Total receipts	1 090	1 152	1 222	1 758	. . .	2 004	19 916
Materials	622	570	589	979	. . .	900	9 633
Wages	170	170	170	170	. . .	195	2 125
Taxes	126	126	126	126	. . .	144	1 578
Rents			204		. . .	204	816
VAT		118		173	. . .	354	1 495
. . .							
Total payments	1 191	1 313	1 362	1 774	. . .	2 168	19 312
Net change	−101	−161	−140	−16	0	−164	604

banker that there will be a cash problem in April, he is likely to be awarded the loan he might need.

1.5 Grondal Industrial Rolls

We need to follow up a budget to see what went right or wrong. But nobody knows everything. We have to point out who should explain what. Here's how.

Grondal Industrial Rolls, a company in the Grondal Group, produces two types of large industrial rolls. These rolls are sold to automotive and steel industries all across Europe.

In the Grondal Industrial Rolls company there is one production department, one sales department and an administrative department handling premises, personnel matters and accounting. There is one department head in each department and a managing director in charge of the whole company.

In recent times, demand has been highly volatile and recession has been threatening. Therefore the managing director has made the basic decisions on volumes and customers, but the head of the sales department has negotiated prices and all other details in sales contracts. The production volume was designed to follow the sales volume without any important changes in inventories.

The group CEO, Victor Sjolkov, has recently received a budget report and an income statement for the latest quarter at Grondal Industrial Rolls. He is worried because of the big differences between the budget and the actual outcome. Table 1.6 shows the main budget and outcome figures for the latest quarter.

Table 1.6 Budget and outcome figures for the last quarter

	Budget €000	Actual €000	Variance €000
Sales			
Cluster mill rolls	108 000	96 000	−12 000
Section mill rolls	104 000	106 000	2 000
Total sales	212 000	202 000	−10 000
Production			
Direct wages	30 000	36 000	−6 000
Material cluster mill rolls	54 000	39 000	15 000
Material section mill rolls	72 000	84 000	−12 000
Total production	156 000	159 000	−3 000
Administration	30 000	30 000	0
Total company	26 000	13 000	−13 000

Table 1.7 Number of rolls sold

	Budget €000	Actual €000
Cluster mill rolls	3 600	3 000
Section mill rolls	4 000	4 200
Total, all rolls	7 600	7 200

Direct wages are variable costs and they are seen as proportional to the total number of rolls produced.

There is also a separate report on the physical quantities of the rolls (Table 1.7).

After seeing the reports, the group CEO was very concerned about the outcome and felt that the managing director, in charge of volume, as well as the head of sales would have to provide detailed explanations. The managing director would have to explain why the profits had diminished so much while the head of sales was responsible for most of the losses. 'Only production and administration,' said Mr Sjolkov, 'appear to have done their jobs reasonably well!'

In this situation, Mr Sjolkov will need some help to further analyze the budget and the outcome in order to be more precise in his criticism and to make clear what needs to be explained by whom.

Please prepare the material further. Bring in an adjusted variable budget and perform a proper variance analysis, finding out which department heads are actually responsible for what!

Solution: Grondal Industrial Rolls

Finding out what really happened can be quite a tricky business when there are very many products and departments. In this particular case, things are not very complicated, but we can show that the intuitive opinion of the group CEO might not have caught the true essence of the problem. However, the following analysis can be used even in a more complicated case.

First, the volume of the company is a very important variable. It affects almost everybody although volume decisions are normally made by quite a small number of people. In this case the managing director is said to have made the main volume decisions, but in many other cases these decisions are made by the sales department. When production is strained to the limit, volume decisions might be made by the production managers.

In either case, it is normally a good thing to find out the impact of the volume changes. We can do so by creating a variable budget adjusted to actual volumes. This is how:

For cluster mill rolls, the actual volume was 3000 units instead of 3600. Then, other things (especially prices) being equal, sales would fall to:

$$\text{Sales, cluster mill rolls (€000)} = 3000/3600 \times 108\,000 = 90\,000$$

For section mill rolls the actual volume was 4200 instead of 4000. Then, other things (especially prices) being equal, sales would rise to:

$$\text{Sales, section mill rolls (€000)} = 4200/4000 \times 104\,000 = 109\,200$$

Thus, total sales of our adjusted variable budget will be:

$$\text{Total sales (€000)} = 90\,000 + 109\,200 = 199\,200$$

In the production department, direct wages are said to be proportional to the total number of rolls. Then, the adjusted variable budget for wages will be:

$$\text{Direct wages (€000)} = 7200/7600 \times 30\,000 = 28\,420$$

Material will have to be calculated for one type of roll at a time. For cluster mill rolls, volumes fell from 3600 to 3000. Here is the adjusted variable budget:

$$\text{Direct material, cluster mill rolls (€000)} = 3000/3600 \times 54\,000 = 45\,000.$$

The volume of section mill rolls rose from 4000 units to 4200 units. The adjusted variable budget will look like this:

$$\text{Direct material, section mill rolls (€000)} = 4200/4000 \times 72\,000 = 75\,600$$

Altogether we have the following adjusted rolling budget for production:

$$\text{Total production (€000)} = 28\,420 + 45\,000 + 75\,600 = 149\,020$$

In administration we do not know of any relationship between costs and the volume of production. Therefore our adjusted costs of administration are equal to the costs of the original budget.

Bringing all these calculations together, we put the adjusted variable budget between the original budget and the actual outcome and we get the results in Table 1.8.

But in addition to the columns of budget, adjusted budget and actual outcome there are now two additional columns in the table: variance I and variance II.

Table 1.8

Sales	Budget	Adjusted budget	Actual	Variance I	Variance II
	€000	€000	€000	€000	€000
Cluster mill rolls	108 000	90 000	96 000	−18 000	+6 000
Section mill rolls	104 000	109 200	106 000	5 200	−3 200
Total sales	212 000	199 200	202 000	−12 800	2 800
Direct wages	30 000	28 420	36 000	1 580	−7 580
Material cluster mill rolls	54 000	45 000	39 000	9 000	6 000
Material section mill rolls	72 000	75 600	84 000	−3 600	−8 400
Total production	156 000	149 020	159 000	6 980	−9 980
Administration	30 000	30 000	30 000	0	0
Total company	26 000	19 020	13 000	−5 820	−7 180

In the variance I column we calculate what the volume decisions meant for each activity in the company. We can see that so much volume was lost that sales declined by 12 800. But, on the other hand, lower volume means lower production and, hopefully, lower production costs. Further down in the variance I column we can see the likely savings in wages and material in production that ought to occur when the production volume diminishes. On the whole, production costs ought to come down by €6.98 million. Since the costs of administration were not expected to change, the total change in profit due to the change in volume is −€5.82 million.

Now, variance I, the difference between the original budget and the adjusted budget, is due to the manager(s) in the company who make volume decisions. In this case these decisions were made by the managing director.

The numbers in the variance II column are not due to variances in volume, but to other factors in each of the departments. In the sales departments the main explanation would be prices. Since variance II is positive in the sales department we can assume that prices were higher, which will increase the profit of the company by the same amount.

On the other hand, in the production department, the total variance is negative, −€9.98 million. We do not know very much about the reasons for this large deviation, but we know that it will have to be explained by the head of the production department.

There could be several reasons for the variances in the production department. First, the large negative variance in direct wages could be due to a larger number of hours than was assumed in the adjusted variable budget. We assumed that direct wages were variable and this was perhaps not quite true. Changes in production procedures might even have caused the number of hours to increase. Secondly, the wage rates may have risen during the period. Only the production manager can explain these factors.

In production we also have variances in direct material. It appears that money was saved on material for cluster mill rolls, but there are negative variances in

Table 1.9 Summary of responsibilities

	Variance I	Variance II	Managing director	Sales	Production
	€000	€000	€000	€000	€000
Sales					
Cluster mill rolls	–18 000	+6 000	–18 000	+6 000	
Section mill rolls	5 200	–3 200	5 200	–3 200	
Total sales	–12 800	2 800	–12 800	2 800	
Direct wages	1 580	–7 580	1580		–7 580
Material cluster mill rolls	9 000	6 000	9 000		6 000
Material section mill rolls	–3 600	–8 400	–3 600		–8 400
Total production	6 980	–9 980	6 980		–9 980
Administration	0	0			
Total company	–5 820	–9 180	–5 820	2 800	–9 980

the section mill rolls. These variances could be due to changes in the quantity of materials used, or they could be due to changing prices materials. Only the production manager can provide us with those details.

All told, we can summarize the responsibilities as shown in Table 1.9. In this table we can see clearly that Victor Sjolkov was not quite right in his original intuitive understanding of the case. The volume decision was clearly a very expensive one, costing the company almost €6 million after considering likely savings in production.

Given the volume decision, however, the sales manager appears to have done a good job in pricing the sales contracts. On the other hand, there are problems in production, which is contrary to the group CEO's original belief. Costs of production, according to variance II, increased considerably and contributed most of the losses compared with the original budget.

1.6 Forest Wheels

There was once a small company way up in the Scandinavian forests. They made lightweight aluminum wheels for modern cars. Their four regular customers were well-known European car makers. They were not exclusive suppliers, but they were quite good and they were continually trying to expand by finding new customers. At the time of the following events they were trying to woo a fifth regular customer. Being located so far away from most business events, they had difficulty convincing new customers that they were truly dependable suppliers.

At the start of the case, the Forest Wheels company had a very unusual set of owners. A few years before, the original company had got into financial difficulties and new owners stepped in and took over the whole thing. Our story doesn't relate exactly how this all came about, but starts with two owners, each with 50 percent of the equity capital. One was the local municipality and the other was (oh, yes) a foreign investment company. The municipality wanted to save the jobs and the foreigners wanted to get a fair return on their money.

The management of Forest Wheels felt that they were good at making aluminum wheels but they also felt that they did not have a very good planning system. Their traditional budget worked reasonably well, but they wanted some more explicit numbers to be checked regularly. And they knew that they would have to plan for some quite important changes in several areas. So they sent their chief accountant to a conference on balanced scorecards.

At the conference the chief accountant found a consultant who appeared to know a bit about the subject and he brought the consultant back for a 2-day meeting with the company's management. He asked the consultant to give them all a short introduction to balanced scorecards.

■ Criticizing traditional budgeting

The consultant started by explaining why traditional management control systems were not good enough any more. He emphasized the following points:

■ *In traditional budgeting there is too much looking back instead of planning ahead.* This happens because traditional accounting reports mainly emphasize what happened during the last month or the last quarter. Managers tend to study the reports and discover that things did not come out as they might have wished, but they do not always have explicit goals to be reached in every planning period, such as a month or a quarter. The budget is typically defined over a year, which might be too long a period for regular follow-up and too short for strategic planning.

■ *Managers tend to forgets customers' opinions and qualitative needs.* The reporting system typically deals mainly with the quantitative economic outcome of activities during the latest period. But customers' needs might not be reported at all. If a customer wants a different quality or a larger quantity during the next period, we would need a report making those wishes explicit to our own planning system.

　Also, our reporting system does not show if a customer is happy or unhappy. But because of Forest Wheels' special situation, with only a few very important customers, reporting and managing the satisfaction and needs of customers would actually be much more important to the company than merely analyzing the latest accounting outcome. We cannot trust customers to increase their orders in the future unless they are happy now and feel that their ever-increasing needs of aluminum wheels can be safely net.

■ *The traditional system creates short-sighted managers, always trying to manage the present quarter.* The quarterly reports to the owners are not very useful in terms of future profitability. In fact, now is already too late to manage the present quarter, or even the next quarter, very well. We should be planning those things that are needed for next year even if this requires measures that do not show up very well in accounting reports. If we need to change quality or increase volumes in the future, we have to plan for those changes now to make sure they can be carried out in time.

- *Management accounting has become subordinated to financial accounting.* As in many other companies, Forest Wheels does not have any separate reports for management accounting. All regular reports are designed according to the rules and needs of financial accounting. While those rules have a lot of support among accountants, they are normally very conservative, which might not be a good rule for managers who need to know the true state of things in order to make wise decisions.

- *Most reports are inward-looking instead of open to changes in the surroundings.* Almost all planning deals with the company *per se*, but very little planning deals with the surroundings of the company and the need to accommodate change.

What to do?

Considering all that criticism it should be quite clear that the present system creates distorted information for managers' decision-making. We therefore need to plan in a different way. Instead of just trusting old-fashioned reports, we need to realize that:

- there are many goals in the long run; and therefore,
- we need to prepare for the future.

We can do those things by consciously and systematically

- raising competence
- improving customer relations
- modernizing systems of production.

By doing so, we can ensure that today's profits are not allowed to disturb future profits or working conditions. But to get all these things right, we need a plan to co-ordinate goals so that each goal can be reached at the proper time without affecting the other goals. There are many ways to achieve this, one of which is by creating a balanced scorecard.

To make a balanced scorecard instead of budgeting or as a complement to budgeting, you need a vision that tells everybody as clearly as possible what is supposed to be done. Considering Forest Wheels' special situation with two very different owners, management felt that in the long run both owners would have to be kept reasonably happy. So the vision was not really a problem.

Company vision

'We want to create and maintain a company that will be profitable for very many years and there should always be at least as many employees as today.'

If this vision can be realized, both owners will be reasonably happy.

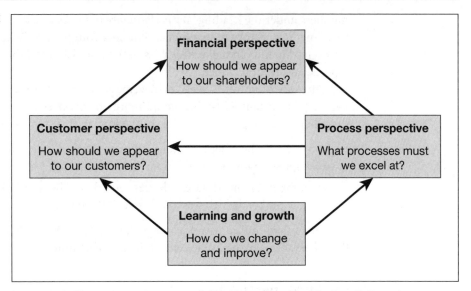

Figure 1.9 The balanced scorecard (first suggested by Kaplan, R.S. and Norton, D.P., 'The Balanced Scorecard – Measures that Drive Performance', *Harvard Business Review*, Jan–Feb., 1992, pp. 71–9). Used with permission.

■ Components of the balanced scorecard

In Figure 1.9 you will find the original design of the balanced scorecard, presented by Kaplan and Norton in the early 1990s. As can be seen, the writers suggest four major perspectives for planning:

- A *financial perspective*, usually describing economic or other variables that are important to the owners.
- A *customer perspective*, indicating what needs to be done in order to keep customers loyal to the company and to retain their business in the future.
- A *process perspective*, focusing on what needs to be done to improve the working process through upgrading business procedures and machinery.
- A *learning and growth perspective*, indicating the needs to further develop competencies of employee and procedures.

In some companies that have introduced balanced scorecards they have also added an 'employee perspective' in order to make really sure that employees are well treated and happy with the overall situation. In the case of Forest Wheels, the managers felt that these issues were as important to the company as to employees and therefore they felt that all employee needs would be taken care of in the learning and growth perspective.

Solution: balanced scorecard at Forest Wheels

■ Financial perspective

In the financial perspective many companies include a large number of variables, such as sales numbers, profit numbers, profitability ratios and perhaps be even cost numbers under the heading '*key performance indicators*' (KPIs). Discussions can be very lengthy and they quite often end up in a compromise, where several KPIs are introduced mainly to make all parties in the discussion feel that their own favorite aspects have been included.

In the case of Forest Wheels, management decided that there were actually only two very important KPIs: one would represent the needs of the municipality and the other would represent the aims of the foreign investor, as follows:

- profits should be at least X million during the first year and later grow in order to compensate for yearly inflation;
- the number of full-time employees would not be allowed to fall below the present number (which was a little over 300 people).

After those two indicators were accepted, the next issue would be about organizing the others to make the fulfillment of the financial indicators possible.

Customer perspective

In order to keep a constant number of employees and still keep the real profit constant or even growing, it was obvious that the annual volume of business would need to grow. Since productivity would grow all the time, it would take a bigger and bigger volume to keep the employees busy.

Therefore, on the customer side they needed to define KPIs that would ensure a growing business. In a way, management defined only one goal around the customers, but an important one:

Always deliver ordered quantities, spotless quality, and keep up acceptable lead times.

Always delivering ordered quantities could be quite a problem. The business was already running at a fairly high percentage of capacity most of the time. One large customer had a tendency to order new wheels without really considering the situation at the Forest Wheels plant. In some seasons, this was all well and good, but it was quite difficult to increase volumes suddenly during the hunting season in the fall. Not all employees felt that the production of aluminum wheels had a higher priority than the annual moose hunt.

Spotless quality was another matter! There was a quality inspection team scrutinizing every wheel before delivery, but there was a problem keeping the scrap rate low enough. Every time a faulty wheel was identified by the quality inspection team, there was an efficiency problem. Faulty wheels needed to be identified and scrapped as early as possible in the chain of production, thus avoiding spending a lot of time and effort on those wheels that would be scrapped anyway. But not all employees felt that way. Some of them just kept passing wheels on to the next department although they should have been scrapped; to some individuals it was a matter of not being identified as the one who caused the damage. It turned out to be quite a challenge to get everybody to co-operate in the scrapping of wheels when faults were discovered, rather than just passing them on to the next department down the line.

So bringing these things together, the attitudes of employees would have to be changed and the capacity of machinery increased in order to fulfill customer demands – which leads us to the process perspective.

■ Process perspective

In the process perspective, two major points came out of the discussion around the customer perspective. The company had to:

- create technical capacity to make 1.3 million good wheels per year;
- introduce a process such that one department would never again pass faulty wheels on to the next.

At the time of the study the technical capacity was something like 950 000 wheels per year. Therefore bringing capacity up to 1.3 million would be quite a demanding task. But management could identify those situations when the higher capacity would be an absolute necessity, especially if it meant the possibility of adding a new company to the list of customers.

Buying machinery, of course, would be quite expensive. But whatever the technical capacity, there would be a need to make sure that the capacity could be used at all times irrespective of the season. But if faulty wheels continued to be passed on to the next department there would be a big loss of working time for employees as well as for machinery. Thus, a big 'change of attitude' project would have to be created to ensure that everybody understood the need to scrap faulty wheels as early as possible. Of course, nobody objected, but not everyone really internalized the issue and thus the problem remained for some time.

But then along came a completely unforeseen capacity problem, when the local supplier of raw aluminum politely refused to deliver a larger quantity of raw materials.

■ Learning and growth perspective

So what? If the local supplier didn't want to sell aluminum to Forest Wheels, they could buy it from somewhere else! True, but then the aluminum raw material would also be produced somewhere else and by someone else and in this case that meant a Russian supplier to the world market. They had never done business with the Russians before, but they could, couldn't they?

The situation presented at least two new difficulties. One was the cultural problem in dealing with businessmen from a very different country. What is obvious to one is not always obvious to the other, and vice versa! Writing a contract becomes more difficult than before and making sure that the right goods arrive on time is even more problematic.

The other difficulty was of a technical nature. Russian aluminum does not follow exactly the same chemical norms as domestic aluminum. Forest Wheels would

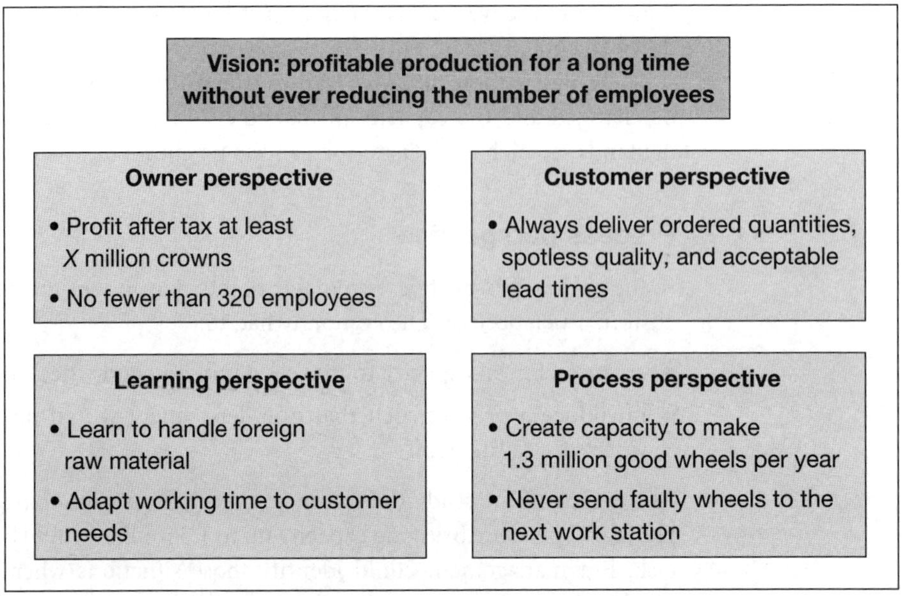

Figure 1.10 Balanced scorecard for Forest Wheels

have to learn to compensate for that difference in order to keep working with the new raw materials. And if they had to shift back and forth between local and Russian aluminum, could they manage that?

They had to learn – that is why this perspective is called learning and growth! But learning those things turned out to be more difficult than they imagined.

Adding the pieces together

After working through the whole scorecard, the final picture emerges (Figure 1.10). We did not think it was necessary to retain the arrows, but the boxes have been filled out in roughly the usual way.

Happily ever after . . .?

Changing the attitudes of employees in the local neighborhood and learning to work with Russian aluminum proved quite demanding. These issues were easily identified during the process of creating the balanced scorecard, but solving them was not as easy as hoped. And then, on top of it all, the financial crisis struck, resulting in falling volumes instead of rising volumes. How then does one ensure that profits remain high?

You may have heard the line about the hospital: the surgery went well, but unfortunately the patient still died! In this case, the planning system was logical and good, but perhaps not powerful enough to solve all the difficulties to the full satisfaction of the foreign investor. They encountered further difficulties and had to be reorganized once more.

1.7 Three budgetary processes

In large companies budgeting is not that simple!

This section contains overviews of budgetary processes in three large industrial companies. Let us study those processes and clarify the differences between them. It will be helpful to draw diagrams showing how working procedures shift between managers in different positions. We can then classify working procedures according to the main types of procedure.

Finally, we will discuss the differences between them in order to find out if they could be caused by:

- different budgeting aims
- different industries
- different owners
- different personalities of leaders.

■ Budgeting in Company A

In Company A, there is a long-term plan, which is revised every year, usually in the spring. This plan is originated by the company's budget committee. There, division managers and managers of the main HQ staff meet regularly to discuss the future. Once they have designed a preliminary overall plan encompassing major investment projects, they send the outcome of their discussions to each of the divisions. Each division manager then adds the necessary details for his or her own division, before sending the document down to the next level of managers for comments. After receiving their comments, the division manager produces a final document to bring before the budget committee for approval.

In the shorter term, this company has an annual fixed budget. In the early summer the budget committee reconsiders the long-term plan in order to create a starting point for the annual budget. After considering expected business conditions, costs, prices and wages, the budget committee creates a suggested 1-year budget for each division. These suggested budgets are usually sent to the divisions at the beginning of August.

Division managers develop detailed goals for each department in their division to hand over to the department heads. At the departmental level, the main details of the budget are worked out. Budgets for production and investment are developed in detail. When these budget sections are available, there is a period of discussion between department heads and division managers. During these discussions, the final numbers for production and investment are decided for each division within the limits of the suggested allowance for capital investment.

About 1 month before the start of the budget year, division managers present their budgets to the budget committee. In cases where one or more division managers feel that they are unable to reach the profits specified in the original plan from the budget committee, all divisions have to review their budgets in a final attempt to achieve the original goal.

Budgeting in Company B

In this company, a yearly budget is produced every autumn. In fact, the work starts in the late summer. At that time the CEO meets with each division manager for an introductory discussion. During those discussions, the managers work out some flexible goals for sales, investments, research and profitability of each division.

After discussions are over, the CEO's staff inform the HQ's budget department of the agreements reached. Now, the budget department produces a plan for the budgeting process, which explains in detail what is to be done, by whom, and when.

Later in the fall, all divisions start the real budget procedure by forecasting sales and personnel budgets. Later, budgets for all different functions are developed, and comparisons between functions are done regularly.

Towards the end of November, all budget sections in each division are set to work compiling a complete divisional budget to be presented to the division management. When the division manager is satisfied, the budget is sent to the central budget department for consolidation into a company budget.

All division managers present their suggested budget to the HQ management. The central budget department provides a general overview in order to provide insights into the overall situation and into the group budget.

If the CEO is not satisfied with a divisional budget, this particular budget has to be revised. If the revision is not good enough, other divisions might have to revise their budgets too. However, this does normally not happen. The budget department usually keeps the CEO well informed throughout the budgetary process. To do this well, they regularly create budget forecasts that show the progress of the budget all through the fall. Thus, if something goes wrong along the way, the CEO has the opportunity to take action long before the final presentations.

Budgeting in Company C

During the summer, foreign sales units compile their market estimates for the following year. Even domestic units do some preliminary planning in order to be able to present their main thoughts to the budget department toward the end of August. Because there are no budget instructions available in the summer, each unit does some thinking on its own, sometimes using last year's instructions or perhaps no instructions at all. In this way, there is no central control over the initial thinking and no bias is introduced through common instructions.

At the beginning of September the budget department collects opinions from all parties abroad and from most domestic production units. Forecast prices, volumes and the anticipated development of costs are carefully studied. A very preliminary profit budget is developed, and it is presented to the budget committee in the middle of September. Thus, the budget committee can see a preliminary overview fairly early in the fall. Normally, this profit budget is not thought to be good enough. Quite often production costs and the costs of central HQ staff have been rising too fast. In recent years, costs of research and development have normally been too high.

At this point, the budget committee develops a set of assumptions on business conditions, prices and volumes in various markets. In addition, they outline goals for each division in areas such as sales and marketing, production and product development. The budget department will add instructions on forms to use, time limits to uphold and procedures to be followed. After that, the real budgeting starts in all units.

According to the instructions, all units should submit their budgets by the end of October. When these documents arrive, the budget department creates a revised profit budget for the group, to be presented to the budget committee. Normally, at this point, budgets for product development and central HQ staff are renegotiated and then confirmed.

Budgets for sales and production, however, are normally not yet acceptable. After production budgets reach the sales departments, all these units need to renew their discussions in a final effort to reach the profit goals of the budget committee. The outcome of this final round is communicated to HQ towards the end of November.

In a late November meeting, the budget committee accepts and confirms most divisional budgets. However, if some divisions still are not good enough, there will still be time for a final revision before the board meets to confirm the final budget just before Christmas.

Comments on the budget processes

Company A

The budget process in Company A actually starts with long-term planning. You don't see this kind of planning as often nowadays as a number of years ago. But in some cases it appears to be needed and this is such a case. The procedure is illustrated in Figure 1.11.

This kind of budgeting is quite close to what theoretical books call 'break-down budgeting'. The planning process originates at the higher levels of the company and planning documents are broken down in several steps, from the budget committee at the top of the diagram to departments inside divisions at the bottom. This planning process is repeated twice, first for the long-term budget and then for the regular annual budget.

In fact, there is an explanation for the design of this budgeting process in the industrial setting of the company in the first paragraph of the budget description, in relation to the long-term budget. There we can see that major investments are discussed in the budget committee, probably because such projects are so important and so expensive for the entire company that they have to be agreed upon and allotted between divisions at a very early stage. This characteristic could be the reason for having a long-term budget.

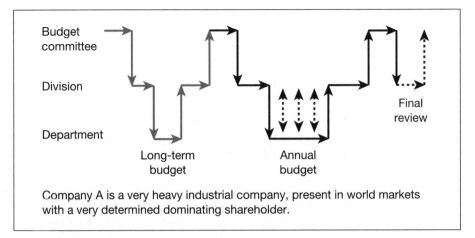

Company A is a very heavy industrial company, present in world markets with a very determined dominating shareholder.

Figure 1.11 Budgeting in Company A

Such a situation indicates that centrally made decisions are very important for the company. This is also why the breakdown budgeting routine is acceptable to managers and employees in the divisions. They know that the big investments and the overall production plan dominate, and therefore have to dominate the planning process. In such a case, breakdown budgeting is normally widely accepted and works reasonably well.

An industrial entrepreneur, Rune Brandinger, once showed me an earlier version of Figure 1.12 in order to explain why companies plan in different ways. On the horizontal axis there is the certainty of forecasting and on the vertical axis there is flexibility in the working situation. The diagram indicates, fairly obviously, that companies in the lower right will need a long-term plan. If you work in an industry

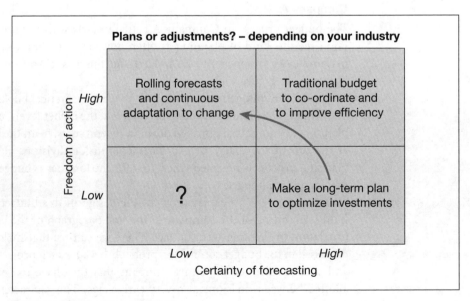

Figure 1.12 Planning methods

where forecasts can be made with reasonable certainty and your daily flexibility is low, clearly you will need a long-term plan.

There are many industries in this situation, e.g. mining and steel industries, forest industries of several kinds, railroads and electricity generation. They are all tied to their equipment and cannot be easily transformed into something else. Therefore, their flexibility is low. Luckily, in many of these cases, certainty of forecasting is quite high, and therefore a long-term plan to optimize investment projects will normally be a rewarding procedure.

But things change over time. Traditional telephone companies used to be found in this corner, but the industry started to move away from that position with the arrival of mobile telephone systems.

In fact, many industries used to sit in this corner, but technical improvements have increased their flexibility of action and decreased the certainty of forecasting at the same time. In recent years, a lot of industries have been moving toward the upper left (as shown by the arrow). Some of them are now in the upper right-hand corner and some have moved all the way to the upper left.

As has already been mentioned, one of the main features of the design of the planning process in Company A is the breakdown approach. This is a dangerous approach, because it can easily alienate certain managers, leaning them feeling they are not being listened to. On the other hand, it is a very good planning process if the main marketing and technical knowledge is to be found in the budget committee rather than in the divisions or departments. This is quite often the case in companies with very heavy technical structures and very expensive production equipment.

If central units are better informed than divisions or departments and everybody understands this and agrees to it, then the breakdown budget may actually work quite well.

Another interesting feature of this budgetary process is the final revision of the budget. This can be done mainly because there is a very strong owner (either a single owner or a dominating shareholder) who demands a good return on the money invested.

Company A exemplifies an unusually efficient breakdown process.

Company B

At first sight, the planning process in Company B might look fairly similar to that of company A. But after studying it more carefully you will see that it is not.

First, there is only one annual planning process and, consequently, there is no long-term budget. Of course, there could be long-term planning at HQ, but there is not a common long-term planning process as there was in Company A.

Secondly, this is a build-up instead of a breakdown process. There is an initial discussion between the CEO and all division heads leading to a set of basic assumptions and instructions. In Figure 1.13 these discussions are indicated by dotted arrows on the left of the diagram. During this process, the CEO meets personally with all division heads in order to make clear what is expected of every division and how those expectations can be met. After that initial planning process, build-up budgeting starts in the departments within divisions.

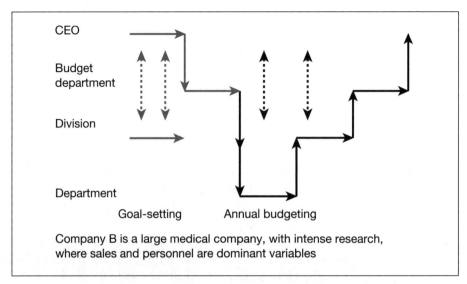

Company B is a large medical company, with intense research, where sales and personnel are dominant variables

Figure 1.13 Budgeting in Company B

When I had the opportunity to interview the CEO, he emphasized the importance of the initial planning process. It takes him a long time, but he meets with all division heads and tries to make sure that all parties understand each other.

The third interesting point in Company B is indicated by the dotted arrows in the middle of the diagram. This is an unusual feature that originates in the budget department. The staff of the budget department will follow the work of divisions and departments very closely in order to have an advance picture of the likely future budget. Then, if there is a deviation from what is expected they will inform the CEO and, if needed, take action long before the budget is formally presented to the budget department.

Clearly, this company operates in an industry in the top-right corner of Figure 1.12. Forecasts are not as reliable as in Company A, but they are still there. They form one of the foundations of the discussion between the CEO and the division heads at the beginning of the planning process. Flexibility, on the other hand, is much greater here. Research goes on all the time and the company can easily switch between products if there are changing needs in the market. The CEO has a very strong personal influence. This company is quoted on the stock exchanges in several countries and there is not one single dominating owner.

Company B exemplifies a very efficient build-up process.

Company C

In Company C they start in quite an unstructured way. There are no budget instructions, but still the budgeting process for the following year starts in the summer, which is very early. We are now in the top left-hand corner of Figure 1.12. Here there are no reliable long-term forecasts at all. On the contrary, every year they need to understand what is happening in the markets and in technical development. Therefore the process will now look like Figure 1.14.

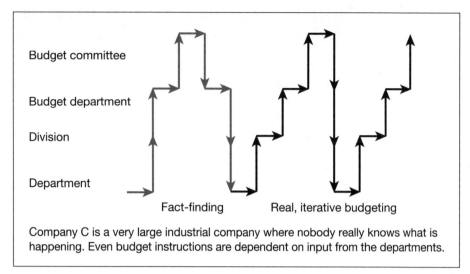

Budget committee

Budget department

Division

Department

Fact-finding   Real, iterative budgeting

Company C is a very large industrial company where nobody really knows what is happening. Even budget instructions are dependent on input from the departments.

Figure 1.14 Budgeting in Company C

In this new situation, the central units do not want to give out any instructions at an early stage. They want to collect information and, after pondering it, give instructions as to the continuation of the budgeting process. This is why there is a fact-finding phase before the real budgeting starts in the fall.

When the real budgeting starts, there is a very clear build-up process. But as the company is so big, and the environment changes all the time, nobody expects the first budget to fulfill everyone's needs. There are so many divisions and departments that need information or components from each other that complete budget instructions cannot be finalized until the first round of budgeting has already been done. Therefore, the budgeting process becomes iterative, meaning that it has to be done several times over, the divisions successively adjusting to each other's needs.

This company has a fascinating history. Now and then it has been extremely successful. But at other times is has been very close to bankruptcy. Market changes and technical changes just come too quickly! In fact, what is portrayed here may not be the optimum solution for a company in the top left corner of Figure 1.12. Their iterative budget is an attempt to achieve continuous adaptation to change. But the solution might instead be found among the techniques of truly rolling forecasts. The next case is an example on that very theme.

1.8 Worldwide Group, Inc.

In companies that need to continually adapt to change (see Figure 1.12 in Case 1.7), the decision is sometimes taken to introduce rolling forecasts. Several Scandinavian companies were among the first ones to make a serious attempt at this. This case describes the reasons behind the change from a traditional budget to rolling forecasts in a large company with its headquarters in Scandinavia and subsidiaries in many European countries.

There are two documents describing the change. The first (Document 1) was issued at group HQ and sent to all regional companies fairly unexpectedly. The second (Document 2) was produced by a regional subsidiary after receiving the directives from HQ. The documents are unedited and the company will remain anonymous. Please read the documents and consider the following issues:

1 Find the most important criticism against budgeting.

2 Describe the new system of rolling forecasts. State both strong and weak points. Do you think that the new system will improve management control at the Worldwide Group?

3 What would you like to do in your own organization? Are you going to change your planning system in the near future?

Document 1 (issued by Worldwide Group HQ)

Budget to be replaced by rolling forecasts

Group HQ has decided to discontinue group budgeting. Future budgets will be replaced by 12-month forecasts to be compiled every quarter. The reasons for this decision can be found in the next section.

In the future, rolling forecasts will be presented according to the following plan:

March 29	forecast covering	April–March
June 28		July–June
Sept 30		Oct–Sept
Dec 20		Jan–Dec

During the changeover period the following intermediate forecasts will be compiled:

Oct 26	forecast covering	this calendar year
Nov 06	forecast covering	next calendar year

All forecasts should be specified by month. In each quarter the forecast should be supplemented by comments on the following issues:

• Market development (volumes, prices, and competition)

• Cost development (wages and raw materials)

• Planned investments or other major changes in plant, market or organization

• Margin development and capital balances.

The Group Accounting Department will supply forecasts of currency quotations and prices of raw materials. Revised forms and instructions will be sent out by the end of August.

Signed at HQ in early August

Worldwide Group Controller

▶

Our planning process – living without a budget

Our new planning system starts with strategic planning, defining the general ideas of our business activities. A good period for strategic planning might be 3–10 years, depending on the type of business of individual companies. After a thorough evaluation, the strategic plan should describe the main goods to be produced and the marketing channels that have been selected.

In the next step of the planning process, we need to describe how to find and how to deploy the resources needed to reach those goals and to optimize economic outcome. This is what the budget used to do.

The budgetary process is in essence a long and slow procedure, which is normally overtaken by reality relatively soon. When we designed it, it was a great deed just to produce a consistent budget once a year, even if the content was trivial.

Today there are technical possibilities to plan and to report much quicker. Therefore, a tool that is quicker and better adapted to its purpose should replace the budget.

- *Profit forecasting* will improve if all forecasts are made rolling.

- *Goals of income and cost* can be reviewed in the light of the latest forecast.

- *Capital investment* planning will be based on the strategic plan together with a separate analysis for each project.

- *Production planning*, based on rolling forecasts, will be processed by specialized production planning models.

Our ongoing project, 'Quicker reporting', will lead to systems that are more efficient and to real-time updating of databases. Monthly reporting will follow automatically, and will resemble annual reporting. Decisions based on accounting information can be made immediately.

If necessary, resources for analyses and projects will be made available. Faster information will improve control.

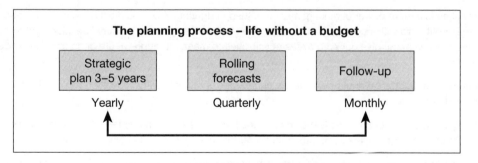

Document 2 (issued by Worldwide Subsidiary)

This company has decided to abolish budgeting starting this fall. At the managers' meeting, we stated the following motives.

1. Budgetary experience

All experience shows that the budget will hold only if things keep going as they used to. On too many occasions, budgeting was just prolonging trends anyway. It is difficult to forecast major changes.

2. The budget as a goal

We used to strive to reach the budget. However, circumstances can change during the year. If that happens it might be wrong to evaluate outcomes by comparison with the budget.

Striving for the budget can be devastating if circumstances change. If orders increase or decrease, the production budget quickly becomes outdated. In addition, if there is a change in competition locally, we do not want to delay appropriate reactions just because they were not in the budget.

3. Aims of budgeting

Budgeting was used to create a starting-point for *profit forecasts*. However, nowadays we can produce those forecasts in a much easier way. In addition, profit forecasts should be improved upon all the time.

Another purpose of the budget was to *influence managerial behavior*. Today, we can do so much more easily by accounting and statistical reports. Everybody should act immediately when needs arise. Do not wait for the next budget! There will not be any!

The budget was supposed to be a tool to *create and conserve central power*. However, using the build-up budgeting method, we do not have that tool any longer anyway!

Through budgeting, you can try to *create participation* in managerial decision-making. We can handle that participation through a far-reaching delegation of power and by working with local profit-centers. Therefore we don't need the budget for this purpose.

Accounting is a more powerful management tool than budgeting. We should tell our employees about our real profit. This will encourage involvement. We shall also emphasize personal development through training programs that give our employees possibilities to meet, although we are geographically widely spread out.

Another aim of budgeting could be to *define boundaries of responsibility*. However, this can be done in other and better ways.

It is very dangerous if employees feel safe once the budget has been accepted. Real safety can be obtained only through our ability to continuously adapt ourselves to a changing environment.

The budgetary process has been a good thing because *it made people understand* our profit reports and the economic consequences of various actions. Therefore we shall continue to improve employee understanding of our reports.

Some people say that everybody involved knows the budget and therefore it can be used as a benchmark for gauging the real outcome. This is not true. Many people feel uncertain of the content of the budget. However, everybody knows what happened last year. We would be better to compare reality with reality!

▶

4. Why no budget?

We know that the budget always follows historical trends. Therefore, if these trends are right, budgeting is a trivial way to consume time and resources. In addition, if the trends turn out to be wrong, it would be dangerous to try to reach the goals of the budget.

The budgetary process is so long and so slow that the budget will soon be too dated to be useful. It was developed before PCs at a time when it was a feat just to create a complete budget document.

5. Working without a budget – controlling by accounting numbers

An important prerequisite for working without a budget is a profit centre organization. For each profit centre, we can measure income and compare it with cost. It is also important for profit reporting to portray correctly the area that each manager can influence. Therefore, our accounts should never contain common costs. Profit goals should be set so high that they will cover these costs.

Our goals should be accounting numbers to be compared with other units (districts, regions, and competitors) and with earlier outcomes for the same unit.

Working without a budget does not mean fewer follow-ups. We shall follow up all reports regularly to see what measures need to be taken. The time we used to spend making a budget in the fall can be used for these discussions.

From now on, a year could be any period of 12 months. The calendar year will be used only for external purposes, i.e. for tax reasons and for our public annual report. Internal accumulated numbers will always show a 12-month period.

6. There will still be planning

Everybody must plan their projects carefully, including what to do, when to do it and who is to be in charge. Since projects seldom last exactly one year, this is another argument to get rid of the traditional one-year cycle.

7. Control and continuous adaptation

What are our goals? We intend to be number one! We have come a long way through our recent reforms. We have realized great cost reductions and we have focused the profit responsibility of local units.

Since we sell our goods and services in strong competition with others, price and quality must be as good as or better than theirs if we are to survive in the end. Therefore, our cost level must be below that of the competition.

A general goal for all managers: make as much money as possible and always more than the competition. That will make us number one! To realize this goal we need to observe the competition and markets carefully and to make appropriate changes whenever needed. We must act quickly and decisively.

Staff units should do a good job at lowest possible cost.

Signed at headquarters of one regional company in September

Regional Company Controller

Comments on the Worldwide case

■ Criticizing budgeting

There is a lot of criticism of traditional budgeting in this case. Personally, I would like to emphasize the following points:

■ *There is too much work and too many details in traditional budgets.* Even when you try to diminish the amount of work, there seem to be forces among employees that keep them going in the usual way. Many people feel that they have to find all the details before they can estimate totals.

■ *Appropriations are always spent!* There is definitely a tendency to treat budgeted amounts as appropriations, even in very profit-conscious private companies. Most employees try to do a very good job in their local environment. To some of them, a good job in the local activity means higher planning quality, but it does not necessarily mean lower costs.

Also, the year-ends are difficult points. If you know that under-spending this year will almost automatically lead to smaller appropriations next year, then you might feel that you need to make the money useful while it is there. Therefore you might prefer to spend it rather that saving it and losing it to other activities. If money could easily be moved from the last quarter of this year to the first quarter of next year, many employees might have a different approach to savings!

■ *Quarters and years are over-emphasized.* Most of us have heard of the big rush to show good results this year even if the activities to do so will make the starting point of next year somewhat more difficult. That tendency has spread into quarters in recent years, probably because of the strong emphasis on public quarterly reporting.

■ *Detailed inputs will quickly be outdated.* This point is especially valid in companies where the traditional budgeting process in the fall dominates the planning system. Planning once a year is just not good enough any more. It is not possible to make a budget this fall which is still useful next fall! Oh yes, I know they have quarterly forecasts to improve planning in the later part of the year. But those forecasts have a lower status than the original budget and they end at the year-end! Therefore, in October and November there is no plan at all for the next few quarters.

■ *Organization and decisions freeze.* The budget is a very strong force in the daily life of companies. Changing plans might be all but impossible because the new plans would contradict the budget. Changing the organization might be totally impossible because some of those people who would be affected will refer to the budget as an unchangeable document! These forces are most powerful when the budget has been decided by the board, and that is quite common.

■ *Forecasts are too simplified to be trustworthy for a long time.* We are always making forecasts, and typically those forecasts are wrong, especially at turning points in the economy when it is particularly important to identify what is happening.

Therefore it should be routine to make regular forecasts and also to dump the misinformation in the old ones as soon as possible. We also need to recognize the full consequences of the new forecasts during the ongoing year instead of waiting until they can be fully incorporated in a new budget.

■ The new system of rolling forecasts

To improve some of those weaknesses of budgeting we would need at least the following things:

- We need a shorter planning process to increase timeliness and save planning time.
- We need to plan more often to get closer to changes in reality.
- We need a better grasp of the immediate future and a discussion around the future.
- We need to create a planning process that is actually useful for everybody.

To achieve some of these things, the Worldwide Group adopted a system of rolling forecasts that is quite easy to manage. Plans are monthly and reporting is done monthly but new forecasts are only presented quarterly. The new design can be seen in Figure 1.15.

To make such a process efficient, you need to change people's habits away from the old budgeting routines in several respects. Here are some typical points to be remembered in relation to the design of rolling forecast systems:

- Rolling forecasts include only a limited number of planning variable. To be able to get through the whole planning process in a very short time, the Worldwide Group decided to work with a very limited number of variables.

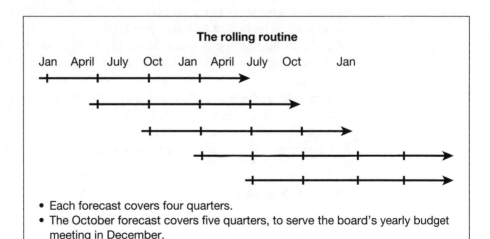

Figure 1.15 Worldwide Group's new system of rolling forecasts

■ First and foremost there needs to be a profit forecast wherever possible, and for every unit that can calculate a profit. When this is not possible, everybody calculates incomes and costs.

■ In addition, for all profit centers, comments are required on each of the following areas:
  – market development
  – sales development and margins
  – cost developments
  – planned investment.

■ Planning is done continuously all year round in local units. Therefore, there is not any real rush to get the forecast ready on time. You can do your part when you have time and when you have access to the material that is needed. Having your planning material on a PC facilitates this kind of thinking very much.

■ Planning documents are submitted at fixed points in time, normally monthly or quarterly.

■ The forecast always covers a certain number of months or quarters.

For this system to work well, managers will have to make decisions on their own in a somewhat more determined way than in the old budget system. When planning material is submitted, there won't be enough time to call a meeting to let everybody have their say. Instead, after receiving forecasts from your staff, you will have to add it up and pass it on to the next level and you will be accountable for whatever you passed on. This is a very different approach from traditional budgeting, where meetings have an important role and tend to delay the process quite a lot.

In the new situation, it will be possible, and almost necessary, to revise company goals quarterly instead of yearly. After all, when does your opinion of the future change? That's right, it changes continuously throughout the year. For technical reasons, we cannot revise company plans every day or week. But we can revise them every quarter. Please take a look at Figure 1.16.

Figure 1.16 illustrates how we start in one place and move towards a goal (goal 1). But after moving in this direction for a while (say, a quarter) circumstances change and we realize that goal 1 either is not good enough or perhaps can't even be reached. We therefore change to goal 2 and start moving our organization in a slightly different direction. After another quarter we make another change and so on. In normal times we can avoid sudden big changes by making small changes much more often. In this way, we do not ever get as far off course as we might with a regular budgeting system.

■ Follow up the future!

When working with rolling forecasts the whole attitude to follow-up and re-planning will change (see also Figure 1.17):

■ Since the first quarter is normally fairly correct, the discussion concerning the latest actual outcome will be less important.

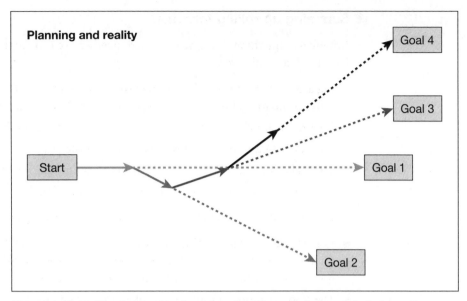

Figure 1.16 Rolling forecasts: changing direction regularly can help keep the organization from going too far off course

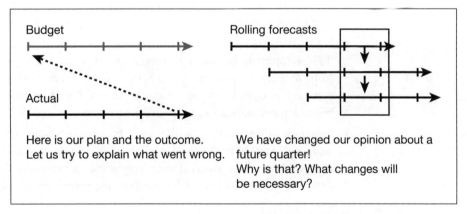

Figure 1.17 Difference in thinking between traditional budgeting and rolling forecasts

- Instead, the planning discussion will focus on changes for future quarters.
- The planning process will really deal with the future instead of looking back and having to defend previous mistakes.

Although this changing attitude to follow-up can be illustrated in a single diagram, it is still one of the most important innovations in rolling forecasts. If we can transform regular follow-up from merely explaining what has happened into a discussion of what to do about future plans, then we have really achieved something.

■ Summing up rolling forecasts

Bringing all the things we have discussed together, we can see that rolling forecasts have the following strengths:

■ They allow the traditional planning process to be speeded up considerably, with most of the formal planning taking a week instead of several months.

■ They allow much quicker adjustment to future changes in the environment.

■ They offer better foresight towards the end of the year.

■ They take account of the fact that the board cannot decide the future.

■ All told, planning will be more realistic using a rolling forecast system.

But there are drawbacks too, compared with traditional budgeting:

■ Very likely, the total planning workload will increase. The actual outcome depends on the particular company and its markets. But if total workload increases, that is probably because the planning situation is demanding.

■ The co-ordination of profit centers might weaken because there is not enough time during the formal planning process to co-ordinate as there is in the traditional system. Consequently, where co-ordination is necessary, that work will have to be done before the formal planning process.

■ The follow-up of past management decisions will be more difficult than with traditional budgeting.

■ Under-performing managers may remain undetected for some time. Scandinavians do not appear to be too concerned about this, but I have heard serious doubts from managers working in southern Europe. Clearly, when there are a lot of consecutive changes in the planning material instead of one large one, it might become more difficult to pinpoint the day when things really went wrong.

■ Demands on personalities will increase because you have to trust each other both ways. You have to trust your superior to really study your forecast before passing it on and you have to trust your subordinates not to exploit the possibilities with many little changes to deviate from the agreed goal. In some cultures these difficulties might be insurmountable.

Chapter 2

Product costing

2.1 Sporting Goods Co.

The Sporting Goods Co. produces and sells three kinds of well-known sports products, namely backpacks, tents and sleeping bags. To simplify our discussion in this case we shall assume that there is only one type of tent, one type of backpack and one type of sleeping bag. Sporting Goods is not a very large company, but there is a good deal of emphasis on profitability and there are regular board meetings every quarter.

■ The quarterly income statement

The accounts for the latest quarter, presented by the CFO, are shown in Figure 2.1. As can be seen, the total costs were greater than the total income. The difference was not in any way disastrous, but the company usually makes a profit and so the board members were naturally concerned about the situation. One was anxious to find out the reasons for the loss. 'What is the profitability for each of the products? Maybe most of the losses come from only one or two of the products?', he asked.

	€000		€000
Labor cost	3 200	Backpacks	2 100
Materials	4 400	Tents	4 400
Production overheads	3 200	Sleeping bags	5 300
General overheads	1 080		
Total cost	11 880	Total income	11 800

Figure 2.1 Sporting Goods' income statement for the latest quarter

The CFO was a little bit concerned, saying: 'Well, you see, we can easily identify labor costs and material for each of the products, but production overheads (for production premises and machinery) and general overheads (for office and administration) are not known for each product.'

The board member was not ready to give in so easily: 'I realize that, but I suppose you could allocate those costs to products in a normal way in order to find the full cost of each product. After that we could compare the full costs to the sales incomes and find out about profitability.'

A full cost statement

The CFO therefore went back to his numbers and produced a full cost statement as seen in Figure 2.2. 'Very good,' said the board member. 'Now we know that sleeping bags are money losers, let's have a discussion about what to do to solve the problem.'

But can we be sure they are right? In this statement of full cost, the CFO has identified the direct labor cost of each product, something that should be easy enough to calculate. Either workers are specialized on one of the products or they would have to write down how many hours they work on each of them. In both cases, the identification of direct labor would be easy.

Furthermore, the products use different materials and it should not be a problem to identify the direct cost of material. Even if they have some material in common, it should be easy to find out how much was used for each of the products.

But, of course, it is not obvious how to allocate production overheads and general overheads. The CFO took the easy way out and used the most common allocation algorithm of all. He allocated production overheads in proportion to direct labor. To do so, we need to compare total production overheads with direct labor. In this case they are the same (€3.4 million), which means that the overhead rate will be 100 percent.

	Packs	Tents	Sleeping bags
	€000	€000	€000
Direct labor	700	700	1 800
Direct material	400	2 000	2 000
Production overheads			
(on labor)	700	700	1 800
Manufacturing cost	1 800	3 400	5 600
General overheads	180	340	560
Full cost	1 980	3 740	6 160

Figure 2.2 Full cost statement by product types for the latest quarter

After finding the overhead rate, we simply apply it to each of the columns, allocating €700 000 to each of the first two products and €1.8 million to the sleeping bags, all in proportion to the well-known costs of direct labor.

Is this a good allocation algorithm? Well, it can be easily calculated because the cost of direct labor should be known by product anyway. Also, according to such an allocation we are quite certain that all production overheads get allocated to the products. After all, we do not really know if there is a more logical way to allocate production overheads. It is for these reasons this routine is the most common way of allocating production overheads all over the Western world!

So what about general overheads? If you look carefully, you will see that a similar rule has been applied: general overheads have been allocated in proportion to total manufacturing costs. More precisely general overheads amounts to 10 percent of manufacturing costs and have been allocated accordingly. Is that a better rule? Not necessarily, but it is even more common than the other one. At this level, there is virtually no other common way to allocate costs.

■ The accounting model of the CFO

In fact, when allocating costs in the way we just have described, the CFO was applying an accounting model that can be presented and challenged. Therefore, let us call it 'Accounting model 1'. You will find it in Figure 2.3.

According to this accounting model, products pass through the company from left to right. As soon as we start working with them we charge direct labor and direct material to them, because those items can be easily identified and they are well known. To keep the reader informed, we have shown these costs below each product box in the figure.

Next, we allocate production overhead in proportion to direct labor. This is because we have a big pool of production overhead and we do not know very much

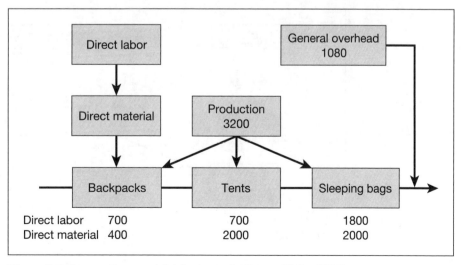

Figure 2.3 Accounting model 1 (one production unit) (in €000)

about it. Finally, at the far right of the figure, we allocated general overhead in proportion to total manufacturing costs.

■ Could there be another accounting model?

Yes, of course. If we look closer at the production process we might find that the tents and backpacks are made from very tough materials. Therefore, they need to be sewn with robust machinery. Sleeping bags, on the other hand, use very soft material and they have to be handled with care during the production process! Recognizing this, we might come up with a new accounting model. Have a look at Figure 2.4.

In the figure we can see that there are two production departments, one producing tents and backpacks and the other producing sleeping bags. We have found out that out of the original €3.2 million of production overheads, €2.4 million applies to Sewing department 1 and only €800 000 to Sewing department 2. Knowing this, of course, we shall allocate the costs of department 1 to packs and tents and those of Department 2 to sleeping bags.

In Department 1, recognizing that there are two types of product, we allocate costs according to direct labor. In Department 2, all costs will be allocated to sleeping bags. Now the cost statement will be revised. The new numbers are shown in Figure 2.5.

So, by studying the production process more carefully, we easily found a revised cost statement, which is probably more precise than the previous one. In this way we can see that the losses are not due to the sleeping bags. Now, it appears that the backpacks are the money losers!

In the cost statement of Figure 2.5 we applied the same costing logic as in Figure 2.2. We assumed that all costs should be allocated to products and that the allocation could be done on the basis of labor. But with more information about the production process, the outcome was very different.

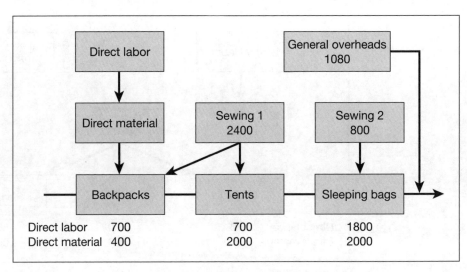

Figure 2.4 Accounting model 2 (identifying departments) (in €000)

	Backpacks	Tents	Sleeping bags
	€000	€000	€000
Direct labour	700	700	1 800
Direct material	400	2 000	2 000
Production overheads			
(on labour, by department)	1 200	1 200	800
Manufacturing cost	2 300	3 900	4 600
General overheads	230	390	460
Full cost	2 530	4 290	5 060
Backpacks are money losers!			

Figure 2.5 Full cost statement by Accounting model 2

What is more surprising, however, is that we appear to have changed our opinion on general overheads. Since those overheads are allocated in proportion to total manufacturing costs, they are also changing. Some of these costs have been moved from sleeping bags to backpacks and tents. The logic of this change is not very convincing, but it is an obvious consequence of the main rules of allocation.

Is this the end of the matter? Well, no it isn't. We can take another step. We could give up allocation on labor, and introduce machine-hours as a basis of allocation. Such a procedure will be more demanding but, again, it will be more precise. Look at Figure 2.6 to see how many machine-hours are used for each product.

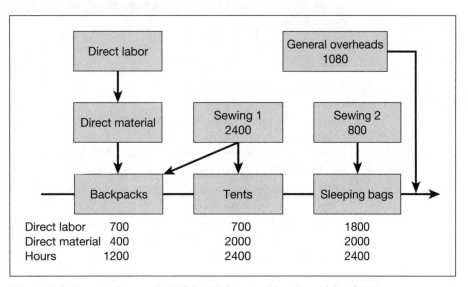

Figure 2.6 Accounting model 3 (identifying machine-hours) (in €000)

	Backpacks	Tents	Sleeping bags
	€000	€000	€000
Direct labor	700	700	1 800
Direct material	400	2 000	2 000
Production overheads			
(by machine-hours)	800	1 600	800
Manufacturing cost	1 900	4 300	4 600
General overheads	190	430	460
Full cost	2 090	4 730	5 060

Tents are money losers!

Figure 2.7 Full cost statement by Accounting model 3 (allocation by machine-hours)

According to the model in Figure 2.6, tents need twice as many machine-hours in Department 1 as backpacks. Knowing that, most of us would feel that it is reasonable to allocate the costs of the department accordingly. In Department 2 there will be no change, because all of those costs will still be allocated to the sleeping bags. Now, we can produce a third statement of full costs, which will look like Figure 2.7. Again, production overheads will be shared among the products. Also again, general overheads will adapt to the total manufacturing costs although we did not intend that to happen.

◼ The moral of full costing

The old philosophy called 'full costing' implies that all costs of the company should be allocated to the products. If we do not know any better, we allocate the costs according to labor time, or labor-hours. With more information we can allocate them according to machine-hours.

In both cases, general overheads are more difficult and tend to move around in proportion to total manufacturing costs.

Full costing is a very common philosophy in reality. At the schools of business we prefer activity-based costing (ABC) and we have difficulty understanding why full costing is still so common out there among companies! In later cases, of course, we shall study ABC very carefully, but we are not yet there. We have a few more traditional cases before we get to the solutions of really modern thinking.

2.2 Little Shop of Pants

At the Little Shop of Pants they make and sell four types of men's pants: superior, first class, regular, and economy. Every type is made in a fair assortment of sizes and colors, which are adjusted every year in response to the trends in society. They have never really worried about profitability, but recently Mr Carling, the CEO and one of the main owners, attended a management training program in Lausanne, Switzerland. There, he learned that you have to know your costs and so he asked the shop accountant to produce a summary statement, describing the profitability of each type of pants.

In Table 2.1 you will see the information Mr Carling received in response to his request. While he was quite happy with the overall situation, he felt that maybe it would be a good idea to get rid of those economy pants once and for all. When considering them, he felt that they did not really match his quality standards and now he could see that they did not even make a profit. So, maybe he felt, it would be a good thing to stop producing economy pants?

What do you think?

Table 2.1 Summary statement for Little Shop of Pants

	Superior €000	First class €000	Regular €000	Economy €000	Totals €000
Direct labor	210	300	240	150	900
Direct material	240	300	180	180	900
Other direct costs	300	300	180	120	900
Total direct costs	750	900	600	450	2 700
Allocated fixed costs	375	450	300	225	1 350
Full cost	1 125	1 350	900	675	4 050
Sales income	1 650	1 400	1 150	600	4 800
Total profit (loss)	525	50	250	−75	750

Solution: Little Shop of Pants

This case describes a very common situation in many mid-sized companies. In very small companies you go by your gut feeling and in large companies there are advanced accounting departments that can present economic facts in a better way than in this case. But before we look at a different model of presentation let us see where the given approach might lead us.

Suppose we accept the indications in Table 2.1 and decide to cease production and sales of economy pants. What will the situation look like now?

Before we really can tell, we will have to study Table 2.1 rather more carefully, noticing the following points:

- First there are three kinds of direct costs. Normally such costs will be variable in proportion to the volume of production. Let us assume this is the case here.

- After total direct costs there is a line showing allocated fixed costs, but we are not told how they are allocated. But looking carefully we can see that they appear to be allocated in proportion to the direct costs of each type of product. They appear to be 50 percent of the total direct costs. In fact, the most common allocation rule is in proportion to labor, but in a production like this one, allocation in proportion to total direct costs might be fairly reasonable. Let us accept the rule and go on from there.

- Finally, we notice that the profit per product type is given after full costs. This is a very reasonable statement, but still, somewhat later in the text, we shall have to criticize it. However, let us accept it for the moment.

Now, let us assume that the production of economy pants is discontinued, leaving only three types of pants. The direct costs will look the same as before for all three types, but the allocation of fixed costs will have to change. Following the same rule of allocation we shall now have to allocate all fixed costs, €1.35 million, to the three remaining types of pants. But while the remaining variable costs are lower than before, the fixed costs (land, buildings, machinery, and administration) would probably not have changed. Therefore fixed costs now amount to 60 percent of direct costs.

Organizing the remaining material in the same way as before, we can now summarize the information as in Table 2.2.

Table 2.2 Summary statement without economy pants

	Superior €000	First class €000	Regular €000	Totals €000
Direct labor	210	300	240	750
Direct material	240	300	180	720
Other direct costs	300	300	180	780
Total direct costs	750	900	600	2 250
Allocated fixed costs (60 percent)	450	540	360	1 350
Full cost	1 200	1 440	960	3 600
Sales income	1 650	1 400	1 150	4 200
Total profit (loss)	450	−40	190	600

Isn't that a strange outcome? We took away a product that made losses and the net profit of the company has become worse! Why is that?

This kind of thing happens because the full costing approach that we showed in those two tables is not very useful information for managerial decisions. When full costs are shown in this way, the tables give an impression that income and costs behave in the same way.

Of course, we can easily stop selling economy pants and the sales income will immediately disappear. But what will happen to the costs?

Direct costs are often proportional to the volume of production. Therefore those costs that occur because of the production of economy pants will quickly disappear.

But the fixed costs of land, buildings, machinery, and administration will not diminish until we make a decision to change them one way or another. Failing to make such a decision, we will probably have to live with the same fixed costs. In this case, following the same rule of allocation as before, the accountant will reallocate costs in such a way that all fixed costs are still allocated to one product or another. If there is no new information, the accountant will probably just raise the overhead rate from 50 to 60 percent, producing the outcome shown in Table 2.2.

The next step

What will happen next if everybody keeps acting in the same way as before?

Studying Table 2.2, we can see that first class pants now look unprofitable. Although we understand that it might not be a clever decision, let us see what happens if we now discontinue those. Doing so, we arrive at Table 2.3.

At this stage, we have all but destroyed the profitability of the Little Shop of Pants. Fixed costs have been reallocated again and now they amount to 100 percent of direct costs. In the analysis of Table 3 we make losses even on regular pants, which used to be so profitable. I shall leave it to the reader to investigate what happens if we now decide to discontinue regular pants and reallocate all costs to the superior model.

Table 2.3 Summary statement with first class pants discontinued

	Superior €000	Regular €000	Totals €000
Direct labor	210	240	450
Direct material	240	180	420
Other direct costs	300	180	480
Total direct costs	750	600	1 350
Allocated fixed costs (100 percent)	750	600	1 350
Full cost	1 500	1 200	2 700
Sales income	1 650	1 150	2 800
Total profit (loss)	150	–50	100

How to present the information?

Although the presentation in Table 2.1 is very common, it was not a good starting point for managerial analyses. In order to see more clearly what will happen if we change our range of brands, let us reorganize it as shown in Table 2.4.

Now, we have brought contribution into the table, and we can easily see that this is positive for all products. This means that it will not be profitable to discontinue a product unless we can also eliminate some part of the fixed costs. Since the contribution is €150 000 we would have to eliminate a similar amount of fixed costs in order to make it profitable to discontinue the economy pants.

Table 2.4 An improved format of presentation

	Superior €000	First class €000	Regular €000	Economy €000	Totals €000
Direct labor	210	300	240	150	900
Direct material	240	300	180	180	900
Other direct costs	300	300	180	120	900
Total direct costs	750	900	600	450	2 700
Sales income	1 650	1 400	1 150	600	4 800
Contribution per type	900	500	550	150	2 100
Allocated fixed costs	375	450	300	225	1 350
Full cost	1 125	1 350	900	675	4 050
Total profit (loss)	525	50	250	−75	750

◼ Could we find a more powerful analysis?

Yes, it is possible. Before we make any changes at all, let us assume that we investigate the company situation very carefully and find that fixed costs can be separated into two main pools:

Automatic sewing	€600 000
Administration	€750 000

Furthermore, we find that automatic sewing takes place in proportion to direct material according to Table 2.1 and that machine capacity is 12 000 hours. Right now, only 9000 hours are actually used for ongoing production and there are 3000 hours left idle. In the administration, managers feel that their efforts are proportional to the number of product types. They could probably take on another type without a rise in costs.

Since only 75 percent of the capacity in automatic sewing is actually used by the products, let us allocate that proportion, i.e. €450 000, in proportion to direct material. The remaining €150 000 will be allocated to idle time. In a similar way, let us allocate €600 000 of administration to the products and leave €150 000 as idle time. Introducing these measures we arrive at Table 2.5.

From this table we can see that there is a good reason to question the value of the economy pants. They are not profitable in the true sense of the word but they still give a contribution of €150 000. Therefore it might be worth giving them up if we could eliminate €150 000 of fixed costs or if we could use that production capacity for something else. However, with quite a lot of excess capacity already, it does not sound likely that the capacity is needed elsewhere. Therefore, from an accounting point of view, we shall conclude that it appears to be a good idea to find out if part of the fixed capacity could be eliminated. After that we would recommend that the decision-makers reconsider the economy pants. However, the loss is not very big and therefore it might also be possible that Mr Carling would like to retain the brand, mainly so he can offer a full line of products at various prices.

Table 2.5 Identifying idle time

	Superior €000	First class €000	Regular €000	Economy €000	Idle €000	Totals €000
Direct labor	210	300	240	150	0	900
Direct material	240	300	180	180	0	900
Other direct costs	300	300	180	120	0	900
Total direct costs	750	900	600	450	0	2 700
Sales income	1 650	1 400	1 150	600	0	4 800
Contribution per type	900	500	550	150	0	2 100
Automatic sewing	120	150	90	90	150	600
Administration	150	150	150	150	150	750
Total costs	1 020	1 200	840	690	300	4 050
Total profit (loss)	630	200	310	–90	–300	750

2.3 Electronic Parts Co.[1]

■ Part 1 – Traditional costing

The Electronic Parts Co. produces components of electronic equipment for several different purposes. In one area, the company is a supplier of one of the big international competitors in the telephone market. In this area the production consists of five similar components with characteristics according to Table 2.6.

Table 2.6 Basic product information

Component no.	Labor cost (€)	Materials cost (€)	Volume (units)
1	115	134	10 000
2	90	142	3 000
3	90	126	500
4	145	154	5 000
5	84	148	20 000

Component 4 is a luxury item to be used especially for those markets where buyers are willing to pay for extra details and extended flexibility. Component 3, on the other hand, was developed as a budget component for certain overseas markets where it is especially important to keep the price as low as possible.

General factory overheads consist of energy, depreciation, interest and maintenance of machinery, general factory maintenance including heating, rent, and indirect labour for production planning and development. These costs amount to €9.34 million.

According to the traditional product costing system of the Electronic Parts Co., general overheads are allocated to products as a percentage of labor costs.

[1] This case (but without a solution) has already been published in 'Accounting for Management Control' (Studentlitteratur, Lund, 2009), by the same writer. It is used with permission of Studentlitteratur.

As an initial step in analyzing Electronic Parts, the company's accountants were asked to calculate product costs in accordance with the traditional costing system.

■ Part 2 – Industrial activity-based costing (ABC)

After realizing that the overhead rate had been rising for a long time and was likely to continue doing so, company accountants decided to study the cost situation of the components department more carefully. They found that the work could be divided into the following activities:

- *preparations (P)* – to make sure the pieces are available and that technical quality is correct;
- *automatic mounting (A)* – where most of the pieces are put together by very efficient machinery;
- *manual mounting (M)* – a tedious process to handle those pieces that cannot be done automatically;
- *testing (T)* – to make sure that finished components work according to specifications.

Next, they identified the time needed to handle each component in each activity. This study produced Table 2.7. They also found total hours and total costs for the activities as given in Table 2.8. Testing, the final activity before delivery, handles the final checking of all the components. Therefore, this activity needs very expensive equipment, as can be understood from the table.

Table 2.7 Hours per product

Component	Preparations	Automatic	Manual	Testing
1	1 600	800	5 000	800
2	540	510	750	510
3	75	100	85	125
4	1 050	250	3 500	650
5	2 200	1 400	8 000	1 000

Table 2.8 Costs and processing time per activity

	Preparations	Automatic	Manual	Testing	Total
Hours	5 465	3 060	17 335	3 085	28 945
Overhead (€000)	1 115	1 417	2 627	3 371	8 530

Accountants also discovered that part of the working time of factory management was spent on production planning when new orders were received. Total order cost amounted to €605 000. In order to allocate the order cost, the accountants investigated the number of orders for each component and found the numbers in Table 2.9.

Table 2.9 Number of orders per component per year

Component	1	2	3	4	5
Number of orders per year	20	20	10	20	25

Finally, the accountants found that a certain amount of management time was spent on the general maintenance of the knowledge of the components, the upkeep of instructions and lists of materials needed for each component. They felt that each of the five components produced should carry an equal share of these costs, which amounted to €205 000. They set out to:

■ find the cost of each component considering all the information they had discovered;

■ assess the managerial consequences of the second cost study.

■ Part 3 – Full ABC

After the second study was completed, the accountants realized that there was a lot of unused capacity in several of the activities. While there was no agreement about what to do with the numbers, they found that total capacities for each of the activities were available in accordance with Table 2.10. Also, the total capacity of the order section appeared to be 120 orders. The accountants needed to decide how to treat the new capacity numbers. If necessary, they would have to reconsider their calculations.

Table 2.10

Activity	Preparations (hours)	Automatic (hours)	Manual (hours)	Testing (hours)
Available capacity (hours)	5 600	4 800	17 400	6 000

Solution: Electronic Parts Co.

Note that a full ABC solution in Excel (without comments) is included at the end of this case for students who wish to perform the calculation is this way.

■ Traditional costing

To solve the case applying traditional full costing, we shall start by finding total costs of direct labor and direct materials (see Table 2.11).

After attributing the direct costs to the products, we now have to turn to the indirect costs. There is no information on how to allocate them between the products, probably because nobody really knows. According to the text, we are dealing with costs of energy, depreciation, interest and maintenance of machinery, general

Table 2.11 Total labor cost and total materials cost

	Volume	Direct labor/unit €	Total direct labor €	Direct materials/unit €	Total direct materials €
1	10 000	115	1 150 000	134	1 340 000
2	3 000	90	270 000	142	426 000
3	500	90	45 000	126	63 000
4	5 000	145	725 000	154	770 000
5	20 000	84	1 680 000	148	2 960 000
Total			3 870 000		5 559 000

factory maintenance including heating, rent, and indirect labor for production planning and development. If we did not expend some effort to write down exactly how this money was spent, there is probably no one who really knows where those costs belong.

If you do not really know how to deal with certain costs, a common way to handle them is allocating them on the basis of direct labor. In this case we can do so by finding out the total overhead costs from the text:

Fetch total overhead from text = 9 340 000

After that, we just need to find the relation between overhead costs and labour costs, by dividing one into the other:

Overhead rate = 9 340 000/3 870 000 = 2.4134

When looking at this number, we can see that total costs of overheads are much bigger than the total cost of labour. In the old days it was not usually like that. Direct labour used to be one of the largest cost items. Therefore many companies decided to allocate overheads to the products in proportion to their shares of direct labour. If we do this, the outcome will look like Table 2.12.

In Table 2.12 we found overhead costs per product by multiplying each entry in the direct labor column by the overhead rate (2.4134). There could be certain

Table 2.12 Total cost or each component and divide by volume to find full cost per unit

Component	Direct labor €000	Direct materials €000	Overheads €000	Total €000	Volume	Per unit €
1	1 150	1 340	2 775	5 265	10 000	527
2	270	426	652	1 348	3 000	449
3	45	63	109	217	500	433
4	725	770	1 750	3 245	5 000	649
5	1 680	2 960	4 055	8 695	20 000	435
Totals	3 870	5 559	9 340	18 769		

effects of rounding. After that we just added the costs of each product together to find total costs per product. Finally, we divided by their volumes to find the cost per unit of product according to the traditional cost accounting technique, full costing.

In full costing, you do not have to allocate overhead costs in proportion to labor. The essence is allocating all costs to the products in one way or another. But very many studies have shown that in the Western world, most industrial companies allocate overheads according to labor, probably because, traditionally, the costs of labor were carefully recorded anyway. Tradition is quite strong here. This is how it is done!

This approach to cost accounting is not a good one. The allocation does not give us any new information. Products with low costs of labor will, apart from the cost of material, remain low-cost products! But some products may need advanced machinery to a greater extent than other products. Such a difference between products could never be shown by this kind of analysis. Instead we would need to know much more about the character of the production activities. And that is exactly where to go from here.

▇ Industrial ABC

When the theory of ABC-costing appeared in the 1990s, many industrial producers had already understood the implications of the previous paragraph. Their accountants knew that allocating in proportion to labor was an easy way out of the cost allocation problem, but they also knew that it was not a very precise method. Therefore, when it was suggested to allocate in proportion to activities going on in the company, they readily accepted the new idea. After all, it was not that new, and you can find allocation according to activities in some of the old full costing methods. But let us start with direct labor (DL) and direct materials (DM) in Table 2.13.

Table 2.13 Fetch total DL and DM from the full cost analysis

Component	DL €000	DM €000	Volumes €000
1	1 150	1 340	10 000
2	270	426	3 000
3	45	63	500
4	725	770	5 000
5	1 680	2 960	20 000
Total	3 870	5 559	

These are some of the original numbers of the case. We will need them when we proceed to summing up the total costs. But first, we are going to find the costs of overheads per activity. Please see Table 2.14 (P, A, M, T are as defined on page 58).

Table 2.14 Use hours and overhead per activity from text to calculate cost per hour

	P	A	M	T	Total
Hours	5 465	3 060	17 335	3 085	xxx
Overheads (€000)	1 115	1 417	2 627	3 371	8 530
€/hour	204.03	463.07	151.54	1 092.71	

In this calculation it is important to observe that total overhead costs are given in thousands of euros in the original text. Here, after the calculation, all numbers are expressed in €/hour. Next, we need to remember how products are using those hours (Table 2.15).

Table 2.15 Hours per unit per activity

Component	P	A	M	T
1	1 600	800	5 000	800
2	540	510	750	510
3	75	100	85	125
4	1 050	250	3 500	650
5	2 200	1 400	8 000	1 000

Now we need to combine Tables 2.14 and 2.15 to find cost per unit of product. For each cell in Table 2.14 we multiply by the appropriate cost per hour from Table 2.15. For example, preparations for component 1 (top left corner) cost:

$$204.3 \times 1600 = 326.4$$

After performing such calculations for all cells in Table 2.15, we find Table 2.16 showing total activity cost for each product.

Table 2.16 Assign costs from activities to calculate total costs per component

Component	P	A	M	T	Total	Volumes	Per unit
1	326.4	370.5	757.7	874.2	2 328.8	10 000	233
2	110.2	236.2	113.7	557.3	1 017.3	3 000	339
3	15.3	46.3	12.9	136.6	211.1	500	422
4	214.2	115.8	530.4	710.3	1 570.7	5 000	314
5	448.9	648.3	1 212.3	1 092.7	3 402.2	20 000	170
Total activity cost					8 530.0		

Now we have handled all the normal activities, allocating their costs per unit of product according to how much time each product needs from every activity. If you compare the numbers, please note that most of these costs are machine costs, not costs of labor. But there could also be some costs of indirect labor, i.e. foremen or experts who are not working explicitly with each unit of product. All regular working time was, as you might remember, included in the first section, dealing with direct labor and direct material.

Before going on, we might also note that the most expensive product in the activity analysis appears to be component 3, the budget product. Actually this is not very surprising, because production volumes are so low that just getting the equipment ready for a series of products will probably influence the total working time quite a lot. This is an important point that was not shown at all in the traditional labor-based full cost analysis.

We still have not dealt with all the costs. The next item will be order costs. According to the text, there were 95 orders to share €605 000 of order costs. Table 2.17 shows this.

Table 2.17 Order cost per order and component

Order cost (€)	Orders	Cost per order (€)
605 000	95	6 368

Component	No of orders	Total order cost (€000)
1	20	127
2	20	127
3	10	64
4	20	127
5	25	159
Total	95	605

Finally, there is the general product cost that was left over. But, knowing that all products have to be designed and budgeted for and entered on to the company price list and costing system, it appears that the accountants wanted to let all components share these costs equally, just because they are there. Table 2.18 shows the outcome. Finally, we have to add all the costs together in our industrial ABC analysis (see Table 2.19).

Table 2.18 General product cost per component

Cost (€)	Components	Cost per component (€)
205 000	5	41 000

Table 2.19 Add ABC costs together

Component	DL €000	DM €000	Activities €000	Orders €000	General €000	Total €000	Per unit €
1	1 150	1 340	2 329	127	41	4 987	499
2	270	426	1 017	127	41	1 882	627
3	45	63	211	64	41	424	848
4	725	770	1 571	127	41	3 234	647
5	1 680	2 960	3 402	159	41	8 242	412
Totals	3 870	5 559	8 530	605	205	18 769	

Studying Table 2.19 we can see that cost numbers have changed a lot. You will easily see there are important changes in cost per unit compared with Table 2.12. Components 2 and 3 have become much more expensive. Components 1 and 5 have become somewhat cheaper. But the unit cost does not show the whole truth. In fact, it looks like the average cost per unit might have increased, and this is actually not the case. That impression occurs because the products with small volumes have become more expensive and the products with large volumes have become cheaper.

If you compare the total costs per component, instead of unit costs, you will see that the most important change has occurred in components 2 and 5 but not in component 3. The total costs (€000) of component 2 have increased by:

$$1882 - 1348 = 536.$$

This is a much bigger change than in any other product. On the other hand, the total costs (€000) of component 5 have decreased by:

$$8695 - 8242 = 453.$$

Those two changes are probably more important for the company than the increase in the unit cost of component 3. Especially in a competitive situation it is important to know that the cost of component 5 is much lower than we thought. If there is intense price-cutting going on in the market, it will be good to know that they can stay in business with their biggest product for longer than we used to think!

But how long can they stay in business if prices fall? For an example, let us look at component 5. If prices were to fall, we now know that they can follow competitors down beyond €435 (Table 2.12) to €412 (Table 2.19). But beyond that, what?

Well, here is one of the problems with our analysis so far. Everybody used to cost analysis according to the full cost method in Table 2.4 knows that the full cost is not a price limit. Since there are allocated fixed costs, it might be a good idea to stay in the market and to sell the product even if the market price falls below €434. Now we know that the firm can follow the price leader at least down to €412. But what then? Could they go down further, if necessary?

Yes, they could, because there might still be fixed costs influencing the calculations. But we do not know the true limit. We need to do some more thinking!

■ Full ABC

At this point, I have to admit to the reader that I have not told the whole truth about this case. There is a story behind it, and now we need to know the story.

Actually I was invited to the Electronic Parts Co. when the above results were to be presented at a manager's meeting. I was sitting at the front, on the right, listening to the young controller who had performed the study in the little company. Beside me sat the chief accountant of the group to which the company belonged, a somewhat elderly, extremely senior person in accounting. We were enjoying the presentation at the beginning, and it was obvious that the controller felt very happy about his findings.

After a while, however, my bench-buddy became uneasy. He was a very determined man and suddenly he took over the whole session and sent the young controller back to his seat: 'Thank you very much, young man. Please sit down! Now, these were some very interesting results! But please, everybody, remember to take responsibility as managers of this company. You see, these numbers may never be known outside this room! Look at those unit costs of component 3! Costs are €848 instead of €433! What do you think our salesmen will do when they learn about that?'

'Actually, I don't even need to ask. Everybody understands that they might stop selling component 3 because they cannot raise the price that much. And then, please look at those order costs in Table 2.17! If they stop selling component 3 there will be only 85 orders instead of 95 and the order costs of all other products will rise. Our volumes will fall and unit costs will balloon. This is a potential disaster for the company!'

Of course, everybody was upset. After all, it was quite a dramatic message and it came from a very influential source. But what did the man say? He said that if one product is discontinued, then the other products will become more expensive. But that is not true. If one product is discontinued, then there will be more unused capacity, but that does not make the other products more expensive. It just raises the cost of unused capacity.

However, if someone decides to allocate the costs of unused capacity to the products, it appears he might be right. That is what they do in traditional full costing and that is why traditional full costing is so dangerous. Unused capacity is a cost to the company, but it is not a cost in terms of the products. Therefore we have to start anew to rework the calculation to eliminate unused capacity altogether. This will give us real ABC.

First, we shall pick up the costs of DL and DM, just as we did in the industrial ABC.

After that, we need to rework the costs of the activities, allocating costs to all available hours instead of just looking at those hours that were actually serving products (see Table 2.20 and remember Table 2.10).

Table 2.20 Available hours per activity

	P	A	M	T	Total
Available hours	5 600	4 800	17 400	6 000	xxx
Overhead cost (€000)	1 115	1 417	2 627	3 371	8 530
€/unit	199.11	295.21	150.98	561.83	

Now the costs per hour are much lower than before. Here we allocate all costs to all available hours irrespective of how those hours are being used. Each product should pay for the the time spent on it, no matter how much time is not spent on it.

Next, bring back the table of hours used (Table 2.21). Combining Tables 2.20 and 2.21 we get a very different allocation of activity costs (Table 2.22).

Table 2.21 Hours per unit per activity

	P	A	M	T
1	1 600	800	5 000	800
2	540	510	750	510
3	75	100	85	125
4	1 050	250	3 500	650
5	2 200	1 400	8 000	1 000

Table 2.22 Assign costs from activities to products and calculate cost per unit and totals per component

Component	P	A	M	T	Total	Volumes	Per unit
1	319	236	755	449	1 759	10 000	176
2	108	151	113	287	658	3 000	219
3	15	30	13	70	128	500	255
4	209	74	528	365	1 176	5 000	235
5	438	413	1 208	562	2 621	20 000	131

Allocated activity cost		6 342
Cost of unused capacity		2 188
Total costs		8 530

In Table 2.22 we have identified the true activity costs of components and also the true costs of unused capacity. We can see that there is a considerable cost for unused capacity which has been messing up our calculations. Now we are almost finished. We need only make a similar adjustment to the order costs and to add the general product cost (Table 2.23).

Table 2.23 Find order cost per order and component, considering total order capacity

Order cost (€)	Capacity	Cost per order (€)
605 000	120	5 042

Component	No of orders	Total order cost (€000)
1	20	101
2	20	101
3	10	50
4	20	101
5	25	126
Allocated costs	95	479
Costs of unused capacity		126
Total costs		605

Note that in Table 2.23 part of the order cost was allocated to unused capacity and only the cost of active hours was allocated to the actual orders. But in the final section, general product cost per component, there is no information about unused capacity. Therefore these costs will again be fully allocated to products. They are shown in Table 2.24.

Table 2.24 General product cost per component

Cost (€)	Component	Cost per component (€)
205 000	5	41 000

Finally, adding all costs of full ABC together, we get the allocation in Table 2.25.

Table 2.25 Add ABC costs together

Component	DL €000	DM €000	Activities €000	Orders €000	General €000	Total €000	Per unit €
1	1 150	1 340	1 759	101	41	4 391	439
2	270	426	658	101	41	1 496	499
3	45	63	128	50	41	327	654
4	725	770	1 176	101	41	2 813	563
5	1 680	2 960	2 621	126	41	7 428	371
Totals	3 870	5 559	6 342	479	205	16 455	
Idle capacity	0	0	2 188	126	0	2 314	
Total costs	3 870	5 559	8 530	605	205	18 769	

When comparing the results of the three calculations, you will find that the full ABC allocation is, on average, lower than the others. Here, costs of idle capacity are not allocated to the products as in the two other models. Because of that we get a much more realistic picture of the true production costs of each product. If a product does not cover its costs in this situation there is a good reason to consider discontinuing that product, unless the lack of profitability is thought to be temporary. This is not the case in either of the two first approaches to costing.

When I lecture on these things and present this solution to experienced managers, they often have difficulties. Almost always someone will say something like: 'Your calculation is wrong because you did not allocate all costs to the products.'

A question like this is quite worrying because it shows that there is some kind of *a priori* assumption that all costs have to be allocated to products. To me it is obvious that the cost of products should comprise the cost of those resources that are consumed in producing the products. On the other hand, the cost of those resources that are not consumed by products will have to be allocated to something else. Otherwise they will just make us confused and, on the whole, inflate our opinion of the cost of the products.

Excel Solution (Full ABC only)

Electronic Parts Co.: Complete ABC

1. Fetch total DL and DM from full cost analysis

Comp	DL	DM	Volumes
1	1 150	1 340	10 000
2	270	426	3 000
3	45	63	500
4	725	770	5 000
5	1 680	2 960	20 000
Total	3 870	5 559	

Be prepared to use these numbers in item 7 below.

2. Use total available hours and overhead per activity from text to calculate cost per available hour

	P	A	M	T	Total
Available hours	5 600	4 800	17 400	6 000	xxx
Overhead cost	1 115	1 417	2 627	3 371	8 530
Cost/unit	199.11	295.21	150.98	561.83	

Please, be prepared to use this information in item 4 below.

Please observe that some overhead costs were not attributed to any particular activity.

3. Use table of hours per unit per activity from text

	P	A	M	T
1	1 600	800	5 000	800
2	540	510	750	510
3	75	100	85	125
4	1 050	250	3 500	650
5	2 200	1 400	8 000	1 000

4. Assign costs from activities to products and calculate cost per unit and totals per component

Comp	P	A	M	T	Total	Volumes	Per unit
1	319	236	755	449	1 759	10 000	176
2	108	151	113	287	658	3 000	219
3	15	30	13	70	128	500	255
4	209	74	528	365	1 176	5 000	235
5	438	413	1 208	562	2 621	20 000	131

Activity cost	6 342
Cost of unused capacity	2 188
Total costs	8 530

5. Find order cost per order and component, considering total order capacity

	Order Cost	Capacity	Cost per order
	605 000	120	5 042

Comp	No of orders	Total order cost (000)
1	20	101
2	20	101
3	10	50
4	20	101
5	25	126
Allocated costs	95	479
Costs of unused capacity		126
Total costs		605

Please note that part of the order cost was not allocated to orders performed.

6. Find general product cost per component

Cost	Components	Cost per component
205 000	5	41 000

7. Add ABC costs together

	DL	DM	Activities	Orders	General	Total	Per unit
1	1 150	1 340	1 759	101	41	4 391	**439**
2	270	426	658	101	41	1 496	**499**
3	45	63	128	50	41	327	**654**
4	725	770	1 176	101	41	2 813	**563**
5	1 680	2 960	2 621	126	41	7 428	**371**
Totals	3 870	5 559	6 342	479	205	16 455	
Idle capacity	0	0	2 188	126	0	2 314	
Total costs	3 870	5 559	8 530	605	205	18 769	

Electronic Parts Co.: final comparison

1. Full costing

Comp	DL	DM	OH	Total	Volume	Per unit
1	1 150	1 340	2 775	5 265	10 000	**527**
2	270	426	652	1 348	3 000	**449**
3	45	63	109	217	500	**433**
4	725	770	1 750	3 245	5 000	**649**
5	1 680	2 960	4 055	8 695	20 000	**435**
Totals	3 870	5 559	9 340	18 769		

2. Industrial ABC

Comp	DL	DM	P	A	M	T	Orders	General	Total	Per unit
					Activities					
1	1 150	1 340	326	370	758	874	127	41	4 987	**499**
2	270	426	110	236	114	557	127	41	1 882	**627**
3	45	63	15	46	13	137	64	41	424	**848**
4	725	770	214	116	530	710	127	41	3 234	**647**
5	1 680	2 960	449	648	1 212	1 093	159	41	8 242	**412**
Totals	3 870	5 559	1 115	1 417	2 627	3 371	605	205	18 769	

3. Full ABC

Comp	DL	DM	P	A	M	T	Orders	General	Total	Per unit
					Activities					
1	1 150	1 340	319	236	755	449	101	41	4 391	**439**
2	270	426	108	151	113	287	101	41	1 496	**499**
3	45	63	15	30	13	70	50	41	327	**654**
4	725	770	209	74	528	365	101	41	2 813	**563**
5	1 680	2 960	438	413	1 208	562	126	41	7 428	**371**
Totals	3 870	5 559	1 088	903	2 617	1 733	479	205	16 455	
Idle	0	0	27	514	10	1 638	126	0	2 314	

2.4 Cost Accounting in Healthcare[2]

This case describes cost accounting in an independent non-profit full-service renal dialysis clinic. The clinic provides two types of treatment. Haemodialysis (HD) requires patients to visit a dialysis clinic three times a week, where they are connected to a special, expensive equipment to perform the dialysis. Peritoneal dialysis (PD) allows patients to administer their own treatment daily at home. The clinic monitors PD patients and assists them in ordering supplies consumed during the home treatment. The total and product-line income statement for the clinic is shown in Table 2.26.

Table 2.26 Clinic income statement

	Total	HD	PD
Revenues			
Number of patients	164	102	62
Number of treatments	34 967	14 343	20 624
Total revenue ($)	3 006 775	1 860 287	1 146 488
Supply costs ($)			
Standard supplies (drugs, syringes)	664 900	512 619	152 281
Episodic supplies (for special conditions)	310 695	98 680	212 015
Service costs ($)			
General overhead (occupancy, administration)	785 825		
Durable equipment	137 046		
Nursing services (nurses, administration, technical)	883 280		
Total service costs ($)	1 806 151	1 117 463	688 688
Total operating expenses ($)	2 781 746	1 728 762	1 052 984
Net income ($)	225 029	131 525	93 504
Treatment level profit			
Average charge per treatment ($)		129.70	55.59
Average cost per treatment ($)		120.53	51.06
Profit per treatment ($)		9.17	4.53

The existing cost system assigned the traceable supply costs directly to the two types of treatment. The service costs, however, were not analyzed by type of treatment. The total service costs of over $1 800 000 were allocated to the treatments using the traditional ratio of cost to charges (RCC) method developed for government cost-based reimbursement programs. With this procedure, since HD treatments represented about 61 percent of total revenue, HD received an allocation of 61 percent of the total service expenses.

For many years, the clinic received much of its reimbursement on the basis of reported costs. Later, however, payment mechanisms shifted and the clinic now

[2] This case has been adapted from T.D. West and D.A. West, 'Applying ABC to Healthcare', *Management Accounting*, February 1997, pp 22–33. Copyright 1997 by IMA, Montvale, N.J., USA, www.imanet.org, used with permission. Some elements are also based on Kaplan and Atkinson, *Advanced Management Accounting*, third edition, 1998, Prentice Hall International.

received most of its reimbursement on the basis of a fixed fee. In particular, because the government regarded HD and PD procedures as a single category – dialysis treatment – the weekly reimbursement for each patient was the same: $389.10. As a consequence, the three HD treatments per week led to a reported revenue per HD treatment of $129.70, and the seven PD treatments per week led to a reported revenue per PD treatment of $55.59. Thus, both procedures appeared to be profitable, according to the clinic's existing cost and revenue recognition system.

The staff of the clinic were concerned, however, that the procedures currently being used to assign common expenses might not be representative of the underlying use of common resources by the two procedures. They wanted to understand their costs better so that managers could make more informed decisions about extending or contracting products or services and about where to look for process improvement. They decided to explore whether activity-based costing principles could provide a better idea of the underlying cost and profitability of HD and PD treatments.

■ General overhead

In a first analysis, staff accountants decided to focus on the general overhead category. They broke down the general overhead category into four resource cost pools. Then, for each pool chose a cost driver that represented how that resource was used by the two treatments. A summary of their analysis is presented in Table 2.27. But then rather than continuing to use the RCC method for allocating equipment and nursing costs, they asked the clinic staff for their opinion on how these costs should be allocated. On the basis of the staff's experience and judgment, they felt that HD treatments used about 85 percent of these resources, and PD about 15 percent.

Table 2.27 General overhead resource cost pool

	Size of pool	Cost driver
Facility costs (rent, depreciation)	$233 226	Square feet
Administration	$354 682	No of patients
Communications and medical records	$157 219	No of treatments
Utilities	$40 698	Kilowatt usage
Total	$785 825	

Accountants then went to medical records and other sources to identify the quantities of each cost driver for the two treatment types (Table 2.28).

Table 2.28 General overhead cost driver

	HD	PD	Total
Square feet	18 900	11 100	30 000
Number of patients	102	62	164
Number of treatments	14 343	20 624	34 967
Estimated kilowatt usage	563 295	99 405	662 700

◼ Nursing services

Clearly, the decision that nursing and equipment costs should be split 85:15 between HD and PD treatments, respectively might not have been very well founded. Actually, the nursing resource category contained a mixture of different types of personnel: registered nurses (RNs), licensed practical nurses (LPNs), nursing administrators and machine operators. It was quite unlikely that each of these categories would be used in the same proportion by the two different treatments. In the next phase of the analysis, they decided to disaggregate the nursing service category into four resource pools and, as with general overhead, selected an appropriate cost driver for each pool (Table 2.29).

Table 2.29 Nursing services resource pool

	Size of pool	Cost driver
Registered nurses	$239 120	Full-time equivalents
Licensed practical nurses	$404 064	Full-time equivalents
Nursing administration and support	$115 168	Number of treatments
Dialysis machine operators	$124 928	Number of clinic treatments

To allocate the costs, accountants selected cost drivers that represented how these resources were used by the treatments (Table 2.30).

Table 2.30 Nursing services cost driver

	HD	PD	Total
Registered nurses	5	2	7
Licensed practical nurses	15	4	19
Number of dialysis treatments	14 343	20 624	34 967
Number of clinical treatments	14 343	0	14 343

Finally, they felt that the 85:15 split was still reasonable for the durable equipment use, and, in any case, the relatively small size of this resource expense category probably did not warrant additional study and data collection.

◼ Durable equipment

The first sections of this case contain material straight from the article in *Management Accounting*. The following section contains some additional material.

In fact, at most European renal clinics, durable equipment is not such a small part of the resource expense as described in the case. There are two possible explanations why the costs in this case are so low:

- ◼ In this particular case, most of the machinery might already have been written off.
- ◼ As in most American costing systems, interest on the equipment is disregarded.

To adjust for those two circumstances, let us add the following assumptions:

- The actual repurchasing cost of durable equipment is $3 000 000. Normal depreciation time would be 10 years. The required real interest at the clinic can be estimated to be around 8 percent.

- Normally each HD patient visits the clinic three times a week, 4–5 hours on each occasion. The rest of the time, other patients can use the equipment. Each PD patient, on the other hand, has his or her own equipment at home. It cannot be used by anybody else.

- In total, there are 125 sets of equipment for the patients, of which 65 are located on the premises and available for HD patients. The remaining 60 units are made available for PD patients in their homes. To simplify, let us assume that both treatments use the same type of equipment.

Solution: Cost Accounting in Healthcare

■ General overhead

To solve the case we need to include all the new information in the solution. Therefore the cost of facilities will be allocated as a cost per square foot, administration as a cost per patient, and so on. Table 2.31 shows the cost per unit of each cost driver. Applying these results to the entire situation we can now find the following outcome (Table 2.32).

When applying cost drivers in this way we can see that we get a very different solution from the traditional RCC method. While not very surprising, this is quite a remarkable outcome. It indicates that the traditional method might not be a very good measure of the costs associated with each type of treatment.

In fact, if the income per treatment is used for cost allocations, the costing system will not give us much valuable information. If costs are allocated in proportion to incomes, then clearly all services will appear to be roughly equally profitable. Therefore, this method of cost allocation will lead us to believe that all services are profitable as long as the clinic as a whole is profitable. But we cannot see differences in profitability between services and so we would be unable to decide which ones to promote if there were a choice. Therefore, the traditional method is quite dangerous for decision-making.

Table 2.31 Cost per unit of each cost driver

Cost drivers	Cost	Number	$ per unit
Area	233 226	30 000	7.77
No of patients	354 682	164	2 162.70
No of treatments	157 219	34 967	4.50
kWh	40 698	662 700	0.06

Table 2.32 Analyzing General Overheads

	Total $	HD $	PD $
Revenues			
Patients	164	102	62
Treatments	34 967	14 343	20 624
Total revenue	3 006 775	1 860 287	1 146 488
Supply costs			
Standard supplies	664 900	512 619	152 281
Episodic supplies	310 695	98 680	212 015
Total supply costs	975 595	611 299	364 296
Service cost			
Buildings	233 226	146 932	86 294
Administration	354 682	220 595	134 087
Communication	157 219	64 489	92 730
Electricity and water	40 698	34 593	6 105
Total indirect costs	785 825	466 610	319 215
Durable equipment	137 046	116 489	20 557
Nursing services	883 280	750 788	132 492
Total service cost	1 806 151	1 333 887	472 264
Total cost	2 781 746	1 945 186	836 560
Profit	225 029	−84 899	309 928
Treatment level profit			
Avg charge per treatment		129.70	55.59
Avg cost per treatment		135.62	40.56
Profit per treatment		−5.92	15.03

But if we decided to perform a careful cost analysis, we should study all cost components of the company. Therefore we shall now go on to nursing services.

■ Nursing services

When studying nursing services we need to add a few more activities and cost drivers. The new ones and their costs per unit are presented in Table 2.33.

Table 2.33 Cost drivers

	Cost	Number	$ per unit
Full-time nurses	239 120	7	34 160
Assistant nurses	404 064	19	21 267
Treatments	115 168	34 967	3.29
Machine treatments	124 928	14 343	8.71

Table 2.34 Cost accounts per type of treatment

	Total $	HD $	PD $
Revenues			
Patients	164	102	62
Treatments	34 967	14 343	20 624
Total revenue	3 006 775	1 860 287	1 146 488
Supply costs			
Standard supplies	664 900	512 619	152 281
Episodic supplies	310 695	98 680	212 015
Total supply costs	975 595	611 299	364 296
Cost of service			
Buildings	233 226	146 932	86 294
Administration	354 682	220 595	134 087
Communication	157 219	64 489	92 730
Electricity and water	40 698	34 593	6 105
Total indirect costs	785 825	466 610	319 215
Durable equipment	137 046	116 489	20 557
Nursing services			
Nurses	239 120	170 800	68 320
Assistant nurses	404 064	318 998	85 066
Administration	115 168	47 240	67 928
Machine operators	124 928	124 928	0
Total hospital services	883 280	661 966	221 314
Total costs	2 781 746	1 856 364	925 382
Profit	225 029	3 923	221 106
Treatment level profit			
Avg charge per treatment		129.70	55.59
Avg cost per treatment		129.43	44.87
Profit per treatment		0.27	10.72

After including the nursing costs per unit, we obtain the cost accounts per type of treatment shown in Table 2.34.

This analysis shows the dangers of limited cost analyses. Now that we have explored some more activities and found some new cost drivers, we can see that our changes in the beginning perhaps went too far. Having included this new information we see that the HD operations are not as bad as we thought. But perhaps the new information on durable equipment will change our opinion once more.

■ Durable equipment

There are considerable differences in cost accounting between the US and many European countries. While the Americans tend to do cost accounting without treating interest as part of product costs, many European companies prefer to include it.

Therefore, in this section we shall see how things change if there are considerable capital costs in addition to those costs that have already been studied.

Finding capital costs

To follow the reasoning in this section, you might find it helpful to study the capital costs section of the Glamorous Drilling Co. case (page 159).

According to traditional methods, the cost accountant would try to find the original cost of acquisition as a starting point for the analysis of capital costs.

In our case we do not know the original acquisition costs, so we have to find them through some intermediate calculations.

Now if the equipment lasts for 10 years and they replace it regularly, the average age of the machinery will be around 5 years. Therefore, let us assume that all equipment is 5 years old. But over those years there would very likely have been some price changes. If inflation is assumed to be some 2 percent per year (in line with the ambitions of the European Central Bank) that means that the original price would have been around $2.7 million instead of today's $3 million. Half of that amount should have been written off by now. Therefore today's remaining value might be estimated to amount to $1.35 million. Consequently we can find depreciation and interest in the following way:

$$\text{This year's depreciation (\$000): } 2700/10 = 270$$
$$\text{This year's interest on remaining value (\$000): } 1350 \times 10\% = 135$$

We found the interest rate by adding 2 percent inflation to the real rate of interest, 8 percent, which was given in the case.

According to this analysis, we ought to add $270\,000 + 135\,000$ of capital costs to our cost analysis and to allocate those costs between the two kinds of treatment.

An alternative method to find yearly capital costs is a 'real annuity'. To find a real annuity we start from today's actual value of the machinery and today's real rate of interest, 8 percent. According to the regular tables, the accumulated present value of a series of payments lasting for 10 years at 8 percent real interest is 6.71. Applying that number to today's value of the assets we get ($000):

$$3000/6.71 = 447$$

Therefore the yearly capital cost of the equipment, calculated as an annuity will be $447\,000$.

Cost allocation

The easiest way to allocate the costs among the treatments is in proportion to the number of machines used for each kind of treatment. Since there are 65 machines for HD patients and only 60 for PD patients we allocate the capital costs – and the maintenance costs – in those proportions. When doing so we shall assume that all the original costs of durable equipment were maintenance costs. The outcome of such an allocation can be found in Table 2.35.

Table 2.35 Including durable equipment

	Total	HD	PD
Revenues			
Patients	164	102	62
Treatments	34 967	14 343	20 624
Total revenue	3 006 775	1 860 287	1 146 488
Supply costs			
Standard supplies	664 900	512 619	152 281
Episodic supplies	310 695	98 680	212 015
Total supply costs	975 595	611 299	364 296
Cost of service			
Buildings	233 226	146 932	86 294
Administration	354 682	220 595	134 087
Communication	157 219	64 489	92 730
Electricity and water	40 698	34 593	6 105
Total indirect costs	785 825	466 610	319 215
Durable equipment			
Real annuity 8% on $3 000 000	447 088	232 486	214 602
Maintenance	137 046	71 264	65 782
	584 134	303 750	280 384
Nursing services			
Nurses	239 120	170 800	68 320
Assistant nurses	404 064	318 998	85 066
Administration	115 168	47 240	67 928
Machine operators	124 928	124 928	0
Total hospital services	883 280	661 966	221 314
Total costs	3 228 834	2 043 625	1 185 209
Profit	−222 059	−183 338	−38 721
Treatment level profit			
Avg charge per treatment		129.70	55.59
Avg cost per treatment		142.48	57.47
Profit per treatment		−12.78	−1.88

Since total costs have risen quite a lot and there was no change in incomes the clinic is now losing money on both products and, of course, on the total business of the clinic.

Finally, the reader will observe that there might now be overcapacity in HD machines. There is not much information in the case, but we are told that an HD machine will serve a patient in 4–5 hours. If we assume that each machine can serve two patients a day, there will be 12 treatments in a week and 600 treatments per year for each machine. Thus 24 machines would be enough to manage the total number of treatments in a year and we will find that we have a considerable cost of overcapacity (see Table 2.36).

Table 2.36 Identifying idle time

	Total	HD	PD	Idle
Revenues				
Patients	164	102	62	
Treatments	34 967	14 343	20 624	
Total revenue	3 006 775	1 860 287	1 146 488	
Supply costs				
Standard supplies	664 900	512 619	152 281	
Episodic supplies	310 695	98 680	212 015	
Total supply costs	975 595	611 299	364 296	
Cost of service				
Buildings	233 226	146 932	86 294	
Administration	354 682	220 595	134 087	
Communication	157 219	64 489	92 730	
Electricity and water	40 698	34 593	6 105	
Total indirect costs	785 825	466 610	319 215	
Durable equipment				
Real annuity 8% on $3 000 000	447 088	85 841	214 602	150 222
Maintenance	137 046	26 313	65 782	46 047
	584 134	112 154	280 384	
Nursing services				
Nurses	239 120	170 800	68 320	
Assistant nurses	404 064	318 998	85 066	
Administration	115 168	47 240	67 928	
Machine operators	124 928	124 928	0	
Total hospital services	883 280	661 966	221 314	
Total costs	3 228 834	1 852 029	1 185 209	196 269
Profit	−222 059	8 258	−38 721	
Treatment level profit				
Avg charge per treatment		129.70	55.59	
Avg cost per treatment		129.12	57.47	
Profit per treatment		0.58	−1.88	

In fact, the products are not really profitable, but they are not that bad either. The problem of the clinic is the overcapacity in HD equipment. Such an important point, however, is well beyond the logical capacity of the traditional full costing analyses performed in the first few sections of the case.

2.5 Metropolitan Transfer

In the 1990s a Nordic government decided to allow full competition in the country's mail services, even for regular letters. As that had never before been tried, many economists were very interested and were looking forward to seeing how things would develop.

In fact, there had been a lot of competition in the postal sector for some time (for parcels, heavy documents and cash transfers) but this was the first time there would be competition for standard letters.

In the beginning nothing much happened. But after a while an experienced entrepreneur started a company called Metropolitan Transfer and they offered a very low price for industrial mail.[3] Metropolitan Transfer's price was offered on the condition that the mail was already sorted by the sender, something which is quite easy to do using modern computer systems. But they added another special condition. All recipients had to be located in or around a fairly big city, and letters would not be delivered every day. Each local district would be serviced only 2 or 3 days a week instead of the old National Mail tradition of delivery at least once a day. Metropolitan Transfer also did not accept any letters bound for medium-sized or small cities.

National Mail understood that Metropolitan Transfer could be highly competitive in the big cities so they – of course – developed a similar system of their own. But while cost accounting at Metropolitan Transfer was quite simple, it turned out to be quite difficult at National Mail.

For many years National Mail had a routine of delivering A letters (overnight mail) every day in every district all over the country. The system was called 5A (5 days a week overnight). To compete with Metropolitan Transfer they introduced a 2B system (2 days a week – but it could take up to 3 days for a B letter to reach its recipient). The B service is much cheaper than the A service, because B letters can go by train or truck instead of airplane and they can even wait until the next day to be delivered if there is congestion at their destination.

■ Determining the cost of B letters

Now, in order to find the cost of delivering a B letter at National Mail we need to consider the situation in Figure 2.8. In a local district there are 60 million A letters to be distributed. The total cost of distribution is SEK 120 million. Since all A letters are equivalent, a simple full cost analysis will tell us that the cost per A letter is SEK 2. In the same district they could organize a 2B distribution system to distribute 40 million letters of industrial mail for SEK 40 million. This will be equally simple and these letters will cost SEK 1.50 each since they are also all equivalent.

But, of course, they are going to pool the two systems. After pooling they will have one distribution system that can distribute 100 million letters. Because of the

---

[3] Industrial mail can be understood as large quantities of letters, sent from one supplier to very many recipients at the same time. It could be banking information from banks to bank customers, insurance information from insurance companies to insurance customers or tax returns from the tax authorities to taxpayers. The sender can organize the mail in large boxes, already sorted according to the addresses (postal codes) of the recipients. In this way, several sorting procedures can be skipped and each box can be taken directly to the transport system and sent to the correct district, ready for delivery.

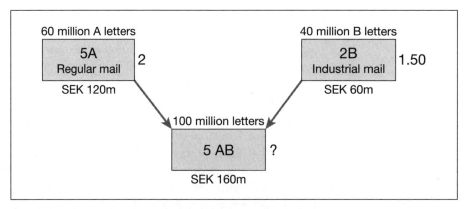

Figure 2.8 Pooling resources for two types of letter

shared resources, the costs of the new system will only be SEK 160 million, SEK 20 million less than the sum of the costs of the two separate systems. Now, let us try to find a fair way to allocate the SEK 160 million to A and B letters respectively!

■ Legal wrangles

Solving this case turned out to be extremely important. After some time there were court cases over National Mail's prices of industrial mail. Metropolitan Transfer asked the court to rule that National Mail was pricing industrial mail too low in order to subdue the competition and order them to raise their prices. On the other hand, National Mail asked the court to rule that they were allowed to price each type of letter in a fair way, knowing that if their price of industrial mail came out too high, Metropolitan Transfer would easily capture the whole market in the big cities – a disaster for National Mail.

External witnesses

When the case was analyzed in court there were two external witnesses present. Before solving the case we are going to hear their arguments.

'This is quite clear,' said the first witness, standing in front of the court officers. 'Right now I hold one letter in each hand [waving letters]. Those letters are equally big and equally heavy. They are delivered by the same postman on the same tour and they are carried in the same box on the same bike or in the same little postal van! But one of them is an A letter and the other is a B letter. Can anybody tell me which is which?'

None of the court officers could. He continued: 'Now, since these letters are completely equivalent, anybody can understand that they are also equally expensive. Therefore the costs of all letters have to be equal in the National Mail system. That cost has to be: 160/100 = 1.60 per letter A and B.'

This statement by the first witness appears to support Metropolitan Transfer. The second witness was an economist from a well-known university in the United States. He had flown over to Europe just to make a statement in court on this particular case.

Here is his main argument: 'According to legal rules, the National Mail are bound by law to deliver A letters overnight whatever happens. Therefore we have to take the A letters and their costs as given and we are going to look at the B letters as a side product that could be added to the main product portfolio on the margin if it is profitable.

'But from such a starting point it should be obvious to everybody that the first SEK 120 million are caused by the A letters only. Therefore, only the additional costs, SEK 40 million, are caused by the addition of the B letters to the product portfolio of National Mail. Consequently, B letters cost:

$$40/40 = 1.00 \text{ per B letter.'}$$

This witness clearly supports National Mail.

Solution: Metropolitan Transfer

To solve the case, we have to consider a large number of possibilities, which are presented in Figure 2.9.

The table starts with the so-called stand-alone costs (SAC) of each type of letter. This is the cost that would occur if that product were the only one in the product portfolio. These can be found in the original introduction to the case in Figure 2.8.

In the second row is the suggested solution of the first witness, 'full average cost'. According to that solution all letters should be seen as being economically equivalent. If we accept this approach, the full cost of each letter will be SEK 1.60. If this view were accepted by the court, National Mail would be ordered to raise its prices of B letters to SEK 1.60. If that happened, Metropolitan Transfer would price their offer at around SEK 1.55 and capture almost all the market.

	A letters SEK	B letters SEK
Stand-alone cost (SAC)	2	1.50
Full average cost	1.60	1.60
Direct costing A + B	2	1
Direct costing B + A	1.67	1.50
Paying back per unit	1.80	1.30
Proportional costing	1.78	1.33
Shapley value	1.83	1.25

Figure 2.9 Suggested solutions to determining the cost of A and B letters

But very likely this is not going to happen, because there are two mistakes in the reasoning of this witness:

■ A letters and B letters may look alike and they might be equally heavy, but they are not economically equivalent. A letters have to be distributed overnight and B letters have to be delivered within 3 days of receipt by National Mail. Therefore, regardless congestion, the A letters will still have to be delivered, whereas the B letters can be allowed to wait without any violation of the product contract. Clearly, that makes the B letters cheaper than the A letters for the National Mail organization.

■ When pooling the distribution of the two products, the overall organization gains SEK 20 million. Now, if there is one manager in charge of A letters and another in charge of B letters, how would they negotiate the sharing of the gains from co-operation? Would they even consider giving all the gains and some additional compensation to the A letters? No, they would not! The manager of the B letters would prefer to cease co-operation and operate alone rather than losing money. On a stand-alone basis, B letters cost only SEK 1.50. Sharing the costs equally is an option only if it brings gains to everyone, and in this case it does not. Therefore the full costing suggestion would not be considered by serious managers.

The next row has the solution suggested by the second witness. There is a lot of credibility in this argument. If National Mail is obliged by law to deliver A letters, then those letters could be seen as their main product. Then it might be reasonable to think that 40 million B letters can be added at an extra cost of SEK 40 million, which means SEK 1.00 per B letter. This argument is hard to refute.

But wait a minute. There is another similar argument that leads to a very different conclusion. After all, everybody knows that the volumes of mail are changing considerably. The number of individual letters that have to reach their destination in a hurry (overnight) is dropping every year while industrial mail (documenting transactions which are already known) is going up. In the long run, National Mail would barely survive if it only delivered A letters. Therefore, in the long run, the main product will be industrial mail, B letters.

But if B letters are the basic product, then we should start our calculation with them! To start with, we have 40 million B letters at a cost of SEK 60 million. That means SEK 1.50 per B letter. We add 60 million A letters and total costs rise to SEK 160 million. Clearly the additional cost of A letters is SEK 100 million and the cost per A letter could in this case be calculated in the following way:

$$\text{Cost of A letters} = 100/60 = 1.67 \text{ per A letter}$$

Thus there are two ways to define the main product and two ways to identify the extra costs of the additional product. They are equally logical and we cannot really see a reason to prefer one to the other. For now let us just note that they are equally possible.

The 'paying back per unit' solution is preferred by some of the people at National Mail. After all, when you pool the organizations into 5AB, you save SEK 20 million compared with the sum of the costs of the two stand-alone organizations. That SEK 20 million could be reallocated back to all the letters involved in the pooling. Reallocating SEK 20 million among 100 million letters will give you an average reallocation of SEK 0.20 per letter. The costs 1.80 and 1.30 follow from that reallocation.

Thus the cost relationships between the two products remain fairly steady and everybody gains from the pooling. We do not get into any of the difficulties that followed from the first suggestions by the external witnesses. It seems to be a solution that might satisfy everyone.

But this solution has a theoretical difficulty, which is not very clear in this example: we are once again treating A letters and B letters as economically equivalent. We have made the same mistake as the first witness! He said that all letters are equivalent and therefore they should share the costs equally per unit. But they are not economically equivalent and we had to discard that solution. Now we have reallocated 0.20 per unit, a rule that also assumes units are economically equivalent. In this case the rule leads to a very reasonable solution, but in other cases, where products might differ a lot more, such a solution cannot hold. (If we were to assume that Audi makes its A1 cars in the same factory as the A8, should the savings from pooling be shared equally between all the units? That would bring the costs of the A1 close to zero and would not really be noticed in the product cost of an A8!)

Thus we cannot accept 'paying back per unit' as a general rule. But I have to admit that it might work in this particular case!

So, let us go on to 'proportional costing'. This rule says that products should share the pooled costs in the same proportions as their stand-alone costs. Total stand-alone costs are:

$$SEK \text{ (million)} = 120 + 60 = 180 \text{ million}$$

Out of those SEK 180 million, A letters consume SEK 120 million, which is 2/3. B letters consume the remaining 1/3. So out of the pooled costs of SEK 160 million, let us allocate 2/3 to A letters and 1/3 to B letters. That means that we are going to charge $2/3 \times 160 = $ SEK 106.7 million to A letters and $1/3 \times 160 = $ SEK 53.3 million to B letters. We get the following outcome per letter:

$$\text{Cost per A letter} = 106.7/60 = 1.78$$

$$\text{Cost per B letter} = 53.3/40 = 1.33$$

This routine is neutral to the size of the units. It just allocates costs in proportion to the original stand-alone costs. The manager of A letters would gain SEK 13.3 million compared with the stand-alone costs of A letters, and the manager of B letters would gain SEK 6.7 million compared with the stand-alone costs of B letters. The gains are proportional to the original sizes of the two fields.

Thus the biggest gains the biggest part. Is that a fair way to share the gains? This formula will probably readily be accepted by business managers, but that does not necessarily make it fair. If one manager were to make his own stand-alone costs higher, he would increase his share of the gain. That could not be said to be fair. Still, this formula is probably the one that will find the greatest support among managers and at the same time everybody will share in the gain from pooling.

However, there is one final possibility in the figure: the Shapley value, which is a theoretical solution originating from game theory. The Shapley value rule originates from research into coalitions among a number of parties. It stipulates that all possible orders of forming coalitions should be investigated and then the solution will be found by computing the average payout for each party after considering all possible orders. The interested reader is referred to the theory of coalitions in game theory.

In our particular case, it turns out that there are two possible orders of coalition. We could start with A and add B (see 'direct costing A + B'). Or we could start with B and add A (see 'direct costing B + A'). These are all the possible orders of coalition with only two products. With three products there would be six possibilities.

In our case we find the Shapley value solution by averaging rows A + B and B + A. The costs of the letters will now be:

$$\text{Cost of A letters} = (2.00 + 1.67)/2 = 1.83$$
$$\text{Cost of B letters} = (1.50 + 1.00)/2 = 1.25$$

In this scenario, the total savings from pooling are shared equally between the two contributing departments (SEK 10 million per type of letter). This solution could be seen as fair in a theoretical sense, but I am not convinced that all managers would prefer it to the proportional solution we discussed earlier.

Personally, in theory I think the Shapley value is a very good solution. Unfortunately it is difficult to explain and, when there are many parties involved in the co-operation, it is also time-consuming to compute. Regular business managers are normally quicker to adopt the proportional costing allocation. After all, both rules of allocation fulfill the basic rules of cost accounting for co-operation among several products (Figure 2.10).

- All the final costs should be assigned to some product
- Every product should gain something compared to its SAC
- Every product should pay more than its direct cost
- Every product should carry a fair share of the total cost

Figure 2.10 Basic cost accounting rules when there is co-operation among several products

2.6 Road Connections at Barken Lake

(Readers might find it useful to study case 5.1, the Glamarous Drilling Co., before solving this case.)

A large international company decided to locate its new research facilities close to Barken Lake to provide excellent and charming surroundings for its research personnel. A nice new hotel was about to be built in a nearby location so it was felt that access to the area would prove to be not too difficult.

While investigating the prospect in more detail, the project team found that the road to the Barken Hotel was to be private, wholly owned by the Barken Hotel Co. But as building a completely new road of their own would be quite expensive, they decided to negotiate sharing most of the road and found the following information on the technical situation.

The road to the Barken Hotel will be a modern, two-lane permanent road. The distance from the public road to the hotel is 3 km. Building the road will cost €900 000. The road can be used for at least 25 years provided yearly maintenance is done correctly. General maintenance will average around €12 000 per year plus additional snow-clearing costs (€6000 per year).

Considering these facts, the research team felt that a similar road to their own research facility could be built for €600 000 since the distance was only 2 km. Also, regular maintenance and snow-clearing costs were expected to come out in proportion to the length of the road.

On the other hand, if the research company negotiated an agreement to share the hotel road, they would only need to build an extra 1 km of their own. Building costs would be €300 000 plus €82 000 for a new crossing. Maintenance would be €4000 a year plus snow-clearing costs of €2000 per year. If that was done they would need permission to drive regularly along the hotel road, increasing maintenance costs (but not snow-clearing costs) of the hotel road by 50 percent.

We will assume that the volume of traffic to the research facility amounts to 50 percent of the volume to the hotel. In order to prepare for a negotiation, we will find the costs of the different alternatives according to the following plan: when performing the calculation we will assume that both companies will apply 8 percent nominal cost of capital and that inflation will average 2 percent a year in the future. We aim to find:

- the annual costs of each road if they are built separately according to the original plans of each company;

- the total annual costs of the combined system if the research company is allowed to drive along the hotel road to the hotel and then on their own road from there;

- a cost allocation, distributing the total costs of the combined system in a reasonably fair way between the two companies.

Solution: Road Connections

For each road there will be capital costs as well as operating costs. Since we are dealing with a large number of years we need to calculate the real costs of each road and adjust them for inflation in the long run.

Applying 6 percent real interest over 25 years, the hotel road will cost (in €000):

Annuity = 900/12.78 =	70.4
Regular maintenance	12
Snow-clearing costs	6
Total annual costs	**88.4**

Calculated in the same way, the separate road to the research facility will cost (in €000):

Annuity = 600/12.78	46.9
Maintenance	8
Snow-clearing costs	4
Total annual costs	**58.9**

Thus the total costs for two stand-alone projects will be:

$$\text{Total stand-alone costs} = 88.4 + 58.9 = 147.3$$

The combined system will be 4 km long. The costs can be found in Table 2.37. Thus we can see that the total costs of the combined system will be much lower than the sum of the costs of the two private roads. Now let us discuss how to allocate those costs between the two parties.

The research company will pay the whole cost of their own connection, which will never be used by the hotel business. Therefore the task will deal only with the allocation of the costs of the hotel road. The various methods of allocation are shown in Table 2.38.

Stand-alone costs are included mainly for comparison and as a starting point for the following calculations.

Sharing the full costs of the hotel road according to traffic is one solution that might occur to the project group. However, this would be a non-starter because it would be cheaper for the research company to build their own road. Therefore, if the hotel authorities were to insist that the costs of the hotel road should be shared according to such a formula, each company will end up building their own road, a solution that would be very expensive for both parties.

Applying marginal costs, 'hotel + research' implies that the hotel needs its road and pays for it and the research company is just add-on traffic. Such a solution would be very good for the research company and yields no profit for the hotel.

In fact, there is another marginal costing possibility. In the alternative, 'research + hotel', we start by saying that the research company needs a road and will pay for its own. In addition, the hotel will have to pay the additional costs until the total system has been created. It may sound strange but it is equally logical.

Table 2.37 Costs of the combined system

	Hotel road €000	Research connection €000	Total costs €000
Annuity	70.4	29.9	100.3
Regular maintenance after increase in traffic	18	4	22.0
Snow-clearing costs	6	2	8.0
Total costs	94.4	35.9	130.3

Table 2.38 Cost allocation for the combined system

	Hotel €000	Research €000	Total €000
Stand-alone costs	88.4	58.9	147.3
Sharing full cost			
Hotel road according to the volume of traffic	62.9	31.5	94.4
Additional costs for connection to research company		35.9	35.9
Total cost per company	62.9	67.4	130.3
Marginal cost, hotel + research			
Hotel road	88.4		88.4
Marginal cost for research		6.0	6.0
Marginal connection road		35.9	35.9
Total cost per company	88.4	41.9	130.3
Marginal cost, research + hotel			
Research road		58.9	
Marginal costs for total system	71.4		
Total cost per company	71.4	58.9	130.3
Proportional costing			
Hotel: 88.4/147.3 × 130.3	78.2		
Research: 58.9/147.3 × 130.3		52.1	130.3
Shapley value			
Hotel: (88.4 + 71.4)/2	79.9		
Research: (58.9 + 41.9)/2		50.4	130.3

In both marginal cases, one company makes the whole gain. Therefore most managers would probably not be sympathetic to either. Instead, managers are likely to go along with proportional costing where the combined costs are shared in proportion to the stand-alone costs.

The Shapley value is the game theory solution to the case. In this particular case (with only two parties) we can easily find it by averaging the two marginal solutions.

As it turns out, there is a very small difference between proportional costing and the Shapley value. From a theoretical point of view, I think the Shapley value is the preferred solution, but for practical purposes it would probably be easier to negotiate a solution according to proportional thinking.

2.7 Seaside Breweries

(This case was adapted from an original written by Trond Bjornenak at the Norwegian School of Economics.)

Seaside Breweries is one of the main breweries in western Norway. The brewery produces five different types of beer. They used to have a very strong position in the region, but in recent years competition has been increasing. As a result, they now want to calculate the possible cost differences between the various brands in order to take on competition in a systematic way.

The total production of beer according to budget is 50 million liters per year. There are considerable differences between the five brands. The main product, Western Pils, represents 60 percent of the total volume and one of the smaller brands, Eastern Pils, contributes only 10 percent of the total volume.

The brewery has a cost budget (NOK 000) as shown in Table 2.39. Of the indirect costs, roughly 25 percent are variable in the short run. In order to describe the cost situation, Seaside Breweries decides to develop the following cost analyses:

■ direct costing

■ full absorption costing

■ activity-based costing (ABC).

Table 2.39 Seaside's cost budget

	Western Pils NOK 000	Other brands NOK 000	Eastern Pils NOK 000	Total NOK 000
Direct material	60 000	31 000	9 000	100 000
Direct labor	15 000	7 000	3 000	25 000
Indirect costs				100 000
Total costs				225 000

The information available is as follows. Indirect costs have been attributed to activities as shown in Table 2.40. According to the present budget, brands will exploit activities according to Table 2.41.

Table 2.40 Indirect costs of activities

Activity	Costs NOK	Cost driver	Capacity	Per transaction NOK
Materials handling	9 000 000	Buying orders	750	12 000
Production set-ups	13 000 000	Set-ups	1 000	13 000
Bottling	40 000 000	Machine time	40 000	1 000
Quality control	12 000 000	Inspection time	8 000	1 500
Marketing	6 000 000	No of brands	10	600 000
Administration	20 000 000			
Total indirect costs	100 000 000			

Table 2.41 Activities vs brands

Activity	Western Pils	Other brands	Eastern Pils
Buying orders	250	300	150
Set-ups	400	350	200
Bottling time (hours)	24 000	8 000	4 000
Inspection time (hours)	4 000	2 000	2 000

The selling price, excluding taxes, for Western Pils is NOK 4.20 per liter and for Eastern Pils is NOK 4.50 per liter. The other brands are priced between those two levels.

Seaside's accountants are asked to carry out the following analysis:

1 Find production costs and profitability per liter of Western Pils and Eastern Pils for each of the three methods.

2 Discuss the usefulness of the costing models for each of the following decisions:
   - pricing products
   - long-term product mix decisions
   - short-term product mix decisions
   - valuation of inventories
   - introducing new brands.

Solution: Seaside Breweries

Seaside Breweries want to find the possible cost differences between brands because of the intensifying competitive situation.

■ 1. Production costs and profitability

Direct costing

Applying direct costing and allocating the variable part of indirect costs on labor, we get the outcome in Table 2.42.

Table 2.42 Direct costing

	Western	Eastern	Others	Total
Millions of liters	30	5	15	50
Price per liter	4.2	4.5		
	NOK 000	*NOK 000*	*NOK 000*	*NOK 000*
Direct material	60 000	9 000	31 000	100 000
Direct labor	15 000	3 000	7 000	25 000
Indirect costs	15 000	3 000	7 000	25 000
Total costs	90 000	15 000	45 000	150 000
Costs per liter (NOK)	3.00	3.00	3.00	
Contribution per liter (NOK)	1.20	1.50		

According to direct costing, both Western and Eastern give a positive contribution. Therefore, this method indicates that both should remain in the product portfolio.

Variable indirect costs might possibly be allocated according to some other allocation base; in this case I would recommend the total value of prime costs but not the number of liters.

If you decided to leave the variable part of the indirect costs out of the calculation, the costs would be somewhat lower and the contribution somewhat higher. But in that case the value of direct costing for the decisions in the second part of the case would deteriorate considerably.

Full costing

In full costing, all indirect costs should be allocated in a fair way to the products. This might be done according to labor costs or possibly in relation to the value of prime costs. I would not recommend allocation according to the number of liters. Allocating according to labor (400 percent on labor) will give an outcome in accordance with Table 2.43.

Table 2.43 Full costing

		Western NOK 000	Eastern NOK 000	Others NOK 000	Total NOK 000
Direct material		60 000	9 000	31 000	100 000
Direct labor		15 000	3 000	7 000	25 000
Indirect costs	400%	60 000	12 000	28 000	100 000
Total costs		135 000	24 000	66 000	225 000
Per liter (NOK)		4.50	4.8	4.40	
Profit per liter (NOK)		−0.30	− 0.30		

According to full costing, both products make losses. This is a clear indication that things are not quite right in the company. But we do not really know if products are truly unprofitable or if there are inefficiencies in the production system, like idle capacity. There might also be other sources of inefficiency. Definitely, the losses indicated are not big enough to really question the product portfolio. Further analyses would have to be made.

Activity-based costing

In activity-based costing, indirect costs should be allocated to products in accordance with the activities and cost drivers given in the text. This material, including costs per unit of cost drivers, was already prepared for us in Table 2.40. Costs of activities without cost drivers should not be allocated. This gives as the outcome shown in Table 2.44.

From the table we may conclude that Western Pils appears profitable, but that there are certain unallocated costs. Now we can clearly see that the company has a profitability problem. The profit (NOK 000) from Western Pils appears to be $30\ 000 \times 0.41 = 12\ 300$, which is nowhere near enough to cover the costs of administration. Getting rid of all unused resources might not be enough to bring them back to profitability. It is also clear that Eastern Pils is not profitable as things stand. The volumes are too small. Perhaps it would be a good thing to raise the price?

■ 2. Usefulness of the models

Pricing products

If possible, products should be priced according to the market price. If there is no market price, the price should be set by considering full costing and ABC at the same time. Full costing will indicate the necessary average price level, while

Table 2.44 Activity-based costing

	Western NOK 000	Eastern NOK 000	Others NOK 000	Allocated NOK 000	Unallocated NOK 000	Total NOK 000
Direct material	60 000	9 000	31 000	100 000	0	100 000
Direct labor	15 000	3 000	7 000	25 000	0	25 000
Materials handling	3 000	1 800	3 600	8 400	600	9 000
Set up machinery	5 200	2 600	4 550	12 350	650	13 000
Bottling	24 000	4 000	8 000	36 000	4 000	40 000
Quality control	6 000	3 000	3 000	12 000	0	12 000
Marketing	600	600	1 800	3 000	3 000	6 000
Administration					20 000	20 000
Totals	113 800	24 000	58 950	196 750	28 250	225 000
Per liter (NOK)	3.79	4.80	3.93			
Profit per liter (NOK)	0.41	−0.30				

ABC will give the correct allocation between products. Note that professional managers are very reluctant to apply ABC to pricing decisions, as they are convinced it will bring the price down too much. Therefore, when pricing products we need to make sure that necessary common costs, such as administration, can be covered in those prices.

In fact, as in this case, if a product is priced below its ABC cost, then ABC can be a good tool for pricing, because we should never allow a product to be priced below ABC. The only exception to this rule is if there is a short-term campaign or promotion on the go. To really deserve its position in the product portfolio, Eastern Pils has to be priced above NOK 4.80 (its ABC cost).

Direct costing would be dangerous for pricing. As direct costs constitute only a fairly small part of the total costs, this method could easily lead us to a pricing arrangement where the average prices were set too low.

Long-term product mix decisions

ABC was designed to solve this problem. From our analysis we can clearly see that, as things stand, Western Pils is profitable and Eastern Pils is unprofitable. Other brands appear to be profitable on average. In the long run we have to reconsider the volumes and prices of Eastern Pils and we can see clearly that we have a big problem with unallocated costs. Larger volumes would help, provided the additional volumes can be sold at prices above their ABC costs.

Short-term product mix decisions

For short-term product mix decisions, direct costing is superior if you include the variable part of the overheads. In this case, all products give positive contributions in the short run. ABC might be useful to supply a more correct allocation of the variable overhead than is normally done in direct costing. ABC alone would not be efficient, because it might take some time to make those adjustments in capacity that lie behind regular ABC thinking.

Valuation of inventories

For financial accounting, full costing is normally recommended and is preferred. Only manufacturing costs should be included and interest costs on equity capital would have to be eliminated. Most of the interest costs in this case would probably be concealed in the costs of bottling and the set-up of machinery.

For managerial accounting, we prefer ABC and we would include interest on equity. Direct costing would underestimate the fair value of inventories.

Introducing new brands

ABC will indicate clearly what volumes and prices are needed to make a new brand profitable. Direct costing would be downright dangerous, because it appears to indicate that most new brands are profitable even if there is cannibalization among brands.

Chapter 3

Internal transfer pricing

3.1 Premium Motor Co.

At the Premium Motor Co. they have three departments (see Figure 3.1). One department sells new private cars of a well-known brand to regular private customers. They have good times and bad times and sales vary quite a lot depending on business conditions.

Most of the time, when customers consider buying a new car they want to offer their old one in part-exchange. This is a tricky business, because quite often customers have an inflated opinion as to the value of their used cars. They've been driving them for such a long time that they know all the little difficulties that have to be overcome in order to have the car function properly. The do not understand the importance of these problems and some of them are almost offended when salesmen tell them the true value of the old car.

Nevertheless, most deals involve buying a used car from the customer in part-exchange for a new one. The salesman then has to get the used car reconditioned so it can be sold on to another customer, possibly in part-exchange for another, perhaps even older used car.

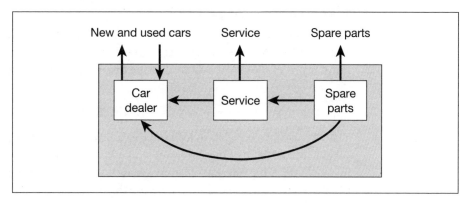

Figure 3.1 Departmental arrangement of the Premium Motor Co.

In order to have the used cars properly reconditioned, the sales department hands them over to the service department, which is part of the same company. This department also services cars owned by customers, most of whom bought them from the sales department one or a few years ago. Many of these cars belong to the main brand of the Premium Motor Co., but there is also a certain inflow of second-hand cars of other brands to be serviced or repaired.

A little more than half the business volume of the service department goes to outside customers, but the internal reconditioning volume is also quite important. The internal volume can be processed when the demand for external business is slow, which happens now and then for no particular reason.

In order to provide secure access to parts and other service materials, there is also a spare parts department. This department was originally set up to supply spare parts to the service department, but over the years the volume that goes straight to the sales department has grown and it is now similar to the volume required by the service department. The spare parts department handles all the 'extras' customers buy for their new cars.

There is also a third group of people who buy spare parts, mainly younger people who are looking to carry out simple repairs and maintenance on their own. While not as important as the other streams of business, this channel adds a considerable sales volume to Premium's total turnover. Also, spare parts to the general public are priced to give a fairly good margin, which is normal for these kinds of sales.

In Premium Motors, operations are run by Mr Nilsson, the owner of the company. He would like a more comfortable life and he thinks he has found a way to get there.

Profit centers and internal transfer prices

Mr Nilsson feels that it is generally a good thing to make employees share responsibilities in a business company. He therefore decided to turn the three departments into complete profit centers and to make one manager accountable for each of them.

Realizing that internal transfer prices will be quite important for their future behavior he invited a consultant to work with his CFO to design a plan for the pricing.

The CFO and the consultant

The consultant brought a textbook on management accounting to his meeting with the CFO. At the first meeting he pointed out a paragraph saying that optimal transfer prices should be designed in the following way:

> Optimal transfer prices should cover directs costs of the products or services supplied plus the opportunity cost of resources used in the process of supplying them.

The CFO could very well understand the logic of the theoretical statement. On the other hand, he felt that the easiest way to find proper transfer prices would be charging the costs of the internal seller, much as they had been charging the costs to each particular order in the old system before the introduction of profit centers. 'Let us see,' said the CFO, 'how various rules might work together to solve the issue.'

In the old days they always tried to find the full cost of every order. After that there was a cost-plus formula to develop prices in the spare parts department and the service shop. A cost-plus formula was also adopted in the sales department, but there the individual salesmen always had to negotiate with customers in order to close a deal at the best possible price.

'How would full cost plus profit relate to your theoretical rule?' asked the CFO, to get the analysis going.

'Well, you see,' replied the consultant, 'according to Kaplan's book on cost and effect, full cost does not have any desirable properties in transfer pricing.'

Actually, as the discussion went on, they found out that full cost is composed of direct costs plus an allowance for indirect costs. Indirect costs, in turn, represent the costs of those people, like management and administration, who do not work on the particular product or service, but they are still needed to keep things going. Also, indirect costs would include costs of the buildings, machinery and equipment that are needed to provide the products and services. Could those indirect costs be similar to opportunity costs?

In some cases they could. One hopes that staff in management and administration provide a value equal to their salaries! If they are in very short supply, the opportunity cost would be higher than their salaries and if they are not very busy their opportunity costs would be lower than their salaries. But if their work rate is reasonable, their costs might be fairly close to the opportunity cost of hiring more of them.

In the long run and on average the calculated costs of machinery and buildings (depreciation, interest and maintenance) might also be quite similar to the costs of using them. If we use them, they will get worn out and we will have to buy new ones. In this case indirect costs might also be similar to opportunity costs.

In some cases we are not going to buy any new equipment because we are going to give up the business altogether. Then it would not matter if the equipment wears out, and the opportunity costs would be zero, leaving only direct costs.

'This is complicated,' said the CFO, 'it means that prices should vary over time! That means a lot of work and a lot of confusion.'

'But it does not really matter,' the consultant explained, 'because in this case we have market prices for all products and services and they are normally better indications of correct prices than are the costs.'

And so they decided to start from market prices instead of cost-based prices because, as the consultant said, there are price lists indicating market prices for all products and services.

'But wait a minute,' objected the CFO, 'selling inside at market prices would be better business than selling to the outside market at market prices. In inside trading there are no selling costs and no credit risks.'

'Rightly so,' said the consultant, 'and because of that we can deduct those savings from the market price when turning it into transfer pricing. If we do so we shall get very close to that optimal rule we started from!'

In fact, market price is equal to the direct cost plus contribution and that contribution is equal to the opportunity costs, if selling inside. But if there are selling costs outside and no selling costs inside then those selling costs could be subtracted from the market price to calculate the optimal internal transfer price. In this case, the internal seller will gain just as much as in external business and the internal buyer will get a small advantage which will promote togetherness and co-operation between profit centers.

'Excellent,' thought the CFO. 'We are done! Let us report to the owner that we have solved the case. We shall trade internally at external market prices less external selling costs.'

So they called a meeting at which the proud project group reported their findings and expected unlimited praise for their analytical ability and impressive shrewdness.

The owner

'What a stupid idea!' complained the owner. 'I just told you to make a fair price list! I want each of these guys to stand on their toes all the time. I don't want any subsidies anywhere. Of course, all trade should take place at full market prices! Please send the consultant back to his theories and print regular price lists that make everybody aware of the full powers of the market. Those who are good will be profitable and the others will notice that they have to improve.'

Exit consultant! Enter independent market-oriented profit centers!

◼ Act II – 2 years later

Meeting at a conference 2 years later, the consultant considered avoiding the dominant owner, but finally decided there was nothing to be gained by running away. He put on a big smile and asked how business was going.

'Most impressive, beautiful volumes and great profits when you helped us along, and we still make a profit now when the market is down and we sell many cars to be serviced in the future. Come and see us if you like.'

'Glad to hear that! But what about the transfer prices? Are you still applying full market prices internally?'

'No, of course not. As you know the market is down right now. All units have to co-operate and we need to promote co-operation.'

'So now they finally give each other discounts as I suggested?' asked the consultant with triumph in his voice, feeling that his theories had been proven right.

'No, of course not. All units are trading at full cost. When business is low we have to support each other to make the whole firm compete in the final market for new and used cars. We do not want service or spare parts to make a profit internally. The car salesmen need to know our costs to the last cent. Every car we can sell now will come back to generate service jobs for many years to come. Good to meet you again. Do come and see us whenever you like.'

Exit owner. Exit consultant.

◼ Whatever you do – keep it simple!

And that optimal rule, what happened to it? Well, the owner might have been right in refusing to let units support each other when business was good. After all, when business is good it might not be necessary to send the internal gains downstream. Let everybody compete in a real market and do not let anybody subsidize anyone else! In an organization where everybody has a market relation, full market prices will put pressure on the units later in the chain.

But when business is poor, it is important not to conceal any profits in the earlier units. Now they will want to sell as many new and used cars as possible. It is important not to overprice them through unduly high costs for service or spare parts. Full costs may actually overstate opportunity costs. Such is the case if there are unused resources in spare parts or services. But still, business managers are almost always hesitant to trade at below full costs. They are afraid they may not be able to raise prices again when business is back to normal.

And what about the independent service shop around the corner? Should the car dealer be allowed to do business there in bad times? No, maybe not, but the internal service shop would have to meet their prices or else the car dealer would have a disadvantage compared with other car dealers a block or two away.

3.2 Cardboard coating

In a large paper-making company there are several divisions, each of which is a complete profit center. The cardboard division produces coated cardboard to be sold to large food producers in the market. They are by far the biggest producer of coated cardboard in their market area.

Accountants of the cardboard division have found that there is a clear relationship between sales price and possible sales volumes. To be precise, they have found the following relationship between price and volume:

Price (€/ton)	1 400	1 600	1 800	2 000
Volume (tons)	58 000	42 000	31 000	24 000

In the following case we shall disregard the possibility of charging prices between those mentioned in the table.

■ Product costing

In the beginning of the case all internal transfer prices are equal to the full cost of the supplier. Under those circumstances, the product costs for 1 ton of coated cardboard are as in Table 3.1.

Paper pulp and coating chemicals are bought from two other divisions within the same group. Internal transfer prices have been suggested by the top management. The product costs of those supplies have been worked out for 1 ton of coated cardboard, as in Table 3.2.

The paper pulp division is working at full capacity and they have a very large market for their products. In the case of lower internal demand, they can easily sell the remaining volumes at list price in the external market.

Table 3.1 Product costs per ton of coated cardboard

	€
Direct materials	
Paper pulp	500
Coating chemicals	150
Other material	100
Direct wages	100
Allocated fixed costs	400
Full costs (€/ton)	1 250

Table 3.2 Product costs of pulp and chemicals per ton of coated cardboard

	Paper pulp €	Coating chemicals €
Direct materials	300	50
Direct wages	50	50
Allocated fixed costs	150	50
Full cost	500	150
Suggested transfer price	600	200
External list price	750	250

The chemicals division, on the other hand, has surplus capacity. If they do not increase their sales soon, they will have to get rid of capacity as well as personnel.

The accountants are asked to consider the following scenarios:

1 Find optimal market price and volume for coated cardboard, assuming that all divisions trade required volumes at full cost of each producer.

2 Since full costs are much lower than external list prices, the controller's department suggests a compromise, pricing paper pulp at €600 and chemicals at €200. Find the optimal market price and volume for coated cardboard, assuming that all internal trade is done at the suggested prices. Find out how decisions might change and what would happen to the total profit of the entire group.

3 It has been said that market-based prices are superior to other kinds of internal transfer prices. Many managers think that market prices are equal to their external list prices. Assume that internal prices are changed into the external list prices of all divisions. Once again, find out how decisions might change and what would happen to the total profit of the entire group.

4 Since the chemical division has surplus capacity, their external list price is not quite relevant for internal pricing. Find the lower price limit per unit of the chemicals sold internally by the chemical division. Also, find out how the decisions might change and what would happen to the total profit of the entire group.

5 After finishing the study above, create a rule for optimal transfer pricing referring to 'direct costs' and 'opportunity costs'.

Solution: Cardboard coating

■ 1. Prices equal to full costs

When the cardboard division accountants look at the situation, from their own point of view, they will start by disregarding allocated fixed costs. This will result in the situation in Table 3.3.

Table 3.3 Prices, volumes, and contribution

	Price (€/ton)			
	1400	1600	1800	2000
Volume (tons, 000)	58	42	31	24
Contribution/ton (€)	550	750	950	1 150
Total contribution (€)	31 900	31 500	29 450	27 600

Optimum price (€/ton) = 1 400
Contribution (€) = 31 900

■ 2. Suggested internal transfer prices

If internal transfer prices are changed into the prices suggested by the controller's department, this will result in the situation in Table 3.4.

Table 3.4 Revised contribution

	Price (€/ton)			
	1400	1600	1800	2000
Volume (tons, 000)	58	42	31	24
Contribution/ton (€)	400	600	800	1 000
Total contribution (€)	23 200	25 200	24 800	24 000

Optimum price (€/ton) = 1 600
Contribution (€) = 25 200

In the new situation the cardboard division cannot make as much money as in the case of full costs. However, if they optimize the new situation they will switch to a somewhat higher price and a smaller volume. For the total group, the changes will be as in Table 3.5.

Table 3.5 Change in contribution

	€000
Cardboard (25 200 − 31 900)	−6 700
Paper pulp (42 × 100 + 16 × 250)	8 200
Chemicals (42 × 100 − 58 × 50)	1 300
Total change	2 800

In the cardboard division the change is just the difference between the contribution levels in the two cases. For the paper pulp division there is a gain corresponding to the difference in prices on two different volumes. First, they get a better price internally on the 42 000 tons which are still sold internally. Secondly, they get a much better price on the 16 000 tons which can now be sold in the market at the external list price.

The chemicals division will also get a surplus of goods when their internal volumes fall. In their market situation, however, they will probably not be able to sell their surplus anywhere. Therefore they will gain an increased contribution on a lower volume, selling chemicals for only 42 000 tons of cardboard instead of 58 000.

As we can see, there is a gain for the total group, because internal prices are now closer to the opportunity costs represented by the list price of the paper pulp division. There is no similar gain for the chemicals division, but their deliveries are smaller and do not dominate the problem.

So far, this case indicates that full costs would not represent good transfer prices for the group. Actually full costs would mislead the decision-makers of the cardboard division and might lead them to setting too low prices in the market of coated cardboard.

◼ 3. List prices of all divisions

If internal transfer prices are changed into external list prices for all divisions, the intermediate goods will become much more expensive than before. Therefore it will appear profitable to the cardboard division to increase the market price considerably, although the sales volumes will fall.

The contribution when internal transfer prices are equal to external list prices can be found in Table 3.6. In the new situation the cardboard division will be worse off and the paper pulp division will gain a lot of money because they finally can sell all their products at the external list price. Table 3.7 shows how contribution numbers will change.

Table 3.6 Internal transfer prices equal to external list prices

	Price (€/ton)			
	1400	1600	1800	2000
Volume (tons, 000)	58	42	31	24
Contribution/ton (€)	200	400	600	800
Total contribution (€)	11 600	16 800	18 600	19 200

Optimum price (€/ton) = 2000
Contribution (€) = 19 200

But this situation is not really profitable. The total gains of the group will go down. This is because the costs of the cardboard division are now so high that they will

Table 3.7 Profit change

	€000
Cardboard (19 200 – 25 200)	–6 000
Paper pulp (+150 × 42)	6 300
Chemicals (150 × 24 – 100 × 42)	–600
Total change	–300

have to charge very high prices to their final customers. The volumes fall to such an extent that the whole group will lose as a result of the change!

But is this really right? Was it not stated in an earlier case that market prices are normally the best indications of direct costs + opportunity costs? But in scenario 3 we did not go for real market prices for the chemicals division. We overstated them, because we applied an external list price that was too high to actually clear the market. Therefore, let us look at scenario 4 in order to find out about opportunity costs.

■ 4. The lowest possible price of the chemicals division

At the chemicals division there is surplus capacity. Therefore their capacity does not have any value in the short run. In fact, to stay in business they must, at the very worst, be willing to supply their products at a price that is equal to direct costs, which is just €100.

Entering those new costs in the cost accounts of the cardboard division means the contribution at all prices will rise by €150 compared with scenario 3. This produces the situation in Table 3.8.

Table 3.8 Transfer prices equal to opportunity costs

	Price (€/ton)			
	1400	1600	1800	2000
Volume	58	42	31	24
Contribution/ton (€)	350	550	750	950
Total contribution (€)	20 300	23 100	23 250	22 800

Optimum price (€/ton) = 1 800
Contribution (€) = 23 250

Here margins are narrow, but if we are very precise we will go for a price of €1800 and a contribution of €23 250 in the cardboard division.

Compared with scenario 3, total contributions will change as shown in Table 3.9. In fact, this is the biggest contribution achieved in the case so far. When going from suggested prices to external list prices the total group lost €300 000, but now, realizing that using the external list prices is not the final solution, we have actually reached optimum.

Table 3.9 Profit change

	€000
Cardboard (23 250 – 19 200)	4 050
Paper pulp	0
Chemicals (–24 × 150)	–3 600
Total change	450

■ 5. Direct costs and opportunity costs

This case describes how different choices of internal transfer price will influence the behavior of managers so as to provide incentives for different external prices and volumes. As seen in scenario 1, full costs did not lead managers to very good decisions. In this case the full costs were too low and the cardboard division produced large volumes at prices that were too low for the group to make a very big profit.

The prices suggested by the controller's department, somewhere between full costs and external list prices, were a great deal better, but then we showed that using everybody's list prices did not improve things. This was because the list prices of the chemicals department did not really reflect the true opportunity costs of their production.

In scenario 4, we set all prices equal to direct costs plus opportunity costs. For the paper pulp division, this price is equal to the external list price. This happens because there are virtually no limits to their sales volume in the market. But for the chemicals division it turned out that there is surplus capacity, and so there are no opportunity costs. The optimum rule merely indicates that the internal transfer price should equal their direct costs. When doing so, we arrived at an optimum for the entire group.

Consequently, we have indicated that if internal transfer prices are equal to direct costs plus opportunity cost for each product or service, then the pursuit of self-interest by all divisions will take the group to a total optimum combination of prices and volumes.

3.3 Super pricing

The Super Co. has several divisions, which are full profit centers. This case deals with two divisions: the Standard division and the Refining division.

The Standard division produces two products, Super and Regular, about which we have the information shown in Table 3.10.

In the Standard division, fixed costs amount to €3 million per year. Total capacity is estimated to be 100 000 working hours and cannot easily be changed. Currently 20 000 units of each product are sold to outside customers. The sales volume of the Super product is expected to remain unchanged for a long time. The demand for Regular at the prevailing market price is virtually unlimited.

Table 3.10 Standard division's products (values per unit)

	Super	Regular
Sales price (€)	600	120
Direct material (€)	20	10
Direct wages (€)	280	70
Working time	4 hours	1 hour

In the Refining division one of their major products is called Perfect (see Table 3.11 for information). There are fixed costs of producing Perfect that amount to €400 000 per year. Expected sales are 3000 units.

Table 3.11 Information on Refining division's Perfect (values/unit)

	Perfect
Sales price (€)	1 400
Foreign direct material (€)	600
Domestic direct material (€)	100
Direct wages (€)	500
Working time	5 hours

In the Refining division, they have found that the Super product might replace the foreign material in the Perfect product. But in such a case, the working time in the Refining division would increase by 25 percent.

As a result, the company wants to investigate:

- The profitability of internal trade in the Super product, including the price limits of each division. What is the likely outcome of a free negotiation between the two divisions?
- The sensitivity of the analysis to changes in the market price of each of the three products.
- How the solution relates to the normally accepted rules of internal transfer pricing.

Solution: Super pricing

■ Basic calculations

In the Standard division, we have the situation in Table 3.12. In addition to what was given in the original case, we have now calculated the total number of working hours used by each of the two products. We can see that 20 000 units of each product will require 100 000 hours altogether. Since the working time is limited to 100 000 hours, increasing production of one product will lead to a decrease in another. Therefore, there might be shortages in working time and so contribution per working hour would be a crucial parameter for the following analysis. We can see that the Super product contributes €75 per working hour while the Regular

Table 3.12 Basic calculations

	Super	Regular
Sales price (€)	600	120
Direct materials (€)	20	10
Direct wages (€)	280	70
Contribution (€)	300	40
Working time per unit	4 hours	1 hour
Total working time	80 000 hours	20 000 hours
Contribution per hour	75	40

product contributes only €40 per hour. Therefore we will prioritize production of Super up to the sales limit of 20 000 units and after that we will employ the remaining capacity to produce the Regular product.

Since all machine capacity is busy, increased production for the Refining division will have to be taken out of what is already produced. Since the contribution of the Regular product is only €40 per hour we could take away four units of those products to make another Super product to be sold internally to the Refining division. We therefore arrive at the situation in Table 3.13 for making extra Super products for the Refining division.

Table 3.13 Costs per unit of making extra Super for Refining

	Super to Refining €
Direct materials	20
Direct wages	280
Opportunity cost (4 × 40)	160
Necessary price	460

The opportunity cost in the table refers to the possible gain from selling four units of Regular in the market. This possible gain will be lost if production of Regular is decreased in order to increase production of Super. Therefore, the minimum price of Super according to the Standard division will be €460.

In the Refining division, we have the situation in Table 3.14, where x stands for the internal transfer price. In this table, we have increased the cost of direct wages

Table 3.14 Calculating Perfect with Super

	Perfect €	Perfect with Super €
Sales price	1 400	1 400
Foreign material/super	600	x
Domestic material	100	100
Direct wages	500	625
Contribution per unit	200	200

in accordance with the original text. This appears possible because there is no indication that labor time is limited in the Refining division. Furthermore, we have to remember that the Refining division wants to gain something from the internal trade. Therefore, contribution per unit will not be allowed to decrease.

By analyzing the table, we can easily see that x, the internal price of Super, will have to be below €475 to make trade profitable for the Refining division.

Price limits and negotiation

The lower price limit of the Standard division is €460 and the upper price limit of the Refining division is €475. The negotiated price is likely to stay between those limits.

Sensitivity to changing prices

If the market demand of Super increases but the volume limit remains unchanged, the logic of our solution remains unchanged. Still, in such a case, the Standard division would probably argue that they deserve a higher price. Since, however, the text makes clear that there is no more demand for Super than what is already being sold, they will probably not succeed to raise the internal price.

If the market price of Super were to fall below €460, negotiations might change. In this case the Standard division would prefer to sell only Regular on the market and to decrease the production of Super. If there is an alternative supplier of Super, the Refining division might choose to buy its components from that supplier.

If the Standard division sells only Regular on the market and the demand is big enough (as was said in the text) then 100 000 units of Regular will give a contribution of €4 million, which is enough to keep the division going with a positive profit.

Changes in the market price of Regular will immediately influence negotiations. If the market price of Regular rises, the price limit of the Standard division will rise by four times as much. Consequently, if the market price of Regular reaches €124 or more, the lower limit of the Standard division will rise to €476 or more, making internal trade unlikely.

If, on the other hand, the market price of Regular falls, then the lower price limit of the Standard division will fall by four times as much. Thus, if the price of Regular falls to €100, the lower price limit of Standard will fall to €380. If the market price of Regular falls below €80, the standard division will stop selling Regular on the market. In this case there is no longer any opportunity cost and the lower price limit of the Standard division falls to €300 per unit of Super. If the price of Regular falls even further, it will not influence the negotiation.

The Standard division can make a profit selling only Super on the market as long as the market price of Super remains at its present level.

Changes in the market price of Perfect will only influence the negotiation if the price falls so much that the Refining division considers discontinuing production. Considering the fixed costs allocated to Perfect, this would happen if the price of the product fell below €1333 and stayed there for a long time. At that price, contribution per unit is only €133, which barely covers the fixed costs. If the market price were to fall further, the Refining division would need to lower its limit below €475.

If the market price of Perfect fell below €1333, the Refining division would need to lower its upper price limit by the same amount. Therefore, if the market price falls to €1318, the Refining division will lower its upper price limit to €460, which is equal to the lower price limit of the Standard division. In this case, internal trade would quickly be endangered. What's worse, the Refining division might decide to discontinue production of Perfect because it will produce losses no matter whether there is internal trade or not.

3.4 Magnetic resonance imaging

To solve this case well you will find it helpful to study Chapter 4 on investment analysis and Chapter 5 on capital costs.

At a large hospital they have a specialized magnetic resonance (MR) center, providing MR photography for the regular hospital clinics. There is a complete MR camera and specialized staff, working Monday morning until Friday afternoon, 8 hours a day. The camera provides highly qualified services for three other departments of the hospital and the MR center assigns all its costs to the recipients of the services.

The three recipients are:

- the medical clinic (regular treatment of many different kinds)
- the oncology clinic (cancer treatments)
- the cardiac clinic (heart treatments).

Last year, there was an economic savings program at the hospital and the number of MR investigations of medical patients had to be reduced in order to comply with the budget. Because of the traditional assignment methods, however, cutting down on the number of medical patients caused the cost of MR services to the other departments to rise, indirectly causing the costs of the oncology clinic to rise beyond its budget. The manager of the oncology clinic was very upset and asked for a study into the costs and cost assignment methods of the MR center.

■ Costs of the MR center

The MR camera was bought 4 years ago. The price at the time was €1 million. After 5 years (= next year) it will be upgraded with modern electronics at a cost of €100 000. After that it will be used for another 5 years and then it will have to be scrapped without any value at all. Buying a brand new MR camera today would cost some €1.3 million. It will have to be upgraded 5 years from now and the full life will be 10 years, just like the old camera.

Variable costs of the camera include chemical material and auxiliaries for €80 per patient. Normally, a patient needs a little less than 1 hour for full treatment. Therefore, the MR center has been designed to treat eight patients a day, 5 days a week, for 50 weeks a year.

Personnel costs of the MR center, including nurses, doctors, technical assistance and administration, amount to €400 000 per year and are completely independent of the number of patients as long as the total capacity remains as described.

■ Demand for MR services (no. of patients)

	Medical clinic	Oncology clinic	Cardiac clinic	Total
Last year's budget	800	800	400	2 000
Last year's actual	500	800	500	1 800

When working with this case, a fair nominal cost of capital can be assumed to be 6 percent before taxes. The hospital, being a government institution, does not pay any taxes. General inflation can be assumed to be around 2 percent per year.

To carry out the study requested by the oncology manager, it is useful to break it down as follows:

1 Find a fair yearly total cost to be assigned to the three clinics. Explain the several different ways to solve this task and justify your choices and working procedure!

2 Identify the traditional assignment procedure which led to the consequences described at the beginning of the case.

3 Show alternative methods of allocation between the three clinics. Describe strong and weak points for each method shown.

Solution: Magnetic resonance imaging

■ 1. The costs of the MR center

The total costs of the MR center could, for example, be estimated using nominal or real depreciation. A nominal linear analysis could be done in the following way. Nominal depreciation could be estimated by dividing the original investment by the estimated useful life. We get (€000):

$$1000/10 = 100$$

In addition, there is interest on the remaining part of the original investment. If the camera was bought 4 years ago, we shall assume that it has already been depreciated four times. Therefore the remaining starting value is €600 000. At 6 percent, the interest cost of next year will be (€000):

$$600 \times 6\% = 36$$

Adding those items together, the capital costs with nominal linear depreciation will be (€000):

$$100 + 36 = 136$$

When using a nominal linear depreciation, there is no good way to take the upgrading into account. This happens mainly because the upgrading has not yet taken place.

Alternatively, we could calculate a nominal or a real annuity of the investment. A nominal annuity be estimated in the following way (values in €000). At the very start of the project there is the original price (1000) plus the discounted value of the upgrading. Since the upgrading will take place 5 years after the original investment, its present value is discounted for 5 years at 6 percent. Its present value will be equal to $0.75 \times 100 = 75$. Therefore the total cost can be estimated as 1075. A nominal annuity (10 years, 6 percent) will be $1075/7.36 = 146$.

If we do the calculation in real numbers we should start from today's price of a new machine, which would be 1300. We add the discounted value of upgrading ($130 \times 0.82 = 107$). Now a real annuity of 1407 (10 years, 4 percent) will be $1407/8.11 = 173$.

	Nominal linear depreciation	Nominal annuity €000	Real annuity €000
Capital costs of investment	136	146	173
Personnel	400	400	400
Chemicals for 1800 patients	144	144	144
Total costs last year	680	690	717

Probably, the hospital would apply the nominal linear calculation. However, we should realize that the nominal linear calculation will make capital costs fall over time. Unless costs of personnel and chemicals rise very fast, this will tend to lower charges over time until a new camera is bought. When that takes place, the costs will suddenly rise.

The nominal annuity will be constant over time. If costs of personnel and chemicals rise at a moderate rate, the total costs will rise at an acceptable speed, which might make a replacement possible without any odd changes in charges.

The real annuity will allow capital costs to rise continually which is a good thing if costs of operations behave in a similar way. But if costs of operations rise much faster than inflation over time, it might be a good thing to have constant capital costs. Those costs might be found through the nominal annuity or through a real linear method.

■ 2. Traditional assignment procedure

Most probably the total costs were assigned to the three clinics according to their actual number of patients. Allocating total costs according to the nominal annuity to 1800 patients we get $690\,000/1800 = €383$ per patient. When allocating those same costs to the clinics we get the following distribution:

	Per unit	Medical	Oncology	Cardiac	Total
Actual number of patients		500	800	500	1 800
Allocation on actual numbers (€)	383	192 000	306 000	192 000	690 000

When the budget was created, probably everybody thought there would be 2000 patients. In such a case, the cost per patient would have been:

$$(146 + 400 + 160) \times 1000/2000 = 706\,000/2000 = 353$$

Assigning €353 per patient to 2000 patients according to the original budget would come out as follows:

	Per unit	Medical	Oncology	Cardiac	Total
Budgeted number of patients		800	800	400	2 000
Allocation on budget (€)	353	282 400	282 400	141 200	706 000

Thus we can see that the costs of the oncology clinic increased by over €23 000 compared with the budget just because the number of patients was reduced at the medical clinic. Clearly, this is not a desirable property of an internal pricing system.

3. Other possible methods of allocation

For an internal pricing system like this there are several possible approaches. The costs could be allocated according to the budget only, even if a clinic needed fewer treatments than budgeted. In this case each clinic would know their own costs all the time and they would not be affected by things that happened in the other clinics. On the other hand, they would not be able to save money during the years by lowering the number of patients.

In this solution we would need a way to make sure that clinics do not intentionally budget using numbers that are too low. Therefore, those clinics that consume more treatments than budgeted would have to pay an additional fee for additional treatments. Probably, such a fee should be somewhat higher than the regular budgeted amount.

Another approach would be to charge costs as standard costs. In this case the normal volume of the MR unit would be calculated in order to find the standard costs. After finding the standard costs, this is what each clinic would be charged for each treatment. In this way every clinic would pay for the treatments they actually buy and their costs would not be influenced by the behavior of the other clinics.

In a solution with standard costs there could be profits or losses at the MR unit even if they stick to their plans as closely as possible. But if the volume rises above the normal volume there will be profits because of the constant amount of fixed costs in the MR business. If volume falls, there will be losses for the same reason.

To solve the allocation problem in a more elegant way, we could allocate fixed costs according to budgeted volume or normal volume, and variable costs according to actual numbers. If we allocate fixed costs according to the budgeted volume we get the following:

	Per unit	Medical	Oncology	Cardiac	Total
Planned numbers; actual numbers		800; 500	800; 800	400; 500	
Fixed costs (146 000 + 400 000)/2000	273	218 400	218 400	109 200	546 000
Variable costs (80 per patient)	80	40 000	64 000	40 000	144 000
		258 400	282 400	149 200	690 000

In this case nobody would be hurt because of the changing volumes of the others. But again, clinics might find it to their advantage to manipulate the budget. If a particular clinic budgets too low a number of treatments, their share of the fixed costs would come down. To avoid manipulative behavior, we would need to charge a higher price (perhaps above full cost) for treatments that exceed budgeted numbers.

If fixed costs are allocated to the normal numbers of each clinic, manipulation can be avoided. Therefore, if normal numbers could be ascertained, this solution is probably the most functional one for management control.

Chapter 4

Corporate investment projects

4.1 Hillary Motors

Hillary Motors is a large supplier of private cars and motorcycles all over the world. In recent years they have tried to find environmentally friendly heating systems for their retailers and they are careful to make use of local sources. The manager of a new retail establishment in a suburb outside the capital is currently considering what kind of heating system to install.

In the local area, the easiest choice is electrical heating using large fans throughout the building. But an interesting alternative is a permanent system of ground source heat pumps channeled through pipes embedded in the floors. This was inspired by the following statement in the annual report of a major supplier:

> Installing a ground source heat pump can lead to a reduction in energy consumption of up to 80 percent. The reason for this is that a ground source heat pump uses the ground, surface soil or nearby lake as the main energy source and all these kinds of energy are free of charge.

For the new retailer and repair shop the cost of the pump (installation included) will amount to €100 000. Energy consumption for heating at other similar retailers in nearby suburbs is around 400 000 kWh per year and the price of that energy is currently around €0.1 per kWh. The manager feels that the actual savings will not be as large as suggested by the supplier, but he believes that a 60 percent reduction may be possible.

According to the rules of Hillary Motors, we need to achieve a 12 percent return on capital before taxes to be allowed to invest. In other words, taxes should be disregarded. Would you then recommend the installation of a system of ground source heat pumps?

Solution: Hillary Motors

When looking at the suggested investment in ground source heat pumps we can describe it in the following way (see Figure 4.1). First, there is the basic investment

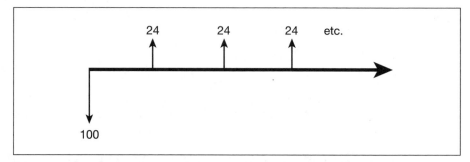

Figure 4.1 Hillary Motors: investment in ground source heat pumps (€000)

of €100 000 which happens at the beginning. We call this time zero. Then there are positive cash flows every year that amount to:

$$400\ 000 \times 0.60 \times 0.10 = €24\ 000 \text{ per year}$$

These payments will last for quite a long time. Let us assume that the manager trusts the equipment to work without any trouble for at least 8 years. Finally, we have not been told that there is any salvage value at the end. Therefore the project just expires without any additional payments.

Three of the most common methods used for cases like this are:

- payback time
- net present value analysis
- internal rate of return.

Payback time

To solve the case many companies would probably calculate the payback time. This involves finding out how many years are needed to get your money back. We find it quite easily:

$$\text{Payback} = 100/24 = 4.2$$

Thus it will take slightly over 4 years for Hillary to earn its money back, and after that the equipment is expected to work without any difficulties for almost another 4 years. Hopefully it will last much longer. Is that good enough? Many people would think so and feel that this is a good investment, especially as it is said to be quite environmentally friendly.

But when companies calculate payback they normally expect payback time to be no more than 3 years. This is because companies have many other uses for their money and feel that other investments might be more profitable than this one. Calculating payback, therefore, many companies would hesitate over this investment.

Net present value

We were told, however, that Hillary Motors wants a 12 percent return on its money before taxes. That means that we could, and should, perform a very different calculation, considering the time value of money.

When calculating net present value, we want to compare the value of cash flows that occur at different points in time. In doing so, we need to consider that most people feel that money now is more important than money later on. The easiest explanation for this is that if we receive money now, we can deposit it in a bank and receive interest. In a year our money will have grown by a certain amount. If the going rate of interest is 4 percent, then €100 today has the same value as €104 a year from now because one can easily be transformed into the other.

Now, in the particular case of energy saving at Hillary Motors, the finance department at HQ has told us that the going rate inside the company is 12 percent, which is much higher than the 4 percent we might get on deposit. This is a common situation in companies, which happens because money is often short and owners feel that investments are risky. Therefore they feel they need extra compensation on top of the going bank rate in order to invest in a risky project. In addition, company taxes will have to be paid before the owners can get their return. Consequently, an allowance for taxes must also be added to the required return.

Accepting the required return of the finance department, we will have to apply 12 percent interest to our transactions. This means that we are required to think that €100 today has the same value as €112 in a year's time after 12 percent interest has been added. In the same way, it means that a future payment will have to be reduced by 12 percent if we want to find today's equivalent.

Considering these circumstances we can now calculate the net present value (NPV) of the cash flow of the investment by finding today's value of all future payments. This procedure is called discounting and we are using 12 percent as our discount rate.

We get the following calculation:

$$\text{NPV} = -100 + 24/1.12 + 24/1.12^2 + 24/1.12^3 + \ldots 24/1.12^8 = 19.2$$

When performing the calculation we can calculate one item at a time in plain mathematics, we can find a table of 'present values' to convert each of the inflows to today's value, or we can find a table of 'accumulated present values' to convert them all in one calculation. Working with regular present values we find:

$$\text{NPV} = -100 + 24 \times 0.89 + 24 \times 0.80 \ldots + \ldots + 24 \times 0.40 = 19.2$$

Working with accumulated present values we find:

$$\text{NPV} = -100 + 24 \times 4.968 = 19.2$$

(Tables of 'Present Value' and 'Accumulated Present Value' are provided at the end of the book.)

After these calculations it appears that the NPV is a fair positive number, which would indicate a good project. But there are many uncertainties around the project and therefore strict economic reasoning is not very conclusive. Instead, sensitivity analysis becomes quite important. We calculated for 8 years. Clearly, an additional good year (which is actually quite likely) will easily take us into positive territory, although not by very much. Assuming 10 good years and applying the table of accumulated present values, we get:

$$\text{NPV} = -100 + 24 \times 5.65 = +35$$

This should be good enough to motivate the investment. Therefore, if the project's life span is greater than 8 years the project appears to be profitable. On the other hand, if the life of the equipment turns out to be less than 6 years, then a similar reasoning will easily show that the project is not profitable enough.

But there is perhaps a worse source of uncertainty. After all, we assumed that the manager was right when thinking that energy savings would amount to around 60 percent of the original consumption. Actually, if we save more than 50 percent of the original consumption, the project will be profitable, but if we save less than half, then the project will be unprofitable. Perhaps should we go back to the supplier to ask if they can really guarantee the energy savings?

As can be understood from our reasoning, if the NPV of a project is positive, then the project is a good one and should probably be carried forward. If not, it should probably not be entertained. But at the same time, the sensitivity analysis should be considered to account for those uncertainties that might remain after the calculations.

■ Internal rate of return

The internal rate of return is used a lot to find profitable investment opportunities. Instead of using an interest rate for discounting, we stipulate a required rate of return and compare that with the internal rate of return (also called 'the yield') of the project we are considering. This can be done by establishing the yield equation as follows:

$$NPV = -100 + 24/(1 + x) + 24/(1 + x)^2 + 24/(1 + x)^3 + \ldots 24/(1 + x)^8 = 0$$

The equation states that there is an interest rate x, which makes the NPV equal to zero. The higher that rate, the better the project.

As you can quickly see, it is not easy to solve the equation. In fact, most equations of this kind (with a degree higher than 3) cannot be solved at all with conventional methods, and a PC or advanced calculator must be used. The program will start by applying an arbitrary rate of interest and calculating the NPV. If this is above zero the interest rate will be raised. If the NPV is below zero the rate will be lowered. After a large number of trials (in a very short time) the solution, the yield of the project, will emerge. In this case the solution is $x = 17.3$ percent.

If the yield of the project is above the required rate, then the project is seen as a good one and if the yield is below the required rate the project is seen as not good enough. Therefore the internal rate of return agrees with NPV in this case.

Academics with training in accounting tend to criticize the internal rate of return. Managers without such training tend to like it because they believe that it clearly indicates if one project is better than another. With a doctorate in accounting and long practical experience as a consultant, I agree with the academics for reasons that will become clearer in later cases in this book.

■ What about taxes?

It was stated earlier in the case that we should perform all calculations before taxes. Many companies tend to do this, possibly because they think that including taxes in the calculations will be very complicated. But taxes are actually quite important payments to most companies and not very difficult to include in the calculations. Therefore we shall include a section on how to account for taxes in a simple investment case like this.

When including taxes in our analysis, we have to allow for three changes:

- tax depreciation on the original investment
- regular income taxes on yearly income
- a lower required discount rate after tax.

Tax depreciation on the original investment will have to be done in accordance with local tax rules in the country where the investment happens. If we assume that tax rules allow linear depreciation of equipment over a period of 5 years, yearly depreciations will be $100/5 = 20$. That amount will be seen as a cost in the company income statement and will lower the taxable profit. Therefore it lowers company taxes in proportion to the corporate tax rate. If we assume that company taxes are 25 percent of taxable profits, taxes will amount to:

$$100/5 \times 0.25 = 5$$

These tax savings will happen yearly for the first 5 years and after that they will end.

The second change refers to regular yearly income, which will now be taxed according to the same rules. We subtract 25 percent tax from all incomes and notice that the remaining income flow will now be only $24 \times 0.75 = 18$ per year.

Finally, we have to reconsider the discount rate. If all payments are constant over time and tax depreciations are distributed over the life of the project, then there is a simple formula saying that discount rate before tax, Dbt, is related to the discount rate after tax, Dat, in the following way:

$$Dbt \times (1 - tax\ rate) = Dat$$

In this case, the assumptions are not quite fulfilled, but still, if we accept the formula, we should change the discount rate to $12 \times 0.75 = 9$ percent.

In the new situation the project looks like Figure 4.2. Calculating NPV at 9 percent interest we get:

$$NPV = -100 + 18 \times 5.54 + 4 \times 3.89 = +15$$

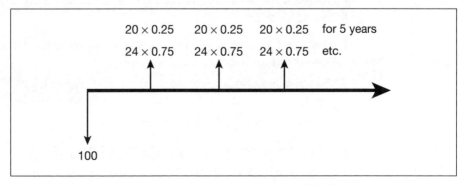

Figure 4.2 Hillary Motors investment, including taxes (€000)

Note here that 5.54 is the accumulated present value at 9 percent for 8 years and 3.89 is the accumulated present value at 9 percent for 5 years.

It appears that the NPV after full taxes is somewhat smaller than before taxes. This is not a very surprising outcome and it indicates that the assumptions for converting the discount rate were reasonably well fulfilled.

In a more ambitious case we ought to find a proper discount rate after taxes right at the start. But in this case we were given the rate before tax by the finance department. In fact, this often happens in the real world.

4.2 Modernizing the Distribution Co.

A division manager of the Distribution Co. has suggested closing down two old terminals (Southern and Eastern), replacing them with a new, larger and more efficient one (Central). In the first analysis, management has decided to disregard inflation and taxes.

The building costs for the new Central terminal are expected to amount to around €120 million. The change is expected to save €15 million a year. It will probably be used for 10 years. After that time it will be sold for €30 million.

If the project is actually carried out, the old Eastern terminal will be offered for rent to outside customers. It is expected to bring in €2 million a year for some time. The Southern terminal will probably be sold for around €25 million. Unfortunately the Southern terminal is only 8 years old. It was bought for €80 million and has been depreciated by €5 million per year. Today it has a book value of €40 million. All efforts have been made to find a seller willing to pay a better price, but these efforts have been in vain. Business in the Southern area is very bad and this is actually part of the reason for closing down the terminal.

Renting and selling transactions will be arranged during the building of the new terminal, but it will probably take most of the first year of operations before they can actually be made available for the new operators.

The owners of the Distribution Co. expect to earn 12 percent on equity capital and the company can borrow from their local bank at 6 percent. In the long run they believe that equity capital represents 60 percent of total capital.

To assess the modernization project, the accountants are asked to carry out the following analysis:

1 Describe the payments of the investment and find the net present value of the project disregarding taxes and inflation.

2 Several assumptions appear to be uncertain. Prepare a sensitivity analysis, showing the consequences of variations in the following numbers:
  - building costs of the new terminal
  - changes in the service level influencing yearly savings (€15 million)
  - the sale price of the Southern terminal (€25 million)
  - the useful life of the new Central terminal (10 years)
  - the annual rent of the Eastern terminal (€2 million).

3 Bring inflation and taxes into the analysis and see how these factors might influence the profitability of the case.

4 Explain the outcome of the analysis and give a recommendation as to what course of action to take.

Solution: Modernizing the Distribution Co.

■ Describing the payments

To start with we can describe the payments in accordance with Figure 4.3. At the start of the project there is the original outlay, €120 million. After that, there is one positive cash flow of €15 million for every year as long as the project lasts. At the end of the first year of operations we assume that we receive payment for the building we sold. At the same time, we assume the rents (paid in advance) begin to appear and keep coming in for as long as the project goes on. Possibly, rents might stop earlier if the old terminal does not function properly for a very long time. We can come back to that issue later. At the very end of the project there is an inflow of €30 million because we are selling the terminal and hopefully receiving payment in the same year.

The item that was left out

Apart from small differences in how we pinpoint rents and selling price in the cash flow diagram, most people would agree on the payments we have included. The problem arrives when someone who has studied a little bit of financial accounting says: 'Hey, you forgot the losses on the old terminal.'

But no, we did not forget it because it does not belong here. The old Southern terminal will be sold for €25 million because there are no buyers willing to pay a higher price. Therefore we shall hopefully receive €25 million and that is exactly what was put into the diagram of payments.

'But we have to write it down from €40 to 25 millions on the books. That is a significant loss!'

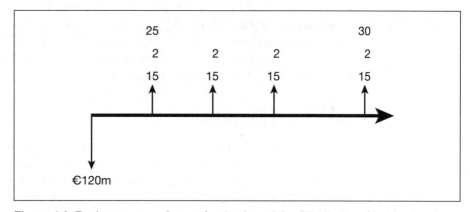

Figure 4.3 Basic payments for modernization of the Distribution Co. (€ million)

Yes, that is right. There is a significant loss on the books because of the old terminal. But that has nothing to do with this project. We have lost that money anyway. Either we sell it for €25 million and save €15 million a year for many years or we keep it. This calculation is being done to find out if it might be profitable to change terminals.

'But if we do not change terminals we do not need to write down the old one.'

Good point. When I play bridge on my computer late at night I also cheat sometimes. I go back and play another card once I have understood my mistakes. Late at night nobody will ever notice. But in business there is no point in fooling ourselves. Keeping a useless asset does not become profitable just because we can fool our readers for a while.

In our analysis we shall include all real payments, but not imaginary ones.

■ Finding the discount rate

Before we can even try to calculate the profitability of the project we need to find a proper discount rate. In a situation like this one, we know the two possible sources of capital and we need to weigh them together. According to our information, the long-term balance between the two sources of capital implies that equity provides 60 percent of all capital and borrowed capital amounts to 40 percent. For the moment we shall accept this information and work from there.

We start by calculating weighted average cost of capital (WACC) in the following way:

$$\text{WACC} = 0.60 \times 12 + 0.40 \times (1 - 0.25) \times 6 = 9.0$$

In the WACC calculation each source of capital is represented in accordance with its share of total capital. For borrowed capital we subtract taxes (somewhat arbitrarily we assume that the corporate tax rate is 25 percent) because those interest payments are deductible when paying taxes. The outcome, 9 percent is a proper discount rate when including taxes in our calculations.

But in this case it was explicitly stated that we should work without taxes in the first preliminary analysis. In such a case, many companies would simply raise the discount rate from 9 to 12 percent, hoping that the higher rate of interest would compensate for the missing taxes. This response is very common but, as was mentioned in the Hillary Motors case, it is not always correct. Still, in the first part of this case we shall accept the rule to avoid long introductory discussions and work with a discount rate of 12 percent before taxes.

■ Discounting payments

Discounting at 12 percent interest and disregarding taxes produces the results in Table 4.1. All items in the table are discounted according to their locations in time. Annual savings and rents are assumed to happen once a year (accumulated present values) for 10 years. Selling the old terminal will happen 1 year from now (present value) and the salvage value of the new terminal is discounted as a

Table 4.1 Discounting at 12 percent

Item	Amount €m	Discount factor	NPV €m
Initial investment	−120	1.00	−120.0
Yearly savings	15	5.65	84.8
Yearly rent	2	5.65	11.3
Selling old terminal	25	0.89	22.3
Salvage value of new terminal	30	0.32	9.6
Net present value			+8.0

one-time payment 10 years from now (present value). Check the tables to confirm the calculations.

It appears that the project has a positive NPV, which means it is profitable. If all assumptions hold and Distribution proceeds with the project, they will gain a value corresponding to €8 million right now compared with not completing the project. The market value of company shares should rise by €8 million if they are a quoted company and all investors fully understand what is happening.

But it has to be admitted that the gain will not show on the books immediately. On the contrary, in the beginning there will be a book loss when we write down the old Southern terminal. But after that, in a typical year, there will be a gain of €17 million a year minus capital costs of the investment. Averaging it all over all 10 years can be done by finding the annuity of the NPV:

$$\text{Yearly annuity (€m)} = 8.0/5.65 = 1.416$$

In other words, a gain of €1.416 million per year for 10 years would correspond to the same NPV as was calculated from the investment.

Some readers might want to see how the income statement changes. To find out we will have to make a few additional assumptions concerning the old Southern terminal. Here are some important ones:

1 Let us assume that the Southern terminal used to be written off by €5 million per year before the project took place.

2 All the new investment (€120 million) was financed by borrowing at 6 percent.

3 The revenue from salvage value in year one (€25 million) is used to pay back part of the initial loan.

If these assumptions hold, this is how the regular income statement will change in year 2 (€000):

	€000
Additional income	17 000
Additional interest costs [(120 − 25) × 6%]	− 5 700
Additional depreciation [(120 − 30)/10]	− 9 000
Disappearing old depreciation	+ 5 000
Additional profit before taxes	+7 300

In my opinion, this is not a very important statement, but some people like to see it to be convinced that in addition to *being profitable* (annuity + €1.4 million per year) it will also *look profitable* on the income statement. In later years, the income statement will improve as the loan is paid back.

▉ Sensitivity analysis

As part of the evaluation we were also asked to perform a sensitivity analysis, to find out what assumptions are the most sensitive ones if things do not turn out as planned. To perform such an analysis, let us work with two different changes in the same table:

- Assume that an item changes by 10 percent.
- Assume that an item changes by €1 million.

Applying these assumptions to Table 4.1 produces the outcomes in Table 4.2. From the first new column we can see that if all numbers grow by 10 percent, so does the NPV. The two most important items are the initial investment and the yearly savings.

Table 4.2 Discounting with new assumptions

Item	Amount €m	Discount factor	NPV €m	10%	€1 million €m
Initial investment	−120	1.00	−120.0	−12	−1
Yearly savings	15	5.65	84.8	8.48	5.65
Yearly rent	2	5.65	11.3	1.13	5.65
Selling old terminal	25	0.89	22.3	2.23	0.9
Salvage value	30	0.32	9.6	0.96	0.3
Net present value				0.8	11.5

In the second new column we can see that if all items grow by €1 million, then the NPV will grow by €11.5 million. The most sensitive items are those that last for a very long time, i.e. yearly savings and yearly rents.

Finally, if the project does not work properly for all 10 years, what then? Well, if we apply a new discount factor referring to 9 years instead of 10, we get the consequences in Table 4.3. We can see that the project loses a little more than half its NPV if it lasts for 9 years instead of 10. Consequently, we may infer that 8 years will not be enough to make the project profitable. On the other hand, if the project lasts for more than 10 years, profitability will increase by around €4 million per additional year.

▉ Inflation and taxes

Nobody knows for certain about future inflation. But most of us think that there will be some inflation and the European Central Bank has been instructed to try to

Table 4.3 Discounting over 9 years instead of 10

Item	Amount €m	Discount factor	NPV €m
Initial investment	−120	1.00	−120.0
Yearly savings	15	5.33	79.95
Yearly rent	2	5.33	10.66
Selling old terminal	25	0.89	22.3
Salvage value of new terminal	30	0.36	10.8
Net present value			+3.7

keep it at around 2 percent a year. Since we do not know any other number, let's assume they are right.

Taxes differ between all European countries. But in this book I normally assume that corporation taxes are 25 percent. That number is lower than the actual European average, but it is a comfortable number for our calculations. I trust the reader to be able to alter it as appropriate.

Also, we assume that machinery and equipment may be depreciated linearly for tax purposes over a 5-year period. Buildings are assumed to be depreciated linearly over a longer time, depending on the kind of building. The reader is advised to find out about local tax conditions as required to make local calculations correct.

In the case of the Distribution Co. it appears that the old Southern terminal was depreciated over 16 years. Since the new terminal will be sold for €30 million in year 10, let us assume that tax depreciation will be $(120 − 30) = €9$ million per year during those 10 years.

Now, adjusting for taxes means that yearly incomes will be reduced to 75 percent of their original values. The €25 million sales value of the old terminal will not be affected but there will be a tax compensation for the loss since its book value was still €40 million. That compensation will amount to $(40 − 25) \times 0.25 = €3.75$ million.

Finally, there will be tax savings because of yearly depreciation on the new terminal amounting to $9 \times 0.25 = €2.25$ million per year.

After those adjustments, cash flows of the project will look like Figure 4.4.

Now, let us evaluate the project again, including tax payments according to Figure 4.4 and, in addition, 2 percent inflation in accordance with the rules of the European Central Bank. But this time, since tax payments are included we shall work with 9 percent cost of capital as was explained in the beginning of the case.

When adjusting for inflation, we start by noticing that the initial investment will not change. Neither will depreciation on that investment. We discount the value of depreciation at 9 percent interest, which means that the accumulated discount factor will now rise to 6.84. A lower discount rate will give a higher accumulated present value.

Next, we have to deal with yearly savings, €15 million per year. Very likely, these will be affected by inflation. Therefore they will get bigger every year in nominal

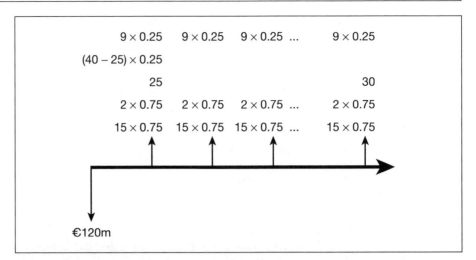

Figure 4.4 Distribution Co. cash flows after adjusting for taxes (€ million)

terms. If inflation changes all numbers in exactly the same way, the evaluation will look like this:

Value of savings $= 15 \times 1.02/1.09 + 15 \times 1.02^2/1.09^2 + 15 \times 1.02^3/1.09^3 + \ldots$ etc

This sequence might create some work for us when evaluating it. Since the individual amounts are no longer identical, we cannot apply the discounting factors from the accumulated present value table as usual. The solution to this problem is to allow the amounts to remain identical, i.e. €15 million per year, and to include the adjustment in the discount rate instead.

In fact, it turns out that $1.02/1.09 = 1/1.07$ (not exactly, but very close). Therefore we can apply a 7 percent discount rate instead of 9 percent. By such a simple step we can adjust for a regular inflation, 2 percent per year. Assuming that yearly rents will also be affected by inflation, we shall treat them in the same way.

The selling price of the old terminal, we can assume, has been agreed between buyer and seller and so it will not be affected by inflation. We discount it as we did last time, but selecting 9 percent instead of 12 percent. However, the sale will incur a book loss of €40 − 25 m = €15 m, which will save a fair amount of taxes.

The salvage value of the new terminal, we suppose, will rise according to inflation. Therefore, we shall discount it at a 7 percent real discount rate instead of the 9 percent nominal rate. We get:

Salvage value $= 30 \times 0.51 = €15.3$ m

We get the analysis in Table 4.4. Here we have added the effects of taxes and inflation. We can see that the value of depreciation more than compensates for taxes on yearly savings. Also, we find that, under the influence of inflation, the salvage value of the new terminal after 10 years is now very much bigger than before inflation was included. Altogether these two factors account for most of the improvement in the analysis.

Table 4.4 Effect of both taxes and inflation

Item	Amount €m	Yearly growth (inflation)	Discount factor	NPV €m
Initial investment	−120	−	1.00	−120.0
Depreciation on investment	9 × 0.25	0	6.42	14.4
Yearly savings	15 × 0.75	2%	7.02	79.0
Yearly rent	2 × 0.75	2%	7.02	10.5
Selling old terminal	25	0	0.92	22.9
Salvage value of new terminal	30		0.51	15.3
Tax gain on old terminal	(40 − 25) × 0.25	0	1.00	3.75
Net present value				+25.85

■ Conclusion

The net present value of the project is now clearly positive. From an economic point of view, the project appears to be quite a good one.

Reservation and warning

Note that our original approach, disregarding inflation and taxes, gave us a much lower value. In addition, those managers who would like to include the loss on the old equipment in a before-tax analysis would very likely think the economic analysis would be negative in this case. They would be mistaken, and they would lose a good investment opportunity.

4.3 Dalecarlia Showboat

The Barken Conference Group has decided to investigate the profitability of investing in a showboat to sail the archipelago of the Barken Lake. In particular, they intend to go into business arranging 'wilderness conferences' and business events on board the boat. During their investigations they have found out the following information (all numbers are given at 2010, prices).

It appears possible to buy a used boat for €5 million. Modernizing it to hold a restaurant and entertainment facilities would cost another €2 million. The boat can be brought into service during the tourist season in the spring of 2011. It can be used for at least 7 years. After that it could probably be sold for around €3 million. For tax purposes the boat can be written off in 5 years according to normal Swedish depreciation rules.

The project will produce an estimated gross income from tourist and conference business of €2.8 million per year. The costs for personnel, raw materials, fuel and sundries will amount to €1.2 million per year. In addition, it will be necessary to tie up around €0.5 million in supplies and receivables.

The company is fairly large and is well established. The average cost of group capital has been estimated to be 10 percent after taxes. The showboat will be a small part of the entire group and will be operated as a separate subsidiary (the 'Showboat Company').

The accountants are required to:

1 Illustrate the payments of the project in a diagram and calculate its profitability.
2 Investigate the sensitivity of the project in case there are changes to the information provided.
3 Present an income statement for the first year of the Showboat activity to the board.

Solution: Dalecarlia Showboat

■ 1. Illustrating the payments

To solve the case we need to start by describing the payments in a systematic way. Such a description could look like Figure 4.5. The payments include, first, a down-payment for buying the boat and doing the necessary renovation (€5 + 2 million). At the start of the project, they will also have to buy some supplies and, as soon as activities begin, they will have to tie up some money in receivables. An investment of €0.5 million is required to cover these.

On the positive side, there are yearly payments for restaurant activities that amount to €2.8 million per year for all 7 years. In addition, there is depreciation on the buying price and on the repairs of the boat. Those items amount to 20 percent per year of the original amount times the corporate tax rate, which in Sweden is 0.263.

Finally, at the end of the project, the boat is to be sold for €3 million. They will have to pay taxes on that €3 million because we have already written the boat off.

At the end of the project they can also sell the supplies and (hopefully) get paid for the outstanding payables, thus receiving back the €0.5 million paid for those things at the beginning of the project. This property has never been written off and therefore there will not be any tax consequences.

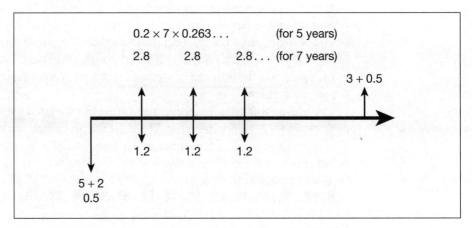

Figure 4.5 Payments for the Dalecarlia Showboat (€ million)

Table 4.5 Calculating net present value

Item	Amount €000	Factor	Present value €000
Buying boat	−5 000	1	−5 000
Repairing boat	−2 000	1	−2 000
Depreciation	0.2 × 7 000 × 0.263	3.79	1 395
Outlay supplies	−500	1	−500
Yearly income	2 800 × 0.737	4.87	10 050
Yearly costs	1 200 × 0.737	4.87	−4 307
Selling boat	3 000 × 0.737	0.51	1 128
Recovering outlays	500	0.51	255
Total NPV			1 021

Calculating profitability

Most of the items in the case appear to be fairly straightforward. But if we depreciate the full price of the boat during the introductory years, taxes would have to be paid on the recovery value at the end of the project. Alternatively, we might limit the depreciation to €4 million, which is the actual loss of value during the activities. Such a solution would be correct, but we would lose part of the present value. After all, saving taxes at the beginning of the project represents an important net gain for us even if those same taxes have to be paid at the end of the project.

Considering these things, the project can be evaluated as shown in Table 4.5. From the NPV it appears that this project is already quite good. But in most companies, the cost of capital is given in nominal terms (inflation included), and in our case we did not include inflation in our payments. Including 2 percent general inflation on all items will take us to an even better NPV calculation.

When including inflation in our payments the following things are likely to happen:

- Yearly income will probably rise by 2 percent per year. Since it is difficult to include yearly changes in the calculation, we choose to lower the discount rate from 10 to 8 percent for those items. The accumulated discount factor changes from 4.87 to 5.21.

- Depreciation will not change because of inflation. Therefore those numbers remain unchanged.

- Yearly costs will probably also rise by 2 percent per year. We change the discount factor in the same way as income.

- Finally, the selling price of the boat and the recovery of working capital will quite likely change because of inflation. Therefore we discount those two items at 8 percent instead of 10 percent just as we did with income and costs.

The revised calculation is shown in Table 4.6. Possibly, the recovery of outlays will incur some taxes that were not included in the table. If certain items are bought for €500 in year 0, then after inflation for 7 years they might sell for around €575 in year 7. But since these goods will probably be bought and sold several times during

Table 4.6 Revised calculation including inflation

Item	Amount €000	Factor	Present value €000
Buying boat	−5 000	1	−5 000
Repairing boat	−2 000	1	−2 000
Depreciation	0.2 × 7 000 × 0.263	3.79	1 395
Outlay supplies	−500	1	−500
Yearly income	2 800 × 0.737	5.21	10 744
Yearly costs	1 200 × 0.737	5.21	−4 605
Selling boat	3 000 × 0.737	0.58	1 290
Recovering outlays	500	0.58	290
Total NPV			1 614

the 7 years, it is very difficult to find out the tax consequences. Therefore, we did not include any taxes in the calculation.

As can be seen from the tables, inflation will increase the accumulated incomes quite a lot. It works to the advantage of the project because future incomes increase whereas the original expenditure to buy the boat does not change.

2. Sensitivity analysis

In the sensitivity analysis we need to find out what happens to the value of the project if one or several of the payments change. Normally it would be useful to study the consequences of two different kinds of changes, namely:

- if payments change by a fixed amount
- if payments change by a certain percentage.

In the following analysis we shall identify consequences of a €100 000 change and a 10 percent change.

Most items are fairly straightforward. But there is one item that needs careful examination: the original outlay for buying and repairing the boat. The original expenditure will influence the amounts of depreciation. As can be seen from Table 4.6, the original outlay is €7 million and the present value of depreciation is €1.395 million. Depreciation will never change in its own right, but it will change in proportion to the possible changes in the original investment.

From Table 4.6 we can see that depreciation relates to the original investment in the following way:

$$1395/7000 = 0.20$$

In other words, the present value of depreciation is almost exactly equal to 20 percent of the original investment. Therefore, if the original investment increases by €100 000 then the value of depreciation will increase by €20 000 and the net effect will be only €80 000.

Table 4.7 Sensitivity analysis

Item	Amount	Factor	PV	Change	
				€100 000	10%
	€000		€000	€000	€000
Basic investment less depreciation	7 000 − 1 395 = 5 605	1	5 605	80	560
Outlay for supplies	500 − 290 = 210	1	210	42	21
Yearly inflow	2 800 × 0.737	5.21	10 751	384	1 075
Yearly outflow	1 200 × 0.737	5.21	4 607	384	460
Salvage value	3 000 × 0.737	0.58	1 282	43	128

There is a similar effect for the outlays for supplies. The original expenditure is €500 000 and the present value of the recovery is €290 000. Consequently, the recovery amounts to:

$$290/500 = 58 \text{ percent}$$

Therefore, if outlays increase by €100 000, the net effect will be only €42 000 after the recovery.

For regular inflows and outflows, we need to bring the present value of the flow into the sensitivity analysis. After that we will study what would happen to the total PV of the flow if the yearly amount changes by €100 000 or 10 percent. Notice that taxes will diminish the effect of changes in those flows.

After considering all these effects, we arrive at the sensitivity analysis shown in Table 4.7. We can see that the most critical payments are the original investment and the yearly flows. But it is very clear that the yearly flows are more sensitive to a fixed yearly amount than the original investment. This happens because the yearly flows will be repeated for a large number of years, whereas the original investment happens only once. Therefore, plans for yearly flows will have to be scrutinized very carefully.

In this case, most of the original investment is buying the boat. We have to assume that there is a contract for the buying price. But the repairs might consist of several separate items or even several little projects and therefore it could be difficult to estimate those costs correctly.

■ 3. First-year profit statement

A profit statement for one or several of the first few years is almost always necessary to convince the board, even if the NPV calculation is clearly positive as in this case. Board members do not always feel comfortable with NPV calculations and they know that a good NPV value can occur even if some years are not as good as the others. Therefore, an income statement for the first year is almost a necessity to convince board members of a project like this one.

However, we have a difficulty in this case because there is not a full description of project financing. It is said that the average cost of group capital is equal to 10 percent after taxes, but we have not been told how the capital for this particular project will be raised. But still, if the company is not issuing new equity capital, they will probably either take the money from available bank accounts or they will borrow what they need for the investment.

To get started, however, let us assume that all the money needed will be borrowed for this purpose and that the borrowing rate is 6 percent before taxes. We will need €5 million to buy the boat and another €2 million to renovate it. In addition, we shall need €0.5 million for operating capital. Altogether, the amount of capital needed will be €7.5 million. In this a case, the first year income statement might look like Table 4.8.

But hold on a minute. This income statement does not look very good at all. There is a loss before taxes and they are depending on income from other projects in order to receive the tax advantage that was mentioned in the beginning. These incomes may well be realized, but the profitability of this project does not look good at all. Did we make a mistake?

No, not really, but we depreciated the boat far too quickly. In fact, the boat can be used for many years and we plan to sell it for €3 million after 7 years. Therefore, we failed to show the full potential of the project.

Many little companies depreciate their assets over 5 years just because the tax authorities will allow it. But, in reality, depreciation should be done over the life of the boat and that time will be much longer than this project. If we depreciate the boat over 10 years instead of 5, the income statement will improve considerably (see Table 4.9).

So, Table 4.9 is the income statement we should show to the board. The higher depreciation shown in Table 4.8 should still be adopted, but only in the tax accounts to keep the company's taxes as low as possible. The income statement in Table 4.9 is probably quite realistic.

Table 4.8 First-year income statement

	€000
Income from sales	2 800
Operating costs	−1 200
Depreciation	−1 400
Profit from operations	200
Interest costs (7.5 × 6%)	−450
Profit before taxes	−250

Table 4.9 First-year income statement, adjusting depreciation

	€000
Income from sales	2 800
Operating costs	−1 200
Depreciation	−700
Profit from operations	900
Interest costs (7.5 × 6%)	−450
Profit before taxes	450

4.4 Paper Pulp Co.

A few years ago there was a surplus of wood in the eastern area of the Paper Pulp Co.'s territory. Accordingly, there was a discussion about a possible new production line to produce sulfate paper pulp at the Eastern plant. The production line was designed to produce 430 000 tons of bleached sulfate pulp after appropriate construction and fine-tuning activities.

As usual, an introductory study was performed, which led to the following description of the situation:

> In order to produce 430 000 tons of pulp Paper Pulp Co. will need to invest around SEK 6000 million, including regular measures for environment protection. Out of this amount, some SEK 2000 million will be spent on building the plant and SEK 4000 million will be spent on machinery.

At the time of completion of the investment, the long-term price trend for bleached sulphate pulp was expected to equal $650 per ton. The exchange rate for dollars was expected to stabilize at around SEK 8 to the dollar. In the long run, the staff expected the market price of pulp to rise in accordance with inflation, i.e. by 4 percent a year (in dollars).

As soon as production starts, there will be yearly fixed production costs (mainly equipment and employees) amounting to SEK 520 million per year. Variable costs (for fuel, chemicals and wood) will be some SEK 2400 per ton. All costs are expressed in SEK and at the beginning of our analysis we shall assume that they will rise over time at the same rate as the market price of pulp.

Without any major reinvestment, the production line would normally last for some 20 years. Thus, the building will be depreciated over this period. For tax reasons, however, the machinery will be depreciated over 5 years, even though it will last much longer. After 10 years the machinery will have to be renovated at a cost of some SEK 1000 million, inflation included.

■ Cost of capital

The board of the Eastern plant normally calculated big investment projects like this one at a cost of capital of 14 percent interest, without considering taxes. There was no very good reason for this discount rate; it was decided by the former CFO, who retired a few years ago.

The new controller, however, felt that disregarding taxes in such big investments might lead to an incorrect conclusion. Therefore, he wanted to include taxes in the analysis. He estimated the cost of capital to be 10 percent after taxes. As a matter of fact, the company could borrow from the bank at only 7 percent interest.

The controller requires an analysis of the project, which it might be wise to carry out in the following order:

1 Calculate the net present value of the project according to the traditional rules of the board, thus using 14 percent interest and disregarding taxes.

2 Discuss how to decide on company cost of capital. In view of the company's traditional approach and the suggestions of the new controller, what is your recommendation?

3 Explain (without calculations) what changes would be necessary in order to include taxes to a full extent into the analysis.

4 Perform the net present value analysis, including taxes, with the appropriate cost of capital.

5 Discuss the sensitivity of the analysis, analyzing possible changes in the assumptions made.

6 Explain (without calculations) how the yearly profit statement of the company will change over time if the project is actually carried out.

Solution: Paper Pulp Co.

This case can be solved very straightforwardly in an Excel sheet, but it can also be solved by regular calculations working with payments and discount rates. In this solution we shall do both alternatives.

■ Excluding taxes

Let us start with the Excel sheet.

Excel solution

Most of the numbers of the case are available in the Excel worksheets 'Capital budgeting: NPV' and 'Capital budgeting: income'. In the NPV worksheet, there are two regular calculations, solving the capital budgeting problem before and after tax. In the income worksheet, there is a description of how to solve the last question dealing with the consequences for financial accounting.

Let us start with the NPV section on page 131. There you will find a top area stating most of the variables of the case. First there is the original investment, SEK 6000 million. Next there is revenue as it would appear at the start of the project. It will be calculated in the following way:

$$430\,000 \times 650 \times 8 = \text{SEK } 2236 \text{ million}$$

We know very well that there will be no income in year 0, but we need this number as a starting point. In the following years we shall apply inflation or other changes to this original number to see where it takes us.

Under the heading 'production' you will find fixed and variable costs, also at year 0 prices and you will find the anticipated growth of each of these numbers.

Further to the right there is a section on cost of capital, which is stated both excluding and including taxes. The first number, 'excluding taxes', is just the number given according the traditional practice of the company. The cost of capital 'including taxes' merely repeats the opinion of the young controller. Later in the solution we

Capital budgeting: NPV

Investment and revenue

Investment year 0	6 000	
Revenue year 0	2 236	
Revenue growth	4%	

Production

Fixed cost year 0	520	
Variable cost year 0	1 032	
Growth fixed costs	4%	
Growth variable costs	4%	

Cost of capital

Excluding taxes	14%	
Including taxes	10%	
Local tax rate	0.263	

			Costs		Excluding taxes					Adjusting for taxes			
Year	Invest	Revenue	Fixed	Variable	Cash flow	Factor 1	NPV	Depr	Profit	Taxes	Cash flow	Factor 2	NPV 2
0	6 000				-6 000	1.00	-6 000				-6 000	1.00	-6 000
1		2 325	541	1 073	711	0.88	624	900	-189	-50	761	0.91	692
2		2 418	562	1 116	740	0.77	569	900	-160	-42	782	0.83	646
3		2 515	585	1 161	769	0.67	519	900	-131	-34	804	0.75	604
4		2 616	608	1 207	800	0.59	474	900	-100	-26	826	0.68	564
5		2 720	633	1 256	832	0.52	432	900	-68	-18	850	0.62	528
6		2 829	658	1 306	865	0.46	394	100	765	201	664	0.56	375
7		2 942	684	1 358	900	0.40	360	100	800	210	690	0.51	354
8		3 060	712	1 412	936	0.35	328	100	836	220	716	0.47	334
9		3 183	740	1 469	974	0.31	299	100	874	230	744	0.42	315
10	1 000	3 310	770	1 528	12	0.27	3	100	912	240	-227	0.39	-88
11		3 442	801	1 589	1 053	0.24	249	300	753	198	855	0.35	300
12		3 580	833	1 652	1 095	0.21	227	300	795	209	886	0.32	282
13		3 723	866	1 718	1 139	0.18	207	300	839	221	918	0.29	266
14		3 872	900	1 787	1 184	0.16	189	300	884	233	952	0.26	251
15		4 027	936	1 859	1 232	0.14	173	300	932	245	987	0.24	236
16		4 188	974	1 933	1 281	0.12	157	100	1 181	311	970	0.22	211
17		4 356	1 013	2 010	1 332	0.11	144	100	1 232	324	1 008	0.20	199
18		4 530	1 053	2 091	1 386	0.09	131	100	1 286	338	1 048	0.18	188
19		4 711	1 096	2 174	1 441	0.08	120	100	1 341	353	1 088	0.16	178
20		4 899	1 139	2 261	1 499	0.07	109	100	1 399	368	1 131	0.15	168
Totals						6.62	-290	7 000				9	605

shall discuss the relationship between these numbers, which is not as obvious as one might at first think.

Finally, there is information on the local tax rate. In Sweden today, the corporation tax rate is 26.3 percent, which is the outcome of a political compromise.

Entering these numbers into the Excel sheet, the year numbers are in column A. In column B we enter investment outlays in nominal numbers. There is the basic investment which is supposed to happen in year 0 and there is a major renovation in year 10.

In column C you will find yearly revenue. It starts from the original SEK 2236 million and each number in the column grows by the revenue growth that was posted in box C6. In column D you will find fixed costs starting from 520 and growing every year according to the growth number in box G6.

Column E displays variable costs, growing every year in accordance with the growth number in box G7.

After those basic entries we calculate yearly cash flows in column F in the following way:

$$F = -B + C - D - E$$

Next, in column G, come the discount factors for each year in accordance with the old recommendation of the board. Box G12 shows the discount factor for year 0 and then they all diminish through dividing by $(1 + L4)$. Box L4, as you will remember, shows the discount rate to be applied before taxes. Box G33 shows the accumulated present value for a 20-year series of payments at 14 percent interest.

In column H we calculate present values of all payments disregarding taxes. The outcome, shown in Box H33, is negative, −290, which means that the NPV of this version of the project is negative. But since we did not include taxes, we know that the outcome is not very trustworthy. Let us therefore postpone discussing the outcome in more detail.

Using a pocket calculator

If you prefer to work the case with a pocket calculator, it might be done as in Table 4.10. When finding the discount factors, I applied a discount rate of 9.62 percent, which corresponds to the relationship:

$$1.14/1.04 = 1.0962$$

Table 4.10 Calculating net present value

Item	Amount SEK m	Growth	Factor	PV SEK m
Basic investment	−6 000	None	0	−6 000
Yearly inflow	2 236	4% per year	8.74	19 541
Yearly outflow, fixed	−520	4% per year	8.74	−4 545
Yearly outflow, variable	−1 032	4% per year	8.74	−9 020
Maintenance in year 10	−1 000	none	0.27	−270
Total NPV				−294

Using my calculator, I found that the discount factor for 20 years and 9.62 percent will be:

$$\text{NPV (20 years, 9.62\%)} = 8.74$$

If you do not have access to a financial calculator, you might instead calculate $14 - 4 = 10$ percent and find the corresponding discount factor in a present value table. It will be 8.51 and the numbers will change to a small extent. The conclusions will remain unchanged.

As can be seen, the NPV comes out to −294, which differs slightly from the Excel sheet. The difference is due to rounding in the manual solution.

■ Cost of capital

Cost of capital should be calculated as weighted average cost of capital (WACC). To do so, we need to find the cost of equity (not given in the case) and the cost of debts (7 percent according to the new controller). After that we need to find, or at least to estimate, the proportion of each kind of capital. Those proportions should be estimated including the full market value of equity and the full market value of debts. Those proportions are not given in the case. Assuming we know all those numbers, WACC can be calculated as:

$$\text{WACC} = \text{CE} \times \text{E}/(\text{D} + \text{E}) + \text{CD} \times \text{D}/(\text{D} + \text{E}) \times (1 - 0.263)$$

In the formula CE is the cost of equity (this number is normally given after company taxes); D and E represent the market values of debts and equity capital; and CD is the cost of debts (this number is normally given before taxes). Because of that, we adjust for taxes in order to find company cost of capital after taxes. Company taxes are supposed to be 26.3 percent.

Since the new controller estimates that WACC is equal to 10 percent after taxes, I think the best alternative would be to follow his advice and accept his estimate.

■ Including taxes

We have to do three main adjustments:

1 Lower the discount rate from 14 to 10 percent.

2 Apply taxes to all regular incomes and costs. Investments should be left unchanged and interest payments should be left out of the analysis just as before.

3 Include depreciation on investments and calculate tax savings on all depreciations.

These adjustments have been introduced into columns I–N of the NPV Excel worksheet.

Excel solution

When including taxes, we start by including tax depreciation in column I according to the tax laws that are applicable in the particular case. In Sweden an industrial building of this type can be depreciated over 20 years, whereas machinery can be depreciated over 5 years. Therefore depreciation during the first 5 years will be (SEK million):

$$2000/20 + 4000/5 = 900$$

In the following 5 years only the building will be depreciated, so we get:

$$2000/20 = 100$$

From year 11 we can depreciate the original building plus the renovation that was done in year 10. Assuming the renovation dealt with machinery, we get:

$$2000/20 + 1000/5 = 300$$

During the final 5 years we shall depreciate the original building only.

In column J we compute yearly profits from the project before taxes in the following way:

$$J = C - D - E - I$$

During the first few years there are losses because the tax depreciation of machinery is fairly fast in Sweden.

In column K we calculate taxes applying the tax rate that was given in box L7. During the first few years taxes turn negative because there were losses before taxes. In some situations, this might cause problems if the tax authorities do not allow companies to even out taxes over the years to come. In this particular case, however, there is not a problem. It was clearly said at the beginning of the case that there was a surplus of wood in the eastern part of the company's territory. Therefore we shall assume that the company has several other plants that make profits and so the negative taxes can be subtracted from positive taxes for other plants.

Column L shows cash flows after taxes in the following way:

$$L = C - D - E - K$$

Column M shows discount factors after tax, accepting the suggestions from the new controller. Column N shows the total NPV of the project including taxes. When working this case including taxes, the analysis comes out at +SEK 605 million. This is a great deal better than the negative number in column H when we were disregarding taxes. Apparently, the tax gains from depreciation and the lower discount rate overtook the losses from taxes on the yearly cash flow. While it is a remarkable conclusion, this is quite a common situation in long-term industrial projects. It shows that including taxes in the analysis is very important.

This is a little known effect of analyses before and after taxes. It happens because interest rates are normally adjusted too much to compensate for taxes. Therefore, when working a case without taxes, companies tend to over-compensate for taxes and to destroy NPVs of many long-lasting projects.

These effects are dealt with in detail in Case 4.8, 'Regulating WACC' (page 147).

Table 4.11 NPV after taxes

Item	Amount SEK m	Growth	Factor	PV SEK m
Basic investment	−6 000	None	0	−6 000
Yearly inflow	2 236 × 0.737	4% per year	11.69	19 264
Yearly outflow, fixed	−520 × 0.737	4% per year	11.69	−4 480
Yearly outflow, variable	−1 032 × 0.737	4% per year	11.69	−8 891
Tax shield depreciating machinery	800 × 0.263	None	3.79	797
Tax shield depreciating buildings	100 × 0.263	None	8.51	224
Maintenance in year 10	−1 000	None	0.39	−390
Tax shield depreciating maintenance	200 × 0.263	None	3.79 × 0.39	78
Total NPV				602

Using a pocket calculator

If you prefer to work the same case with a pocket calculator, it might be done in accordance with Table 4.11. Most discount factors were derived in the same way as in the case before taxes. Depreciating maintenance, however, had to be done in two steps, first discounting the yearly amounts to year 10, and then from there to year 0.

As can be seen, the final outcome differs a trifle from the Excel solution. This difference is due to rounding in the manual solution and is unimportant.

■ Sensitivity analysis

Since NPV is only SEK 605 million, the project will become unprofitable if the original investment rises by somewhat over 10 percent (10 percent × 6000 = 600). If inflation comes down to 3 percent instead of 4 percent, NPV will fall to zero. If costs rise by only half a percent more than incomes, the whole project will become unprofitable.

These changes can preferably be found by varying the numbers in the Excel sheet. In this way we can easily see that the solution is very sensitive to changes in the assumptions.

■ Financial profit statement

In fact, the reported profit statement might not look like the NPV Excel worksheet at all. In financial accounting, we deduct interest payments before paying taxes and reporting profits. In this case we do not know how much money will be borrowed, but we do know that what is not borrowed must be taken out of available cash unless new shares are issued. Therefore, let us assume that some of the capital is borrowed and the remainder is taken out of interest-earning bank accounts. To simplify things, let us assume that the interest rate (7 percent) mentioned by the controller is applicable in both cases.

Capital budgeting: income

	Investment and revenue		Production		Cost of capital	
Investment year 0	6 000		Fixed cost year 0	520	Excluding taxes	14%
Revenue year 0	2 236		Variable cost year 0	1 032	Including taxes	10%
Revenue growth	4%		Growth fixed costs	4%		
			Growth variable costs	4%	Local taxes	0.263

			Costs		Excluding taxes			Adjusting for taxes						Finding the income statement if no more shares are issued				
Year	Invest	Revenue	Fixed	Variable	Cash flow	Factor 1	NPV	Depr	Profit	Taxes	Cash flow	Factor 2	NPV 2	Interest	Profit	Taxes	Net profit	Net cash
0	6 000				−6 000	1.00	−6 000				−6 000	1.00	−6 000					−6 000
1		2 325	541	1 073	711	0.88	624	900	−189	−50	761	0.91	692	−420.0	−609	−160	−449	−5 549
2		2 418	562	1 116	740	0.77	569	900	−160	−42	782	0.83	646	−388.4	−549	−144	−404	−5 053
3		2 515	585	1 161	769	0.67	519	900	−131	−34	804	0.75	604	−353.7	−484	−127	−357	−4 510
4		2 616	608	1 207	800	0.59	474	900	−100	−26	826	0.68	564	−315.7	−416	−109	−306	−3 916
5		2 720	633	1 256	832	0.52	432	900	−68	−18	850	0.62	528	−274.1	−342	−90	−252	−3 268
6		2 829	658	1 306	865	0.46	394	100	765	201	664	0.56	375	−228.8	537	141	396	−2 772
7		2 942	684	1 358	900	0.40	360	100	800	210	690	0.51	354	−194.1	606	159	447	−2 226
8		3 060	712	1 412	936	0.35	328	100	836	220	716	0.47	334	−155.8	680	179	501	−1 624
9		3 183	740	1 469	974	0.31	299	100	874	230	744	0.42	315	−113.7	760	200	560	−964
10	1 000	3 310	770	1 528	12	0.27	3	100	912	240	−227	0.39	−88	−67.5	845	222	623	−242
11		3 442	801	1 589	1 053	0.24	249	300	753	198	855	0.35	300	−16.9	736	194	542	601
12		3 580	833	1 652	1 095	0.21	227	300	795	209	886	0.32	282	42.1	837	220	617	1 518
13		3 723	866	1 718	1 139	0.18	207	300	839	221	918	0.29	266	106.2	945	249	697	2 514
14		3 872	900	1 787	1 184	0.16	189	300	884	233	952	0.26	251	176.0	1 060	279	782	3 596
15		4 027	936	1 859	1 232	0.14	173	300	932	245	987	0.24	236	251.7	1 184	311	872	4 768
16		4 188	974	1 933	1 281	0.12	157	100	1 181	311	970	0.22	211	333.8	1 515	398	1 116	5 985
17		4 356	1 013	2 010	1 332	0.11	144	100	1 232	324	1 008	0.20	199	418.9	1 651	434	1 217	7 302
18		4 530	1 053	2 091	1 386	0.09	131	100	1 286	338	1 048	0.18	188	511.1	1 797	473	1 324	8 726
19		4 711	1 096	2 174	1 441	0.08	120	100	1 341	353	1 088	0.16	178	610.8	1 952	513	1 439	10 264
20		4 899	1 139	2 261	1 499	0.07	109	100	1 399	368	1 131	0.15	168	718.5	2 117	557	1 560	11 925
Totals						6.62	−290	7 000				9	605				10 925	

In this situation the net amount of financial payments will clearly worsen by:

$$6000 \times 7\% = \text{SEK 420 million}$$

See the 'income' Excel worksheet on page 136 to see the consequences.

Profits and taxes will change accordingly and the net profit on the income statement in the very first year will come down from SEK −189 million to SEK −449 million. However, already in the first year cash flow will be SEK 451 million (due to the large depreciation). Therefore, some of the debts might be paid back and so interest costs will fall a little in every year until profits return to positive numbers in year 6 when the main series of depreciation has ended.

In presenting an Excel sheet like this to the board, we should expect difficulties. Board members might not find it very encouraging to see negative profit numbers for the first 5 years of a project. (Maybe this is as long as they actually plan to remain on the board!). Therefore we need to reconsider the presentation and depreciate the original investment in the financial reports over a longer time than in the tax calculation. This can be done by reducing yearly depreciation on the machinery from SEK 800 million to SEK 200 million, thus allocating it over the full life of the project. In this way profits will look acceptable even in the first few years.

Now even the reported profit looks comfortable, and all board members should be happy with the project.

4.5 Buying growing forest

A pension fund manager felt it might be valuable to invest in growing forest in order to have some real and regular income. He investigated the possibilities of buying some forested land (mainly pine trees) in southern Sweden and found the following approximate facts, which are valid in 2010:

- To grow a good pine tree forest, the land should be planted with one plant for every 1.25 meters (m) along each row. After allowing some space at the end of rows, this means that there will be 6400 plants in a hectare (10 000 m^2). The cost of planting pine trees is around SEK 12 000 per hectare.

- Some 10 years after planting, the land will have to be cleared from hardwood plants like birch and rowan trees. The clearing costs around SEK 12 000 per hectare and will yield some firewood, possibly enough to pay half the cost of clearing.

- After another 15 years the area should be thinned. Thinning means taking away 75 percent of the pine trees, yielding on the average 0.03 m^3 of wood per tree, to be sold to a paper pulp factory. The price of paper pulp is around SEK 250 per m^3. The cost of thinning is around SEK 20 000 per hectare.

- Around 50 years after planting there will be a second thinning. Some 75 percent of the remaining trees are cut down. Now they yield on the average 0.2 m^3 of wood per tree. The very best pieces of wood will be treated as timber and the remainder can be sold to a paper pulp factory. Including the timber, the average price will be around SEK 300 per m³. The cost of thinning is still around SEK 20 000 per hectare.

■ Finally, when the forest is fully grown (80 years after planting), the final cutting will be done. The remaining trees yield, on average, 0.7 m³ of timber worth some SEK 500 per m³. In addition, each tree will yield 0.1 m³ of twigs and branches to be sold as firewood, priced at SEK 200 per m³. The cost of final cutting is SEK 15 000 per hectare. After cutting in the winter the area will be planted again in the following summer.

Now suppose our pension fund manager has found a tract of land with a perfectly even distribution of wood of all ages. Thus there is 1 hectare to be planted, another hectare where the forest is 1 year old, 1 hectare where the forest is 2 years old and so on up to 1 hectare which is ready for final cutting. (When evaluating the forest, we disregard the possible value of hunting rights and plots for holiday cottages or other buildings.)

To evaluate the project, the accountants are asked to carry out the following analysis:

1 What is the average value of a hectare of the tract of land if the fund manager wants 6 percent return on his money?

2 Is this 6 percent a nominal or a real interest rate?

3 In the open market, such a tract of land is normally traded at prices of around SEK 60 000 per hectare. What interest rate is applied in the market?

Solution: Buying growing forest

■ 1. The value of an average hectare

If we accept the assumption that the fund manager is buying a tract of land with 1 hectare of each age, then, each year, he will have to plant 1 hectare, clear 1 hectare, and thin 2 hectares. Also there is 1 hectare ready for cutting. Those activities will, in any 1 year, lead to the payments indicated in Table 4.12, all expressed at 2010 prices.

Now, receiving SEK 183 000 each year forever, the value of the whole tract at 6 percent will be:

$$183\ 000/0.06 = SEK\ 3\ 050\ 000$$

Since this value covers 80 hectares, the average value per hectare is 3 050 000/80 = SEK 38 125.

■ 2. What type of interest rate did we apply?

Since all values, old and new, are set at 2010 prices, we are applying a real interest rate for discounting. If the interest rate were nominal we would have to raise prices

Table 4.12 Payments in any year (2010 prices)

Activity	Payments SEK
1 Planting 1 hectare	−12 000
2 Clearing 1 hectare	−12 000
Income from firewood when clearing	6 000
3 First thinning ($0.75 \times 6\,400 \times 0.03 \times 250$)	36 000
Cost of first thinning	−20 000
4 Second thinning ($0.75 \times 0.25 \times 6\,400 \times 0.2 \times 300$)	72 000
Cost of second thinning	−20 000
5 Final cutting ($400 \times 0.7 \times 500$)	140 000
Cost of final cutting	−15 000
Firewood from final cutting	8 000
6 Total payments	183 000

year by year according to expected inflation. After all, we expect to receive SEK 183 000 per year forever applying constant prices.

3. The market price

If the market price per hectare is SEK 60 000, the value of the whole tract would be SEK 4 800 000. Now we get the following valuation:

$$183\,000/X = 4\,800\,000$$

$$X = 3.83 \text{ percent}$$

4.6 Interest rate sensitivity

One dark evening in November 1992 my father came to visit us. He was an old man then (getting close to 90) but still in quite good shape and very clear about what he was doing. He brought me a letter, an old one, enclosed in a sealed envelope without any stamps on it. It looked fairly thick, like there was something more than a regular letter in it.

There was handwriting on the outside: 'To my Grandson Jan, to be received and opened in November 1992'. Inside there was a letter and an additional, smaller envelope:

Hello, Jan, how are you? Do you have a good life? I really hope so. You were born just a few weeks ago and I am not feeling well. We might never find time to see much of each other! But I have done an unusual thing that might improve your life. You see, when I was young I was a stamp collector. And at that time they issued new stamps in two colors. That had never happened before in this country, or anywhere else as far as I know. I felt they might be very valuable in the future. But they were 1 crown apiece, so I could only buy 10 of them for you. I put them in an envelope and I have never touched them since. Here they are.

Some time later I found some more money, so I also bought 10 of the 0.50 crown stamps for you. They will probably never be worth very much, but they have such a lovely lilac color!

Good luck!

Grandfather Albin

Inside was a little envelope with 10 mint stamps of each kind. It turned out that they were issued in 1892. They were called 'circle-type' stamps, a stamp design which was common in those days all over Scandinavia.

Of course, I thought it was a joke, but the stamps were there and they were real. After almost 50 years in the envelope and 100 years since they were issued, they looked as good as new. A few days later I went to a collector's shop and bought a stamp catalog. I found the stamps in the catalog and in Figure 4.6 you can see what it said. If the stamps are still as good as new (mint), they trade for those prices quoted in the column marked 1992. The two-colored stamp was worth SEK 1800 and the other one was worth SEK 3400. That looks like quite an impressive rise in value.

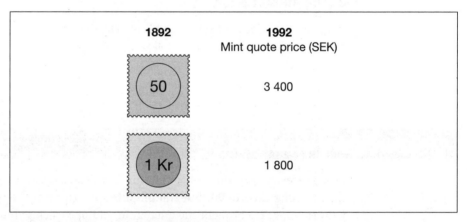

Figure 4.6 Rise in value of 'circle type' stamps

Analyzing the case

Let us start by looking at the two-colored stamp. It was issued in 1892 and it cost SEK 1 at the post office. In 1992 collectors were trading it for SEK 1800 (provided it is in a mint condition). That is quite a good yield, isn't it?

Now, what yield is it really?

Dear readers, before reading on, please have a guess. What yearly interest would have to be compounded on top of the original price to bring us to SEK 1800 in exactly 100 years? Do not pick up your calculator, just have a guess.

Well, if you start with SEK 1 and you get 4 percent interest, in a year you have SEK 1.04. In 2 years you have $(1.04)^2 = 1.0816$. In 20 years you have:

$$(1.04)^{20} = \text{SEK } 2.19$$

This is not very impressive. But wait, this stamp went from SEK 1 to SEK 1800 in 100 years. We thus get:

$$(1 + x)^{100} = 1800$$

Solving the equation, we find that $x = 7.8$ percent.

Now 7.8 percent is a nominal return and in some of those years there was considerable inflation. But this stamp nevertheless gave a fair return over the 100 years. It was probably a great deal better than money in the bank.

When I told the story to students and asked them questions about it, their guesses went in all directions. Some thought that the yearly return was close to zero and others thought it would be as high as 20 percent, or even higher. And after a short session of guessing, I gave them the real answer.

■ The lilac stamp

But now let us turn to the lilac stamp. It cost only 0.50 in 1892 and in 1992 it was worth almost twice as much as the original two-colored stamp. Therefore it would be reasonable to believe that the yield on the lilac stamp was higher than that on the two-colored stamp.

Before going on, have another guess. Now that you know that the two-colored stamp yielded 7.8 percent per year compound interest, and you know that this one was half the price in the beginning and almost double the price by the end, what's the yield?

Now, most students felt better informed and they guessed anywhere between 15 and 30 percent, most of them saying it should be a little less than four times the yield of the other one. But let us solve the equation:

$$0.5 \times (1 + x)^{100} = 3400$$
$$(1 + x)^{100} = 6800$$

The solution is $x = 9.2$ percent. So, when the students were told about the two-colored stamp, they thought they could understand the lilac stamp, but most didn't. Most forecasts were worse in the second case than in the first one.

Why is this? This happens because interest rates and discount factors are not linear functions and most of us try to think in a linear way when we try to be logical. Therefore let us learn from this case that intuition doesn't work very well with interest rates.

Can we learn something else? Well, yes. We can see that just a very small change in the interest rate will make a very big difference over a long period of time.

And my Grandfather Albin? He was born in 1871 and he died in 1945, a little over a year after I was born. I cannot remember meeting him, but I was told that I did. They tell me I sat on his lap and that we liked each other very much! I feel it must be true . . .

4.7 The Beautiful Bridge

At the end of the last century a bridge was built across the narrow waterway between two European countries. The bridge was designed as a four-lane motorway plus a double-track railway line. The following case is based on newspaper articles about the bridge. It might differ from the true situation in certain respects.

Because of the considerable expense of the building project, the national governments were hesitant about the undertaking for a long time. Finally, it was decided to turn the project over to a private consortium of international builders and investors. The consortium undertook the building and the financing of the bridge, including the motorway and railway. In return, the consortium was granted the right to charge a fee for each vehicle crossing the bridge on the motorway for exactly 40 years from the opening date at the beginning of year 2000. After those 40 years, the bridge would be handed over to the two states without payment.

There would be no charge for railway trains except to cover running operating costs and basic maintenance. Thus the motor traffic was expected to pay for the construction of the whole bridge, including the railway part.

The total investment to build the bridge amounted to €2100 million. After opening the bridge to traffic, the consortium determined that there would be operating costs of two kinds:

- general operating cost (€10 million per year)
- maintenance cost per car crossing the bridge (€3 per car).

When the consortium was formed, participating companies stated that they would need 12 percent return on equity after tax. Considering commercial borrowing rates to be around 7 percent and inflation around 3 percent, this reasoning was accepted by the two states. At the start of the project some 80 percent of the investment was financed through borrowing.

We shall assume that the international consortium does not pay any taxes.

During the first year, an average number of 10 150 cars a day crossed the bridge, each paying €30 per trip. The traffic was expected to grow by 2–4 percent per year for a long time.

The following analysis is required:

1 Calculate the required return on capital, make other assumptions as needed, and analyze the profitability of the project. This part should include an NPV calculation, a financial income statement for the first year and some comments on the numbers calculated.

2 For the two national governments it is important to know that the price of crossing the bridge is not outrageously high compared with the costs. Since €30 is a lot more than the maintenance cost (€3 per car), there was considerable concern on the pricing side. Describe how to calculate the full costs of the project and show the outcome for a few selected years during the life of the project. Argue on behalf of the project management to support the price.

3 The chief economist of a European consumer union argued that the project was a disaster for the public, since the price for crossing was much higher than the marginal cost. As a matter of fact, he said, in modern cost accounting, full cost is regarded as old-fashioned and has given way to activity-based (ABC) costing. Consequently, to support the price, he said, an ABC calculation should be done, considering that the capacity of the motorway amounts to at least 60 000 vehicles a day. Find the appropriate calculation and support or refute the arguments of the chief economist.

Solution: The Beautiful Bridge

■ A financial analysis

Cost of capital

A private consortium built the bridge. According to the case, they need 12 percent return on equity after tax. It is known that money can be borrowed at 7 percent, which would normally be before tax. Assuming that the consortium will borrow 80 percent (in the real world they borrowed even more) of the investment, the weighted average cost of capital (WACC) calculation will look like this:

$$\text{WACC} = 0.2 \times 12\% + 0.8 \times 7\% = 2.4\% + 5.6\% = 8\%$$

Thus cost of capital after tax and including inflation will be 8 percent. Inflation is given (3 percent), which will be subtracted from the cost of capital when we are capitalizing numbers that are subject to inflation.

NPV calculation

There is one flow of cash related to the passage of cars across the bridge and another related to the yearly maintenance costs.

Regular income comes from vehicles crossing the bridge. There are 10 150 vehicles a day in the beginning. The price of passage starts at €30 and there is a variable maintenance cost for each car crossing the bridge. Therefore the net inflow per car will be:

$$30 - 3 = €27$$

Daily inflow of money will be:

$$27 \times 10\ 150 = €274\ 050$$

Inflow in the first year will be:

$$274\ 050 \times 365 = €100.02 \text{ million}$$

Calculating the NPV, we notice that the volume is expected to grow by some 3 percent per year and so are prices due to inflation. Therefore we have a series that grows by 6 percent per year. Since the basic cost of capital is 8 percent, we can calculate the present value by applying a reduced discount rate in the following way:

$$\text{Reduced discount rate} = 8\% - 3\% - 3\% = 2\%$$

The accumulated present value factor for 40 years at 2 percent is 27.36. Now we find:

$$\text{PV of income flow} = 100.02 \times 27.36 = €2737 \text{ million}$$

Outlays are €10 million a year. They will grow according to inflation but not in accordance with the growing volume of traffic. We discount the outlays at $8 - 3 = 5$ percent discount rate over 40 years:

$$\text{PV of fixed outlays} = 10 \times 17.19 = €172 \text{ million}$$

Including the original investment (€2100 million), we can calculate the NPV of the entire project in the following way:

$$\text{NPV} = -2100 + 2737 - 172 = €465 \text{ million}$$

When performing this calculation we took at least two shortcuts that might need some explaining. First, we assumed that all volumes and prices were expressed as if they had occurred in year zero. But according to the text, all values were given in the first year of operation. To correct this mistake, all volumes should be reduced by 3 percent, as should all prices, in order to bring the starting point of our analysis back to year zero.

Secondly, we assumed that we can find adjusted discount rates by subtracting growth from the cost of capital. To make things absolutely correct we should adjust discount rates in the following way:

$$\text{Adjusting for inflation} = 1.08/1.03 = 1.0485$$

$$\text{Adjusting further for volume growth} = 1.0485/1.03 = 1.018$$

To get all details right we bring the problem into the corporate investment model. There we find that the true NPV, including those adjustments will be €397 million instead of the €465 million we calculated manually.

Income statement

In the first year, the income statement might look like this (€ million):

	€m
Income from vehicles (10 150 × 365 × 30)	111
Fixed costs	−10
Variable costs (10 150 × 365 × 3)	−11
Depreciation (2 100/40)	−53
Interest on debt (2 100 × 0.8 × 7%)	−118
Profit before tax	−81

Thus, yearly profit will be negative in the beginning. If we add back depreciation we will find that even the yearly cash flow will be negative:

$$\text{Cash flow first year} = -81 + 53 = €-28 \text{ million}$$

Therefore there will be a problem with paying interest during the first few years. Checking with the Beautiful Bridge Excel sheet on page 145 shows that yearly cash flows improve over time, but there will still be negative cash flow for several years at the beginning. Therefore additional cash will be needed, either from the banks or as equity from the members of the consortium.

Capital budgeting: Beautiful Bridge

Investment and revenue		**Production**		**Cost of capital**	
Investment year 0	2 100 000	Fixed cost year 0	10 000	Excluding taxes	8%
Revenue year 0	104 762.47	Variable cost year 0	10 476	Including taxes	8%
Revenue growth	6%	Growth fixed costs	3%		
		Growth variable costs	6%		

Year			Costs		Excluding taxes		
	Invest	Revenue	Fixed	Variable	Cash flow	Factor 1	NPV
0	2 100 000				−2 100 000	1.00	−2 100 000
1		111 143	10 300	11 114	90 366	0.93	83 672
2		117 911	10 609	11 791	95 511	0.86	81 885
3		125 092	10 927	12 509	101 655	0.79	80 697
4		132 710	11 255	13 271	108 184	0.74	79 518
5		140 792	11 593	14 079	115 120	0.68	78 349
6		149 366	11 941	14 937	122 489	0.63	77 189
7		158 463	12 299	15 846	130 318	0.58	76 039
8		168 113	12 668	16 811	138 634	0.54	74 900
9		178 351	13 048	17 835	147 468	0.50	73 771
10		189 213	13 439	18 921	156 852	0.46	72 653
11		200 736	13 842	20 074	166 820	0.43	71 546
12		212 961	14 258	21 296	177 407	0.40	70 451
13		225 930	14 685	22 593	188 651	0.37	69 367
14		239 689	15 126	23 969	200 594	0.34	68 294
15		254 286	15 580	25 429	213 278	0.32	67 234
16		269 772	16 047	26 977	226 748	0.29	66 186
17		286 201	16 528	28 620	241 053	0.27	65 149
18		303 631	17 024	30 363	256 243	0.25	64 125
19		322 122	17 535	32 212	272 375	0.23	63 112
20		341 739	18 061	34 174	289 504	0.21	62 113
21		362 551	18 603	36 255	307 693	0.20	61 125
22		384 630	19 161	38 463	327 006	0.18	60 150
23		408 054	19 736	40 805	347 513	0.17	59 187
24		432 905	20 328	43 290	369 286	0.16	58 236
25		459 269	20 938	45 927	392 404	0.15	57 298
26		487 238	21 566	48 724	416 949	0.14	56 372
27		516 911	22 213	51 691	443 007	0.13	55 459
28		548 391	22 879	54 839	470 673	0.12	54 557
29		581 788	23 566	58 179	500 044	0.11	53 668
30		617 219	24 273	61 722	531 224	0.10	52 792
31		654 807	25 001	65 481	564 326	0.09	51 927
32		694 685	25 751	69 469	599 466	0.09	51 075
33		736 992	26 523	73 699	636 769	0.08	50 234
34		781 874	27 319	78 187	676 368	0.07	49 406
35		829 491	28 139	82 949	718 403	0.07	48 589
36		880 007	28 983	88 001	763 023	0.06	47 784
37		933 599	29 852	93 360	810 387	0.06	46 991
38		990 455	30 748	99 046	860 662	0.05	46 209
39		1 050 774	31 670	105 077	914 026	0.05	45 439
40		1 114 766	32 620	111 477	970 669	0.05	44 681
Totals						12.92	397 428

■ Full cost of operations

The full cost of operations is needed to prove to the governments that the present price, €30 per vehicle, is not outrageously high. A full cost statement would include all the cost items of the income statement above. Thus for year 1:

$$\text{Full costs} = 10 + 11 + 53 + 118 = €192 \text{ million}$$

Dividing by the number of cars we get:

$$192\ 000\ 000/(10\ 150 \times 365) = €51.8 \text{ per car}$$

Therefore the suggested price is actually far below the full costs of operations at the beginning of the project.

Assuming that operating costs follow inflation and capital costs remain unchanged for the first half of the project, in year 21, the number of cars will have doubled to 22 000 a day and the outcome would be:

$$\text{Full costs} = 18 + 53 + 53 + 118 = €242 \text{ million}$$

Dividing by the new number of cars:

$$242\ 000\ 000/(22\ 000 \times 365) = €30.1 \text{ per car}$$

In fact, these calculations show that on a full cost basis, the consortium will just barely cover its costs in the middle years of the project.

Finally, assuming that debts are paid back during the second half of the project, in the final year there will be no (or almost none) interest costs. The number of cars will have doubled again to some 45 000 a day:

$$\text{Full costs} = 33 + 161 + 53 = €247 \text{ million}$$

Dividing by the number of cars we get:

$$247\ 000\ 000/(45\ 000 \times 365) = €15$$

Thus, in the beginning, the price can be easily defended. Later on, cost calculations will probably be forgotten.

■ The economist of the consumer union

In the previous section we found that full costs are €192 million, of which €11 million represent variable costs. This amount corresponds to €3 per car. The remaining €181 million represent capacity costs.

Using ABC in the first year, we substitute 60 000 vehicles into the full cost calculation. Then, the ABC cost per car will be equal to the variable cost per car plus a share of capacity costs:

$$\text{Capacity cost per car} = 181\ 000\ 000/(60\ 000 \times 365) = €8.26 \text{ per car}$$

Consequently, the total ABC cost per car will be:

$$8.26 + 3.00 = €11.26$$

However, while marginal pricing is economically efficient for society, neither it nor ABC is a good pricing instrument for a company in the market. Applying the ABC cost for pricing would take the consortium into bankruptcy very quickly. Thus such a pricing technique would be a disaster for a private company and cannot even be considered. A pricing technique like this would need government support, which is clearly not available in this case.

4.8 Regulating WACC

(The following case is based on reality, but most of the numbers are fictional, mainly to make computations easier.)

During the winter of 2010, the Network Market Authority was busy deciding fair returns on capital invested in the electricity network business. Large private companies (such as Fortum, E.on, and Vattenfall) owned many local networks and each company had a monopoly in each local area. There is free competition in the electricity generation business but there is a monopoly in the network business because you need only one local network in each local area. When there is a private monopoly in a public utility, the law requires the return on capital to be regulated.

Traditionally, the Network Market Authority asked a well-known consulting company to develop a fair WACC to be applied to all local networks. In 2010 the consulting company found that 6.0 percent would be a fair WACC to be applied after taxes. Because electricity companies have to price their services to customers before tax, the consulting company then converted the WACC after taxes to a WACC before taxes through a simplified formula, known from the literature:

$$\text{WACC (before tax)} = \text{WACC (after tax)}/(1 - t)$$

In the formula, the parameter t is the national corporation tax rate.

However, during the discussion, it was suggested that the formula might not always be applicable to all kinds of business. In particular, very long-lasting projects might not be treated correctly when you apply WACC (before taxes) to cash flows before taxes in accordance with the formula.

The following analyses and comments are required:

1 Assist the Network Market Authority in investigating the properties of the formula and, if needed, find an alternative WACC to be applied to calculations before tax in the electric network business.

When solving the assignment it might be useful to assume that a network operator invests €100 million in a network, which can be used for 40 years. Since the network is mainly classified as machinery, it can be depreciated in a linear way over 5 years. To simplify the analysis, assume that the national corporation tax rate is 25 percent. Please assume that there is no inflation at all and that the operator is a large company, paying taxes on other large incomes every year.

To carry out a very thorough study, it might be valuable to compare the usefulness of the formula in the electricity business to a similar situation in a mechanical industry, where capital equipment would last for 10 years instead of 40.

2 If the operator is not a very large company but a smaller one, owning only one investment of €100 million, it might not be correct to treat them as described above. Explain, without calculation, how such a case might be considered.

3 A study such as that in 1 was actually published in September 2010, and one of the large operators hired consultants from a major consulting company to comment on the issue. Among their comments was the following statement:

> It is true that the generous depreciation rules will create a certain tax advantage during the first few years of a project. However, that advantage will have to be repaid in later years when the fast tax depreciation has ended. Therefore the company does not really gain anything. Taxes are just redistributed over time. Consequently, it would not be appropriate to change the traditional formula.

You are asked to comment on this statement from the well-known consultants.

Solution: Regulating WACC

■ Investigation of the formula's properties

A network operator invests €100 million in a physical network. The investment will be depreciated in 5 years according to national tax rules. Since the company has other profits, we may assume that the tax shield from depreciation can be exploited to a full extent. Therefore the tax shield will create the following present value:

$$\text{PV from tax shield} = 100/5 \times 0.25 \times 4.21 = €21.05 \text{ million}$$

In the formula, 100/5 is yearly depreciation, 0.25 is the tax rate and 4.21 is the accumulated present value for 5 years at 6 percent discount rate after tax.

In addition the company will receive an annuity for 40 years which is calculated from the adjusted WACC before taxes. According to the formula we get:

$$\text{WACC before taxes} = 6\%/(1 - 0.25) = 8.0\%$$

If the interest rate is 8 percent, the corresponding 40-year annuity can be found from the table of accumulated present values:

$$\text{PV (40 years, 8\%)} = 11.92$$

Then we can easily find the annuity:

$$\text{Annuity (40 years, 8\%)} = 1/11.92 = 8.39\%$$

Since our original investment is €100 million, our annuity will be $100 \times 8.39\% = €8.39$ million. When evaluating the annuity, we get the following outcome:

$$\text{PV of annuity} = 8.39 \times 0.75 \times 15.05 = €94.7 \text{ million}$$

In the calculation, 15.05 is the accumulated present value for 40 years at 6 percent discount rate after tax. Adding the two items of present value together we get:

$$\text{PV of total inflow after tax} = 21.05 + 94.7 = €115.75 \text{ million}$$

This result means that the network operators get 15.7 percent too high return on their investment just because of the faulty formula of conversion of WACC.

How much would they be entitled to? Well, clearly the total present value of the tax shield plus the present value of the 40-year annuity should add up to the original investment. We find the proper annuity (X) through the following equation:

$$0.75 \times X \times 15.05 + 21.05 = 100$$

$$X = 6.99$$

Thus the yearly annuity needed to get a fair return on invested capital would be 6.99 per year for 40 years. Then, we need to find a number equal to $100/6.99 = 14.31$ in the table of accumulated present values. After some trial and error we find that the proper interest rate is 6.46 percent.

We conclude that the network operators should be allowed to calculate their prices as a 6.46 percent discount rate before taxes. But instead the regulating authority allows 8 percent according to the traditional formula. Thus, operators are paid far too much for their networks, and that happens because of the faulty formula of conversion of WACC.

▦ Smaller operator

If company profits are not big enough for the tax shield to be efficient, the situation will be different. If the company has to slow down depreciation because it would otherwise report losses, the tax gains will be smaller than assumed in the above calculation. In this case, the company will still receive a tax subsidy, but it will not be as big as in the case we calculated earlier.

The proper adjusted discount rate would depend on how fast a depreciation scheme the company can follow. The faster the depreciation, the larger the tax gains for the company.

▦ Comments on consultants' statement

Redistribution of tax payments creates an important advantage to the company. If all taxes are paid later rather than sooner, they mean much less in a calculation of discounted present value. Therefore it is of primary importance to move taxes away from the present and into the future. This important fact ought to have been recognized by the consulting company.

4.9 Parabella Kitchenware

(This case is adapted from one written by Flavio Gabossi.)

Parabella is a leading pottery producer. One of its divisions produces high-quality kitchenware for private consumers. Last year the kitchenware division sold 22 million sets of cups and plates worth €142 million. The export market was very important. Export sales were concentrated on the top-quality and high-priced products. The export market has been very good in recent years and is expected to continue improving. Unfortunately, production capacity in the firing process is already strained to the limit.

The quality of products was one of the of the company's main concerns. Quality was judged on several parameters, such as materials, resistance, colours, etc. In the production process, firing was one of the most delicate and expensive phases.

During an international fair of electronic equipment, the Production Manager of Parabella visited the stand of a company specializing in the automation of the production of pottery and glass.

After discussions with their consultants, he realized that there was an opportunity to automate the Parabella production flow (see the exhibit 'The traditional production process', below). He asked the consultants to study and design an automated production control system in order to:

- collect information in real time
- make all the information on the production flow available in one place
- show all the information on a screen and calculate all the necessary ratios.

The traditional production process

Information on the production process currently collected

Number of sets in production (total, on different lines)

Gas consumption

Conveyor belt speed

Furnace temperature in different furnace sections

Level of activity of different sections of the line

Collecting information

Information concerning these variables is registered in several parts of the line, where workers are present to register information and, if necessary, make adjustments in the process. Workers load information manually on a computer. After loading it is printed and made available for the line operator every hour. To collect all the information, workers have to go through the whole line. Half an hour is needed just to collect the information.

Using the information

The line operator will read the information and eventually decide to correct the production flow (temperature, speed, level of activity). In fact, the line operator used to read the information only sometimes and mainly managed to correct the production process according to his experience and the suggestions of his staff along the line, considering also the kinds of products under production. Each line includes two furnaces and has one responsible operator.

In the long run, he expected the changes to make it possible to read all information and to manage the production flow completely automatically and to predict the impact of possible changes in production variables (temperature, speed of the line, etc.), thus increasing quality considerably.

The consultants carried out the study. Unfortunately, there was a concern regarding the personnel in Parabella. Some people working in production seemed to resent the installation of the control system and refused to give any information to the consultants during the analysis.

Still, the consultants concluded that it was possible to satisfy the manager's request. The result would automate the process, improve quality and could also bring savings to the gas consumption of the line and a reduction in the level of rejected production.

◼ The offer

The consultants offered a control system for one pair of furnaces out of the several pairs in the kitchenware division, presented in Table 4.13. To evaluate the offer, the Financial Controller provided the information shown in Table 4.14.

Table 4.13 The new control system

	€000
Hardware	524
Software	210
Personnel training	16
Total investment	750
Yearly maintenance costs	50

Table 4.14 Direct production costs

	€ per 1000 sets
Material	28
Energy	90
Gas	350
Line operator	70
Workers (two per furnace)	110
Maintenance	25
Total	673
Other information	
Rejected production	5%
Selling price (€ per 1000 sets)	6 500
Variable selling costs (€ per 1000 sets)	1 500
Yearly production per pair of furnaces (1000 sets)	2 700

■ Estimated savings

In addition to automating the process, the production department felt that the new control system could bring:

- an estimated saving of gas of 5 percent of the present consumption
- a reduction of 2 percent in the production rejected (down from 5 to 3 percent).

The financial department of the company expects inflation to amount to 2 percent a year for the near future. Local salaries are expected to rise twice as fast. Company cost of capital is assumed to be 10 percent a year. The national corporation tax rate is assumed to be 35 percent.

The company's accountants are required to conduct an analysis of the situation and to decide under what circumstances it would be profitable to install the new control system.

Warning: There are lots of numbers. Select only the important ones and work with them! See also the exhibit 'The traditional production process'.

Solution: Parabella Kitchenware

■ The project

The present value of investments can be found easily. Assuming that the whole amount, including software and training, will be activated and depreciated in 5 years, we find the cash flows after taxes shown in Figure 4.7 (please note that the tax rate is assumed to be 35 percent).

The present value calculation is done over 5 years, which should be enough for a trial IT project. It has to be profitable in the short run to be accepted at all. Possibly, inflation might influence the maintenance. In this case, we would apply a higher present value factor to the maintenance payments. The NPV value would be a little worse but this is not an important factor in this case.

If you wish to work in a more precise way, you could assume that only machinery will be activated and depreciated. In this case, software and training would be expensed immediately and there would be a small tax advantage in year 0.

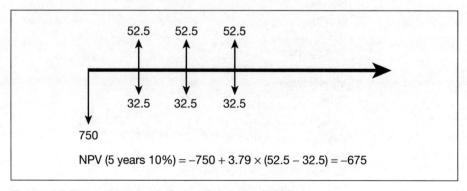

Figure 4.7 The project: cash flows after taxes (€000)

■ Savings from the project

Some savings are explicitly stated in the text. First, there are savings in gas and rejects. Disregarding their possible interaction we find:

$$\text{Savings from gas} = 5\% \times 350 \times 2700 = €47\ 000 \text{ per year}$$

$$\text{Savings from rejects} = 2\% \times 673 \times 2700 = €36\ 000 \text{ per year}$$

$$\text{Total savings from gas and rejects} = €83\ 000 \text{ per year}$$

We do realize that saving 5 percent of the gas bill would lower the direct product costs to a small extent. Then, savings from rejects should be only 2 percent on the remaining direct costs. But as per the warning at the end of the case, we disregard the combined effect of these two variables.

Altogether, those savings amount to €83 000 per year. Their PV after taxes will be:

$$\text{Savings from gas and rejects (€000)} = 3.79 \times 83 \times 0.65 = 205$$

Adjusting for 2 percent inflation and applying 8 percent real interest, we get (€000):

$$\text{Savings from gas and rejects} = 3.99 \times 83 \times 0.65 = 215$$

In both cases the savings are clearly insufficient to justify the project.

However, the essence of the project is automation. Clearly, that means that some workers will be laid off, although we do not know how many or how soon. Let us assume that half the wages can be saved throughout the project. Including 4 percent salary raises we evaluate savings in wages at a 6 percent discount factor, giving:

$$\text{Savings on wages (€000)} = 4.21 \times 110/2 \times 2700 \times 0.65 = 407$$

In the next step let us assume we can eliminate some of the line operators. Saving a full position, we get:

$$\text{Savings on line operator (€000)} = 4.21 \times 70 \times 2700 \times 0.65 = 541$$

Now, we might not be able to save the full value of workers and line operators immediately. But the savings are so large that they will easily cover the full cost of the project. Thus we can conclude that the project appears very profitable.

However, the biggest profit opportunity remains to be considered. If rejects diminish by 2 percent, we can produce and sell 2 percent more sets of kitchenware. Disregarding inflation, the yearly gain will be:

$$\text{Increasing sales (€000)} = 2\% \times 2700 \times (6500 - 1500 - 673) = 234 \text{ per year}$$

We get the following present value from increased sales:

$$\text{Increasing sales (€000)} = 3.79 \times 234 \times 0.65 = 576$$

So, if sales actually do increase, there will be a large gain from this project. It may not even be necessary to lay off workers and line operators to make the project profitable.

4.10 The Superior Power Co.

In light of a worsening domestic power situation, the Superior Power Co. is investigating the possibility of building a large new power plant in a European country.

Applying very modern technical developments, they can see the following two possibilities (all numbers are at 2010 prices):

- A large nuclear reactor producing 8200 GWh per year (1 GWh = 1×10^6 KWh). The reactor will cost €2800 million to build (including interest during the building time). It is expected to keep working for 30 years without any major reinvestments. Yearly costs, including fuel, maintenance and mandatory insurance premiums for dismantling are estimated to be €120 million a year.

- A regular coal-based power plant based on modern 'clean coal' technology. The plant will produce 6200 GWh per year for 15 years and cost €1600 million. After that period of time the plant will have to be replaced (possibly with another similar plant). Operating costs are estimated to be around €60 million a year.

Operations will start on a trial basis at the end of the same year. Commercial operations are supposed to be under way from the beginning of the following year.

The Superior Power Co. is a private international consortium, incorporated inside the European Union. In the local environment, the company expects to find equity capital requiring 12 percent return on equity. Long-term loans are available at 6 percent interest, and some 75 percent of the building costs would normally be financed by borrowing. The market price of electricity, net of production taxes and excise taxes is €0.045 per KWh. Inflation in the European Union is expected to hover around 2 percent a year for quite a long time.

Superior's accountants are asked to carry out the following analysis (all numbers are at 2010 prices; assume that the tax rate is equal to zero):

1 Find the approximate profitability of the two projects according to payback, net present value and the internal rate of return. Compare the outcomes and explain the consequences of the analysis.

2 In fact, there is a problem with the nuclear reactor. By law, it will have to be dismantled after 40 years (10 years after the end of production). The costs of the dismantling, €6000 million (at 2010 prices), are supposed to be covered by the insurance premiums, mentioned earlier. These premiums are paid to the Nuclear Safety Commission. The commission, in turn, lends the money to first-class industrial companies, charging the market rate of interest. Find the appropriate premium (which is already included in the yearly cost given above) to make sure that money will be available for the dismantling when the time comes. The commission does not pay any taxes.

3 If the Nuclear Safety Commission did not exist and there were no insurance premiums to cover the dismantling, what would the payments of the nuclear reactor look like? What would happen to the NPV and the internal rate of return?

Solution: The Superior Power Co.

■ 1. The profitability of the projects

Based on the original text, we can calculate the following income flows in the two cases:

For the nuclear reactor: $8200 \times 0.045 = €369$ million per year

For the clean coal plant: $6200 \times 0.045 = €279$ million per year

Knowing the income flows, we can describe the two alternatives in Figure 4.8 (all numbers are at 2010 prices). By assuming that the clean coal plant is rebuilt after 15 years we may assume that the cash flows go on for 30 years in both cases.

In the short run, the nominal cost of capital of the company can be calculated as the weighted average cost of capital (WACC) in the following way:

$$0.25 \times 12 + 0.75 \times 6 = 7.5\% \text{ (disregarding taxes)}$$

To be able to apply the tables, we round the WACC to 8 percent. Subtracting inflation we find the real rate to be around 6 percent.

In the long run, we assume that the real rate would be stable over time even if the nominal WACC changes with short run inflation. Now, the NPV of the nuclear reactor will be:

$$\text{NPV (nuclear)} = -2800 + 13.76 \times 249 = €626 \text{ million}$$

Payback will be:

$$2800/249 = 11.24, \text{ which is approximately 11 years}$$

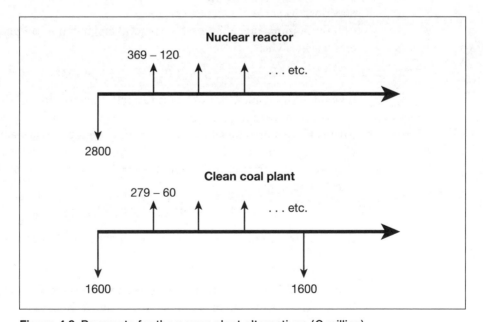

Figure 4.8 Payments for the power plant alternatives (€ million)

The internal rate of return will be found by looking up 11.24 in the table of accumulated present values for 30 years. It turns out to be almost exactly 8 percent interest.

The NPV of the series of two consecutive clean coal plants will be:

$$NPV \ (coal) = -1600 - 0.42 \times 1600 + 13.76 \times 219 = €641 \ million$$

Payback will be:

$$1600/219 = 7.31, \ which \ is \ approximately \ 7 \ years$$

The Internal rate of return will be found by looking up 7.31 in the table of accumulated present values for 15 years. It turns out to be slightly below 11 percent interest.

It looks like the clean coal plant is equal to or superior to the nuclear reactor on all economic indicators. Consequently, on economic grounds we would tend to favor the coal plant. Of course, there could be other reasons (environmental or technical) to favor the opposite standpoint.

▪ 2. The nuclear reactor insurance premium

According to the assignment, all payments reflect the conditions in 2010. Thus the cost of dismantling the reactor, €6000 million, is a real amount in our analysis. But it will not be paid until 2050. Assuming that yearly inflation remains constant, the nominal amount actually needed in 2050 can be found in the following way:

$$6000 \times (1.02)^{40} = 13 \ 248$$

To discount any of those amounts, we have to establish a set of interest rates. Again, according to the brief, the Nuclear Safety Commission will lend money at the market rate of interest, which is 6 percent. This is also the borrowing rate of Superior Power Co.

If the nominal rate of interest is 6 percent and inflation is 2 percent, the real rate of interest will be:

$$1.06/1.02 - 1 = 3.92 \ percent$$

If working with tables, you will have to apply 4 percent to come reasonably close.

Now, to develop a yearly payment, we need to start by converting our future payment into a present value. This is because our tables relate annuities to present values, not to future values. This calculation is shown in Figure 4.9.

If we start from the real amount, €6000 million, we apply 3.92 percent real interest and find:

$$PV = 6000/(1.0392)^{40} = €1288 \ million$$

If we start from a nominal payment, we apply nominal interest and find:

$$PV = 13 \ 248/(1.06)^{40} = €1288 \ million$$

The new number, €1288 million, is the real present value of the cost of dismantling. Because the reactor will operate for 30 years only, we have to turn it into a yearly payment for the production period of 30 years. To do so, we can calculate a real

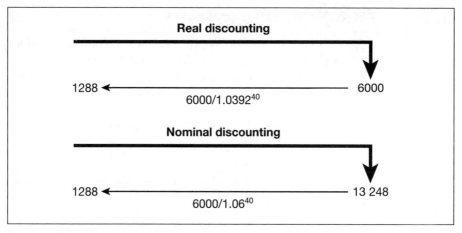

Figure 4.9 Real and nominal discounting (€ million)

annuity at 3.92 percent interest or a nominal annuity at 6 percent nominal interest. See the calculations in Figure 4.10.

In nominal terms, the real payments would start at $73.8 \times 1.02 = €75$ million in year 1 and grow by inflation, to reach €133.7 million in year 30. The nominal payment would remain at €93.6 million all the time. In the real world, the real payments will be used and inflated by 2 percent per year in order to make the insurance premium bearable for the company.

Working with the regular present value table and applying 4 percent real interest we get:

$$17.292 \times X = 6000 \times 0.208 \qquad X = 72.3$$

This is the real value to be paid once a year for 30 years in order to cover the dismantling of the reactor. As time goes by the amounts will rise by 2 percent a year in line with inflation.

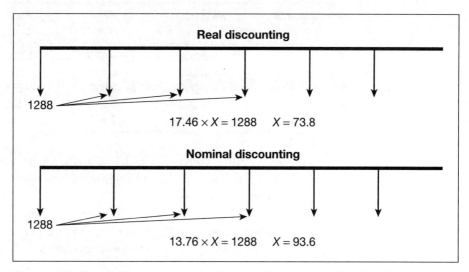

Figure 4.10 Converting present value into yearly payments (€ million)

■ 3. No insurance premiums

If there are no insurance premiums, the yearly surplus of the power company would increase by €73.8 million. On the other hand, they would have to pay for the dismantling in year 40. The payments can be found in Figure 4.11.

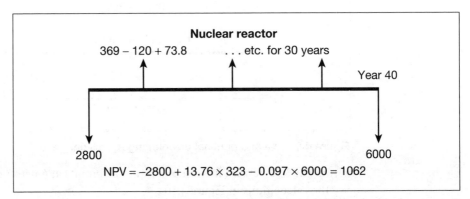

Figure 4.11 Payments without insurance (€ million)

Clearly, the NPV will rise, because the Superior Power Co. will evaluate future payments at 6 percent real interest, whereas the Nuclear Safety Commission used 6 percent nominal interest. To the company, the future cost of dismantling will be much less significant than for the Safety Commission.

Calculating the internal rate of return will bring difficulties. Since there are negative payments in the end as well as in the beginning, there might be two internal rates of return. They can be found by investigating the NPV at various interest rates (see Table 4.15).

Table 4.15 NPV at various interest rates

Interest rate %	Investment €m	Flow €m	End €m	Total NPV €m
0	−2 800	9 690	−6 000	890
6	−2 800	4 444	−583	1 061
8	−2 800	3 637	−276	561
10	−2 800	3 046	−132	114
12	−2 800	2 590	−66	−276

In fact, there is only one solution, which happens at roughly 10.5 percent interest. Thus, the IRR calculation confirms our finding that the project will look better to the company without insurance.

But still, of course, the government will tell the company to pay the insurance. If not, it would be profitable for the consortium to forget about the insurance and let the company go bankrupt after 30 years of operations.

Chapter 5

Capital costs

Get ready for a tough ride. This little case has been presented to hundreds of managers and almost every breakout group on MBA programs came up with their own solution. In some cases, groups could not agree among themselves but presented several solutions. It is a very short case followed by a number of fairly long solutions. Here we go!

■ Drilling equipment

The equipment department of the Glamorous Drilling Co. owns a drilling rig for heavy duty which is 3 years old. When it was bought, the price was $260 000. The rig is used for certain drilling projects, which are supposed to pay the costs for using their equipment. Today a similar rig costs $300 000. During the period the yearly inflation has been 5 percent.

A drilling rig of this type can be worked for 5 years. Then, for safety reasons, it has to be scrapped with zero scrap value.

Company financing comes from:

- 50 percent equity costing 20 percent per year
- 50 percent bank loans costing 10 percent per year.

Glamorous's accountants are asked to carry out the following analysis:

1 When using the rig, the project leader typically pays all operating costs. Therefore, the equipment department would need to recover its capital costs only. Find those costs in order to make a price list for using the rig in year 4.

2 It might not always be efficient to revise cost calculations every year. Could these be generalized into an internal price list that is valid for the whole life of the drilling rig?

3 Now, assume that the engineers suddenly discovered that this particular type of rig is safe enough to operate for 8 years instead of 5. What difference would this make to the capital costs for year 4?

Solution: The Glamorous Drilling Co.

■ Nominal depreciation and interest

To visualize the situation, let us assume that the capital providers supply the capital that is needed to buy the drilling rig. During the life of the machine the company has to pay back the money to them and, in addition, interest on the amount that has not yet been paid back. It might be sensible to pay back the money at the same rate as the equipment wears out. Thus, there will be capital costs for depreciation. In addition, the capital providers will need to be paid for interest costs.

Depreciation in financial accounting would typically be done in 5 years in the following way:

$$\text{Depreciation} = 260\ 000/5 = \$52\ 000$$

If depreciation is included in the rental price, then the capital owners could be paid back the same amount when the year is over. But, in addition, they would need to be paid interest on the capital that had not been paid back at the start of the year. If we assume that all capital is pooled, and that there are equal shares of equity and borrowed capital, then the average cost of capital (WACC), disregarding taxes, can be calculated in the following way:

$$0.5 \times 10\% + 0.5 \times 20\% = 15\%$$

Let us now assume that depreciation has already been going on for 3 years. In this case the remaining capital is:

$$260\ 000 - 3 \times 52\ 000 = \$104\ 000$$

A quicker way to the same outcome might be to identify the remaining time, which is 2 years out of 5, and to calculate:

$$260\ 000 \times 2/5 = \$104\ 000$$

Anyway, these calculations mean that the outstanding debt of the drilling rig is $104 000 at the start of the fourth year.

Normally interest rates are stated in a nominal way, i.e. including inflation. Therefore we assume that these interest rates are nominal and that they include 5 percent inflation, as mentioned in the brief.

Given those assumptions, the interest costs in year 4 will be:

$$104\ 000 \times 15\% = \$15\ 200$$

Therefore the total capital costs are found to be:

	$
Depreciation	52 000
Interest	15 200
Total capital cost	67 200

If we can recover this cost during year 4 we can pay back this years's part of the loan and in addition pay interest on the amount that was outstanding at the start of the year.

Dealing with depreciation and interest in this way is fairly common thinking and it is called *nominal linear depreciation* (NL). There are also other methods, which we shall deal with later in this case.

■ The NL method over time

Before we turn to the other methods, it might be useful to look into the profile of capital costs over the life of the drilling rig. When using the NL method, the capital cost will appear fairly high in the beginning. In year 1 the company would have to pay interest on the full original price of the drilling rig. After that interest would fall every year until the equipment has been fully depreciated in year 5. But after that, the company will have to buy a new drilling rig, and then, very likely, the price will be higher.

Capital costs would appear to change over time as in Table 5.1. The table starts in year 1 and shows that the starting value of the drilling rig would be $260 000. Then interest on the full value would be ($000) 260×15 percent $= 39$. Depreciation is 52 and so the total capital cost will be:

$$39 + 52 = 91$$

The end value of the rig is found by subtracting depreciation from the start value.

Table 5.1 Change in capital costs over time

Year	Start value $000	Interest $000	Depreciation $000	Capital cost $000	End value $000
1	260	39	52	91	208
2	208	31.2	52	83.2	156
3	156	23.4	52	75.4	104
4	104	15.6	52	67.6	52
5	52	7.8	52	59.8	0

Looking at these values over time, we can see that the total capital costs get cheaper every year. Then, if a new drilling rig were bought at the end of year 5, the price would be much higher, and the capital costs would jump. In fact, if prices keep rising by 5 percent a year, the price of the new equipment will be $331 800. To be able to buy it, the company would have to find a new round of complete financing among its equity holders and lenders. If that can be done, the following years will look like Table 5.2.

Now we can see that the capital costs not only fall each year at the beginning, but they also suddenly jump in year 6 when the new equipment is acquired.

So, do you feel that this method of finding capital costs is a good tool for pricing? In my opinion, it is not. It is true that all money was paid back to shareholders and

Table 5.2 Cash flows up to year 8 including purchase of new equipment

Year	Start value $000	Interest $000	Depreciation $000	Capital cost $000	End value $000
1	260	39	52	91	208
2	208	31.2	52	83.2	156
3	156	23.4	52	75.4	104
4	104	15.6	52	67.6	52
5	52	7.8	52	59.8	0
6	331.8	49.8	66.4	116.1	265.4
7	265.4	39.8	53.1	92.9	212.4
8	212.4	31.9	42.5	74.3	169.9

lenders, but unless the operating costs rise fast enough to compensate for the falling capital costs, I think customers will be quite puzzled when prices fall year by year. Despite this, they would probably accept it for years 1–5, but what about when new equipment is bought and prices suddenly rise considerably in year 6? I don't think customers would like this at all! We need to calculate capital costs in a way that will help to set prices that are stable over time or perhaps rise in line with inflation.

Changing methods

In fact, we can quite easily find a way to even out capital costs over time. Let us simply apply the annuity method mentioned in the section on corporate investment analysis (page 119) to find capital costs that are the same for each of the 5 years ($000):

$$260/3.352 = 77.57$$

In the formula, the factor 3.352 represents the accumulated present value factor for 5 years at 15 percent.

These costs are called *nominal annuities* and the method is sometimes shortened NA.

Thus, if we were to charge capital costs amounting to $77 570 in every year we would have a flat series of capital costs. Furthermore, this series of payments would be big enough to pay back the loans and to pay interest on the outstanding amounts.

Checking the present value of capital costs

If we calculate the present value at 15 percent (WACC) of all the capital costs we shall find that in both cases (NL and NA) it corresponds exactly to the value of the original equipment. This is shown in Table 5.3, where we can see the present values of the yearly capital costs discounted to the beginning of the process, i.e. to the end of year 0.

Because the present values of all the yearly payments add up to an amount identical to the original investment, both these methods will recover the nominal

Table 5.3 Present value using nominal linear depreciation (NL) and nominal annuities (NA)

| Year | Capital cost | | PV factor | PV NL | PV NA |
	NL $000	NA $000		$000	$000
1	91	77.57	0.87	79.13	67.45
2	83.2	77.57	0.76	62.91	58.65
3	75.4	77.57	0.66	49.58	51.00
4	67.6	77.57	0.57	38.65	44.35
5	59.8	77.57	0.50	29.73	38.57
				260.0	260.0

value of the original investment. After the process is over, all borrowed money could be paid back to shareholders and lenders, should we choose to do so. Also, during the process, owners and lenders will be compensated for inflation through the high rate of interest.

However, neither method allows for inflation very well. Could we not find a method of calculation where costs rise over time so as to follow inflation more closely?

Calculating a real annuity (RA)

The costs will follow inflation much more closely if we calculate real annuities and inflate them year by year to adjust for prevailing inflation. To do so we take inflation out of the interest rate and allow the basis of depreciation to grow over time. In daily life we would say that if the nominal interest rate is 15 percent and inflation is 5 percent then the real interest rate is $15 - 5 = 10$ percent.

(Those readers who have studied interest rates very carefully might know that this simple calculation of real interest rate is not quite correct. Instead we are supposed to divide the yearly nominal growth into the full inflation factor to receive the real growth, as follows:

$$1.15/1.05 = 1.0952$$

Consequently, the correct mathematical real interest rate is not 10 percent but 9.52 percent. Now that we know this fact we are going to overlook it for the remainder of the chapter, although we will return to it briefly at the end of the discussion.)

Let us now assume that we can apply 10 percent interest as the real interest rate. In this case we can calculate a real annuity instead of the nominal one, as follows ($000):

$$260/3.791 = 68.58$$

In this calculation 3.791 is the accumulated present value factor for 10 percent and 5 years.

Table 5.4 Capital costs using inflated real annuities

Year	Start value $000	Real annuity $000	Inflated real annuity $000
1	260	68.58	72.01
2		68.58	75.61
3		68.58	79.39
4		68.58	83.36
5		68.58	87.53
6	331.8	87.52	91.90
7		87.52	96.50
8		87.52	101.3

This real annuity, $68 580 is actually valid in year 0. As soon as we start business in year 1 we have to add 1 year of inflation to convert the annuity from a real number to a nominal number. (All business is done in nominal numbers.) In the second year we add another year of inflation and so on for all 5 years. The capital costs will develop in accordance with Table 5.4.

Look at that series of numbers! It will follow inflation beautifully, and in year 4 of the case our capital costs should be $83 360 instead of our original $67 600. Note that there is no sudden change when new equipment is bought at the end of year 5. The inflated real annuity just keeps rising in accordance with yearly inflation exactly as before.

Now the calculation is finally giving a cost distribution that can be applied as an input to pricing the services.

However, this method is not always used in this way in the real world. Instead of inflating the real annuity by yearly inflation, companies tend to inflate the original starting value of the asset involved in order to find its replacement value at the start of each particular year. In this way they can find annuities through a yearly calculation, by dividing the latest replacement value into the present value factor (see Table 5.5).

Table 5.5 Capital costs using inflated replacement values

Year	Replacement value $000	Real annuity $000	Inflated real annuity $000
1	260	68.58	72.01
2	273	72.01	75.61
3	286.7	75.61	79.39
4	301.0	79.39	83.36
5	316.0	83.36	87.53
6	331.8	87.52	91.90
7	348.4	91.90	96.50
8	365.8	96.49	101.3

If we want to calculate only the costs of year 4, we could do the following analysis:

$$\text{Replacement value (\$000)} = 260 \times (1.05)^3 = 301$$
$$\text{Real annuity (\$000)} = 301/3.791 = 79.39$$

Finally, we find the inflated real annuity by multiplying by 1.05:

$$79.39 \times 1.05 = 83.36$$

When we inflate replacement values instead of annuities we get exactly the same numbers as before if the price of equipment follows inflation exactly. But if the price of equipment rises faster or slower than general inflation, this method will allow us to adapt to the real price changes.

■ But of course there has to be a real linear method too?

Yes, of course. To use real linear depreciation we take the replacement values from Table 5.5 and charge depreciation and interest costs to them. Simplified real interest (10 percent, not 9.52 percent) should be charged to the starting value in each year and depreciation should be calculated as a share of the replacement value at the end of the year, if we assume that depreciation happens at the end of the year.

To find the capital costs of year 4 according to the real linear method we would start with the replacement value at the beginning of the year, and calculate 10 percent interest on the part that has not yet been depreciated:

$$\text{Interest costs (\$000)} = 301 \times 2/5 \times 10\% = 12.04$$

To find depreciation we divide the replacement value at the end of the year by five:

$$\text{Depreciation, year 4 (\$000)} = 316/5 = 63.2$$

Consequently, our total capital costs during year 4 would be \$75 200. This number is lower than the inflated real annuity, but much higher than the original numbers according to the NL method.

The outcomes over time are shown in Table 5.6.

Table 5.6 Capital costs by the real linear method

Year	Replacement value $000	Remaining value start $000	Interest $000	Depreciation $000	Capital costs $000
1	260	260.00	26.0	54.6	80.6
2	273	218.40	21.8	57.3	79.2
3	286.7	171.99	17.2	60.2	77.4
4	301.0	120.39	12.0	63.2	75.2
5	316.0	63.21	6.3	66.4	72.7
6	331.8	331.80	33.2	69.7	102.9
7	348.4	278.71	27.9	73.2	101.0
8	365.8	219.49	21.9	76.8	98.8

Table 5.7 Present values using the two real methods

1 Year	2 Inflated real annuity $000	3 Real linear capital costs $000	4 PV factors	5 PV of column 2 $000	6 PV of column 3 $000
1	72.01	80.60	0.87	62.6	70.1
2	75.61	79.17	0.76	57.2	59.9
3	79.39	77.40	0.66	52.2	50.9
4	83.36	75.25	0.57	47.7	43.0
5	87.53	72.69	0.50	43.5	36.1
				263.2	260.0

As can be seen, this calculation gives a little bit of room for increasing costs of operations, which was not the case with the inflated real annuity.

Finally, before leaving the theory, we need to find out if the two real methods also have present values that add up to the original cost of the equipment (see Table 5.7). The figures in the table look pretty good! But wait, there is a deviation in column 5: the sum of PVs of the inflated real annuity is $263 000 instead of $260 000. Why is that? This has happened because we solved the example with 10 percent real interest instead of 9.52 percent, the correct real rate. Readers will have to forgive me for this simplification. Alternatively, you could rework the inflated real annuity at 9.52 percent to see that this adjustment corrects the problem.

◼ Discovering that the rig can be used for 8 years instead of 5 years

If engineers unexpectedly discovered that these rigs can be used for 8 years instead of 5 years we will have to do the same calculations with different numbers.

Working out the NL method for year 4 out of 8, we get the following numbers ($000):

$$\text{Depreciation} = 260/8 = 32.5$$
$$\text{Interest} = 260 \times 5/8 \times 15\% = 24.38$$
$$\text{Total capital costs} = 56.88$$

At this point those readers who know financial accounting might be a little concerned, thinking that we ought to pay attention to the depreciation that was done under a different scheme at the beginning of the life of the rig. But, in fact, we don't. As soon as we know that the rig lasts for 8 years, we calculate as if we had known that all the time. Mistakes in the beginning cannot be corrected by more mistakes later. In bookkeeping they can, but in the real world of business we do not go back and change old prices.

Working out the NA method for 8 years we get the following numbers:

$$\text{Nominal annuity (\$000)} = 260/4.49 = 57.91$$

Because we are very close to the middle of the life of the drilling rig, the NL method and the NA method give very similar answers. Their outcomes would differ much more if we were close to the beginning or to the end of the life of the asset.

Working out the inflated RA method for 8 years we get the following numbers, valid at year 0:

$$\text{Real annuity (\$000)} = 260/5.335 = 48.73$$

After inflating it to year 4 we get:

$$\text{Inflated real annuity (\$000)} = 48.73 \times (1.05)^4 = 59.24$$

Finally, working out the inflated real linear analysis, we get the following numbers ($000):

$$\text{Depreciation} = 316/8 = 40$$

$$\text{Interest } 301 \times 5/8 \times 10\% = 18.81$$

$$\text{Total capital costs} = 58.81$$

As can be seen from all these numbers, all methods are fairly similar at the middle of the expected life of the equipment.

■ A theoretical note on these methods

At the start of the case, we were asked to find a good starting point for pricing. Since prices have to be adjusted for inflation, we investigated how inflation was taken care of by each of the methods. But we also took care to check that the total present value of capital costs would add up to the original buying value of the equipment.

As a matter of fact, there are three requirements to be fulfilled when we calculate capital costs:

1 We want the profile of costs over time to go reasonably well together with pricing even if there is inflation (pricing and competition requirement).

2 We want the total present value of capital costs to coincide with the original investment (paying back the original amount with proper interest to capital providers).

3 We want the total depreciation to be just right for buying a new piece of equipment at the going price when the old equipment wears out (replacing equipment).

If the real costs of operation are fairly steady over time, the inflated RA method will give us an almost perfect starting point for pricing our goods and services. The RL and NA methods will also work reasonably well, especially if the real costs of operations rise over time. But the NL method will seldom meet the first condition. Since capital costs according to the NL method tend to fall all the time, the real costs of operations must rise considerably to give us a gentle slope of total costs that might match inflation.

If the price of equipment follows inflation, then all methods will fulfill the second condition. But for the inflated RA method to be absolutely correct we have to work with the exact real interest rate (9.52 percent in the case). If not, there will be a quite small deviation (see Table 5.7). If the price of equipment rises faster or slower than inflation, both real methods will give us too much, or too little, compensation for general inflation. That might be necessary to meet the third criterion.

The third condition can normally only be fulfilled by the two real methods. Since real depreciation means that depreciation at any point in time should be directly related to the price of a new piece of equipment at that very time, the methods have been designed to meet the third criterion. The nominal methods can meet this criterion only if prices of equipment are constant over time.

5.2 Deregulating telephones

When the telephone market was deregulated in a European country, the government felt a need to break up the old state-owned monopoly without wasting available resources. Therefore, they decided to give new operators access to the existing local networks of the old monopolist. In this way, there would be no need for new operators to build their own local networks.

After the decision, the Telephone Authority was instructed to manage the daily regulation of the network market and to make sure that local access was made available for all operators on a shared full cost basis.

For one local area of the country, there was a fairly new and well-functioning local network to be shared. The network had been built by the old monopolist 5 years previously. The investment amounted to €100 million. The monopolist originally treated the network as machinery and depreciated it all in 5 years in accordance with the tax rules of the country. Consequently, when the new rules were introduced, this network had just barely been written down to zero, although everybody knew that such a network would be useful for at least another 15 years. Due to inflation during recent years a similar network would cost €120 million today.

There was a discussion between the old monopolist and the new independent operators concerning the full cost of the network to be shared. The following opinions were presented to the Telephone Authority.

To calculate full costs of the network, the old monopolist suggested the following procedure:

	€m
Depreciation (20 percent of 120)	24
Interest on remaining value (15 percent × 0.75 × 120)	13.5
Yearly maintenance costs	8.5
Full cost to be shared	**46**

In the accompanying notes, the old monopolist explained that 15 percent was the required return on equity capital of the owners of the company. (The bank lending rate was 8 percent.)

The union of independent operators emphasized that the network had already been fully depreciated and was carried at zero value in the balance sheet of the old monopolist. Thus neither depreciation nor interest on capital were meaningful elements of full costing. They were, however, willing to share yearly maintenance costs.

After seeing these opinions, the representatives of the Telephone Authority realized that 'a shared full cost basis' was perhaps not as easy to manage as it may have sounded at the start.

A firm of accountants is asked to evaluate the project, as follows:

1 Discuss the consequences of each opinion for the monopolist, other operators and general telephone customers.

2 On behalf of the Telephone Authority, suggest a solution to the conflict. Support your solution with appropriate calculations.

Solution: Deregulating telephones

As can be seen, the old monopolist wants to calculate depreciation on today's acquisition value of the network. This is a reasonable start to a calculation of real depreciation and interest, but the depreciation time should be 20 years, and thus the depreciation rate should be 5 percent only instead of 20 percent.

In the next step, the old monopolist calculates interest on remaining value, which is also correct, but now the interest rate is wrong. Among the comments from the monopolist it is said that equity owners demand 15 percent return on invested capital, which might be a reasonable nominal return if there is inflation in the market. But if depreciation is calculated on replacement cost, then we need a real cost of capital. Considering the good potential to borrow money in the telephone business, we could guess that at least 50 percent of financing will come from borrowed money. In this case a nominal WACC could be estimated in the following way:

$$0.5 \times 15\% + 0.5 \times 8\% = 11.5\%$$

Looking at the price of a new network we can see that investment costs rose by 20 percent in 5 years. That corresponds to almost 3.7 percent a year. If we subtract 3.7 percent for inflation, we find that a fair real WACC is only 7.8 percent instead of 20 percent as suggested by the monopolist. But as we made certain assumptions that might not be absolutely correct, let us adjust it to 8 percent. Consequently, the monopolist is overstating the full costs by a considerable amount.

The union of independent operators has quite an interesting point. Since the old monopolist depreciated the network over only 5 years, it probably charged the full costs (depreciation, interest and operating costs) to customers. These customers paid the amount in full, and therefore they could be said to own the network in a moral sense. In a way, then, it would be fair to suggest that customers should no longer pay any capital charges at all for the network.

On the other hand, in a legal sense, the network belongs to the old monopolist and the Telephone Authority is concerned with trying to create a market, where companies can compete for customers and still share the costs of the network.

When creating a market, we have to realize that a resource that can be used for providing telephone services for a long time has a value today. That value should be written off over the expected useful time (15 years in this case) and interest should be charged every year on the remaining value. Therefore, it would not be reasonable to assume that the network belongs to consumers. But it might be reasonable to conclude that customers have paid too much for network services during the previous 5 years. Therefore they should be entitled to a refund before the new market really starts.

Unfortunately I have never seen a market where customers were given a refund for such reasons! When monopolies are broken up, typically whatever customers have paid in the past is forgotten and authorities concentrate on creating a workable market for the future.

To create such a market we will need to remember the three requirements that were mentioned in the case on the Glamorous Drilling Co.:

1 We want the profile of costs over time to go reasonably well together with pricing even if there is inflation (pricing and competition requirement).

2 We want the total present value of capital costs to coincide with the original investment (paying back the original amount with proper interest to capital providers).

3 We want the total depreciation to be just right for buying a new piece of equipment at the going price when the old equipment wears out (replacing equipment).

Considering these rules we can start answering the questions of the case.

■ Consequences of the opinions

The monopolist appears to do real linear depreciation (the most expensive depreciation system) with nominal interest on remaining values (the most expensive interest calculation). If the monopolist has its way, it will make a great profit. The depreciation time is much too short and the interest rate is much too high to match a real calculation.

But we have to ask ourselves what the monopolist intends to do after 5 years' time. If depreciation is completed in 5 years, then the book value of the assets will again be equal to zero! If the price (apart from operating costs) is then lowered to zero, the first of the above rules will be broken very flagrantly. On the other hand, if the prices are not lowered to zero, the monopolist will make good profits and earn much more than is needed to follow rules 2 and 3.

The new competitors will have great difficulty competing at all. Their costs to access the network will be so high that they might even decide to build their own networks. In this case the ambition of the government to create a market will not be fulfilled. Prices will remain very high and the customers will not see any improvement in the market.

If the independent operators have their way, the monopolist will give away valuable network access almost for free. The price will fall very much and the monopolist's profit will deteriorate. There will be intense competition and low prices for a period of time, and the new operators will be fairly happy, because they will probably have slimmer organizations than that of the monopolist.

The public will benefit from very low prices for a period of time and many new operators will enter the market.

In the longer run, there will be trouble, because the going price of capacity is far below the building costs. Therefore, everybody will hesitate to build until there is an obvious lack of capacity and prices start to rise again.

■ Solving the conflict

Since the monopolist appears to be ready to introduce the real linear depreciation method (RL), we could work it out in a correct manner. In this case, depreciation could be based on today's real value and on the full real life of the network. Interest could be based on real average interest on remaining value at any one time. For the next year we might do the calculation in the following way:

	€m
Depreciation (120/20)	6.0
Interest (8 percent × 0.75 × 120)	7.2
Yearly maintenance costs	8.5
Full cost to be shared (RL)	**21.7**

Alternatively, we could calculate a real annuity of today's acquisition value, assuming 8 percent real interest and 20 years lifetime. We get:

	€m
Capital cost 120/9.82 (now) = 12.2	
Inflating the annuity to the first future year (12.2 × 1.037)	12.5
Yearly maintenance costs	8.5
Full cost to be shared (RA)	**21.0**

The final adjustment for inflation in the RA method is really a minor point. To solve the case we need to make it clear that both real methods are much more realistic than the traditional nominal approach. Fine-tuning is less important.

Sharing these costs will create a well-functioning market for the network at the correct price level and will show consumers the advantages of competition in full as opposed to both suggestions by the conflicting parties.

5.3 Warm and cosy

In a middle-sized city in a cold northern country, there used to be a municipal distance heating network. The municipality erected a building with a big boiling plant to heat regular water. They also built a network of pipelines to distribute the hot water to most of the buildings in the central part of the city. Most of the property owners in the city found it profitable to connect to the network and arranged heating systems in their buildings accordingly.

Some inhabitants did not connect to the system. Either they lived too far away from the boiling plant and found the connection too costly, or they were already well equipped with alternative heating systems (oil or electricity or even wood-burning fireplaces in outlying areas).

In order to treat all citizens fairly, it was decided to provide hot water to all property owners at full cost, no more and no less. When analyzing the situation, accountants found that there were several kinds of costs involved:

- cost of energy to heat the water
- cost of operations and maintenance
- capital costs, i.e. depreciation and interest on the plant and the network.

Since the cost of energy has to be paid to external sources, it is completely uncontroversial and will be left out of this case. To simplify the situation we shall assume that the boiling plant and the network can be used for 40 years.

When the plant and the network were originally built in 1988, the cost was €60 million. The municipality decided to depreciate it over 40 years. They estimated their nominal cost of capital to be equal to the market rate of interest plus 2 percent. In every year for 20 years they charged prices to cover the capital costs as well as the costs of operations and maintenance.

■ Selling the heating system to save the municipal budget

However, in 2008, the municipality ran into economic difficulties due to the financial crisis and decided to sell the plant and the network to the highest bidder. Several large private companies participated in the bidding. The final buyer – The Heating Company – paid €75 million. At the time the actual building costs of a new plant and a new network were estimated to be around €100 million. The Heating Company promised to apply the same cost of capital as the municipality, at least for a few years in the beginning.

Still, by 2009, the property owners in the city and the Heating Company already had very different opinions on the pricing. The National Competition Authority was called in to mediate and decided to arrange hearings on the case. At the hearings, the following opinions on yearly costs were presented:

	Full capital costs €m
Property owners	3.30
Invited municipal experts	4.50
Experts at the Competition Authority	5.05
Invited private financial Expert	6.54
Heating Company Chief Accountant	8.25

In 2009, the nominal market rate of interest was around 4 percent. Long-term inflation is expected to come out at around 2 percent. Let us assume that everybody accepted those rates of interest and that each of the above calculations is correct from its own particular point of view.

Accountants are asked to perform the following analysis:

1 Find out how each party calculated the capital costs for 2009.

2 Explain the calculations and write comments that could be used to justify each approach.

3 In fact, you should not completely leave out the cost of operations and maintenance. The reason for this is that those costs tend to rise over time even in a real sense. Ideally, total real costs should be approximately constant over time. Find out which, if any, of the previous calculations would help to make total real costs approximately constant over time. Also, explain why total real costs should be constant over time.

Solution: Warm and Cosy

■ 1. Identifying the methods of calculation

Let us first assume that everybody made a correct calculation according to their own theory. In that case we will find:

The private property owners probably investigated how the municipality used to organize depreciation and interest. When doing so they might have found that the municipality applied the nominal linear (NL) method of calculating capital costs. Starting from the data given in the case, that method would yield the following numbers:

	€000
Depreciation (60/40)	1 500
Interest (60 × 20/40 × 6 percent)	1 800
Total capital cost	3 300

Applying this method means that capital costs are falling all the time until the big boiling plant has to be rebuilt. Clearly, private customers feel that they paid very high dues to the municipality during the first few years, and that therefore they are now entitled to lower dues as the plant is getting older.

The invited municipal experts from the National Association of municipalities would probably be quite good at cost accounting theory. Furthermore, they understand that the municipality ought to prepare for reinvestment in a new boiling plant sometime in the future. Therefore they are likely to apply the real linear (RL) method of capital costs to make sure that money for reinvestment is set aside to such an extent that there will not be economic difficulties when the plant wears out. Starting from the basic data in the case they might think in the following way:

	€000
Depreciation (100/40)	2 500
Interest (100 × 20/40 × 4 percent)	2 000
Total capital costs	4 500

The experts at the National Competition Authority have an inclination towards annuities because, using annuities you need not really make yourself a lot of trouble to find the true ages of all items. A real annuity needs only a small number of variables compared with the other methods, and, when looking at the functions of a market, a method like this will be quite sensible. This is how they might have done their calculation:

	€000
Real annuity (100/19.79)	5 050

Here 19.79 is the accumulated present value factor at 4 percent real interest and with a life of 40 years. Possibly, the number should have been inflated into the next year. Also, the interest rate should probably not have been exactly 4 percent, but instead the exact mathematical real rate of interest, 3.92 percent. However, the capital cost would change very little as a consequence.

The private financial expert was probably invited by the Heating Company to support their case. Someone like this (being paid by the Heating Company) would be anxious to give a true picture, which proves that he knows the subject well, but would want to offer something that would support the calculations of the Heating Company. He could go for a nominal annuity on the actual buying price. Noticing that now the buying price is €75 million and the expected remaining life is only 20 years, this is what it would look like:

	€000
Nominal annuity (75/11.47)	6 540

Here 11.47 is the accumulated present value factor at 6 percent nominal interest and with 20 years of remaining life.

The CEO of the Heating Company does not have a very difficult task. He will do exactly the same calculation as was done in the municipality when they built the big boiler, but he will start from the buying price of the Heating Company and not from the historical municipal numbers. He will want to earn a lot of money as soon as possible and he wants to bring this calculation in line with all other calculations that are done in nominal terms at the Heating Company. Here is his calculation:

	€000
Depreciation (75/20)	3 750
Interest (75 × 6 percent)	4 500
Total capital costs	8 250

2. Justifying the calculations

Private property owners probably know that the municipality has been applying the NL method for the past 20 years. During those years, in the first half of the project, the NL method tends to yield quite expensive yearly capital costs. But now that the first half of the project is over, the property owners probably feel that it would be unfair to them to change the method of calculation in such a way that the remaining years become more expensive than they would have been had the NL calculation continued for the remainder of the life of the project.

In fact, there are property owners who feel that during the first half of the project they paid off half the plant on behalf of the municipality. Therefore, from a moral perspective, half the plant is theirs and whoever manages it should not be allowed to arbitrarily change their conditions.

On the other hand, the property owners, while paying the full cost of the capital and operations, did not take economic responsibility for the plant and were, at least in a legal sense, free to switch to some other kind of energy for their houses.

The municipal experts, as was mentioned in the previous section, understand that the municipality ought to prepare for reinvestment in a new boiling plant at some time in the future. Therefore they feel that the RL method of capital costs is a good way to make sure that money for reinvestment is set aside to such an extent that there will not be economic difficulties when the plant wears out. In fact, they do not plan to hoard the money over the years, but rather invest some of it in one year and some of it in another year to keep the entire plant in a good shape.

Theoretically, if a company had 40 boiling plants and 40 networks of different ages, applyiong the RL method for depreciation to all of them would make sure that one whole plant could be exchanged every year, which is exactly what is needed. Therefore the RL method will focus on the need for replacement capacity, one of the rules mentioned in the first case in this section.

Also, municipal experts would be concerned with rising real costs of operations because of rising leakages and rising maintenance costs over time. In such a situation they know that the slowly falling capital costs of the RL method will make it possible to make room for rising costs of operations without rising prices to customers.

The invited experts from the National Competition Authority have an inclination towards annuities because, using annuities, you do not really need to find the true ages of all items. To calculate a real annuity you need only a small number of variables compared with the other methods, and, when looking at the functions of a market, this approach will be quite sensible.

The real annuity will create the same real capital costs for all items of the same kind, irrespective of how old they are. But if there are rising real maintenance costs over time, total costs will also rise over time, making the heating service more expensive to the customers as the years go by. Still, in a system like a distance heating plant and network, the rising maintenance costs will probably not make themselves felt very much until a much later point in time.

(Between ourselves, they are probably not going to change the pipes after 40 years; instead they will keep them as long as they possibly can, charging successively higher costs for losses to the customers as the years go by!)

The invited private expert will be anxious to show some knowledge of these methods and, therefore, he will feel that he needs to find a more moderate alternative compared with the very hefty price rise suggested by the CFO of the Heating Company. That could be the reason why he is advocating the NA method, which is not used very much in real companies, but it is well known in theory.

But the expert is also doing something else, which has very broad implications in this kind of case. He states that capital costs of the Heating Company should be calculated on the basis of the money they spent for the current used plant rather than calculating capital costs on an original new plant. This position might appear very reasonable, but let us look at the likely consequences.

If the Heating Company is allowed to base its tariffs to customers on the price they really paid instead of a fair price for the assets, then any price would be legalized for a local monopoly. In the next step, the Heating Company could resell the plant at any price they want to another company (maybe to their own subsidiary or to another company in a related industrial group) and pocket the gains, knowing that the buyer will be allowed to charge the customers for his own real buying price. All buyers and sellers will make large gains, and the monopolized customers will have to pay.

As long as there is a partial monopoly, as in this case, almost any price will have to be accepted by the customers. If not, customers will have to change the whole heating system of their houses to some other type of energy, something that is probably prohibitively expensive. Still, managers of the Heating Company will feel that they are entitled to a fair return on the money they spent.

If this kind of calculation is allowed, then the damage is already done to local consumers. The municipality solved its economic problem by selling to the highest bidder and they will claim that they were well paid. But the true payers are their own inhabitants, who are now going to be charged a very high price for the heating plant, which, in a moral sense, was already to 50 percent their own!

The CFO of the Heating Company, of course, notices that the company paid €75 million for something that will last for 20 years. He will pretend to be in good faith when he wants to charge depreciation over and above the depreciation that was already applied and interest costs on recreated debts, 50 percent of which were paid back a long time ago.

Note that the municipality depreciated €30 million and now the Heating Company will attempt to depreciate another €75 million on an asset whose buying price was originally only €60 million.

My own opinion will be offered in the final section of the solution.

■ 3. Keeping real costs constant over time

If total real costs are kept constant over time, then nominal costs will follow inflation. Both customers and competitors will feel that the prices are fair and the market situation will have certain similarities to a competitive market. In many cases, this is what authorities are looking for when they privatize general utilities like municipal distance heating.

In most large technical systems like this one, real operating costs (leakages and maintenance) will rise over time. When pipes get older, there will be more leaks and consequently the operator will either lose hot water on its way to the customers or will have to maintain the pipes at ever rising real maintenance costs, unless there is a sudden technical improvement.

In a situation like this, the inflated real annuity will contribute to overstating the costs in the later years of the project. The real value of capital costs remains constant over time, which would be ideal if there were no operating costs. But if real operating costs rise over time, we would need capital costs which are slowly falling to get it all right. This can be achieved using the RL method or the NA method. But of those two, only the RL method will ensure that depreciation is large enough to manage reinvestment in case of inflation. Therefore I believe this case should be regulated using the RL method and the municipal experts ought to have their way.

But what about the poor managers of the Heating Company: are they then not entitled to a fair return on the money they invested? No, they are not! They spent money on a monopoly and we do not want to legalize monopoly gains. Let them suffer in order to learn the fair price of assets that constitute a partial monopoly utility.

Chapter 6

Inventory management

6.1 The Garage at Korsheden

The Garage at Korsheden is the last filling station at the limit of civilization in the Finnmark area in middle Sweden. They sell 4200 liters of petrol a week all year round. Ordering costs are SEK 1500 per order. Delivery will take exactly 1 week.

The buying price of petrol is SEK 9 per liter including petrol taxes. There is only storage space for 15 000 liters. Financing is difficult. Therefore, Garage management has decided that they need 15 percent returns on all investment before taxes. If that cannot be achieved, they will go fishing. Income taxes are disregarded.

The firm's accountants are asked to perform the following analysis:

1 How many liters of petrol should be included in each order? Also find the yearly order costs and the yearly holding costs and compare them.

2 The size of the storage tank might need to be increased. Assume that the extra space could be used for a long time. Determine how much space to add and how much could be paid for building it. Of course, the builders would work in the black economy (no income tax, no tax depreciation).

3 Assume that the expansion in scenario 2 has not been done. If management turns to a low-price chain instead, the price of petrol will fall to SEK 8.80 per liter. The order cost will rise to 2500 SEK per order and they will have to buy at least 30 000 liters each time. Under what circumstances would such a move be profitable?

Solution: The Garage at Korsheden

■ 1. Optimum order quantity

Finding the optimum order quantity is a classic problem, which can be solved quite quickly and easily by applying the EOQ (economic order quantity) formula.

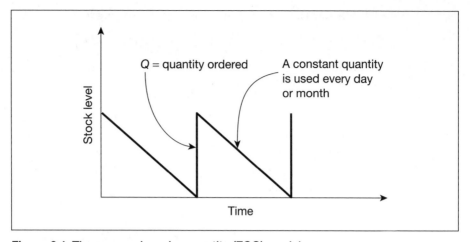

Figure 6.1 The economic order quantity (EOQ) model
Source: The EOQ model was developed by F.W. Harris in 1913 ('How Many Parts To Make At Once' *Factory, The Magazine of Management*, 10(2), 135–136, 152 (1913)), and further developed by R.H. Wilson ('A Scientific Routine for Stock Control' *Harvard Business Review*, 13, 116–128 (1934)).

To apply the simple formula it helps to assume that customers arrive at a well-defined rate, which is known in advance. In this case it is said that sales are 4200 liters a week and it takes exactly a week between placing an order and the new load of petrol arriving. Furthermore, there is an order cost to be paid along with every order (in this case, mainly for transport) and there is an interest rate or some other reason why it is expensive to hold very large quantities in store for a longer period.

Selling and replenishing are assumed to take place according to Figure 6.1. The following parameters need to be specified:

- demand, D, for the period studied, usually a year;
- ordering cost, O, every time an order is made, irrespective of the quantity;
- holding cost, H, including opportunity costs, insurance, warehousing and storage, materials handling and possible costs of obsolescence for the same period as demand.

In this case, we have the following information:

$$D = 4200 \times 52 = 218\,400 \text{ liters per year}$$

$$O = \text{SEK } 1500 \text{ per order}$$

$$H = 15 \text{ percent} \times 9 = 1.35 \text{ per liter per year}$$

To solve the case we need to find the lowest possible total cost for order costs and holding costs together. To find it we can create the following equation, showing how total costs vary with quantity ordered:

$$\text{Total cost for a period (TC)} = DO/Q + QH/2$$

Next, we can differentiate the total costs with respect to Q to find:

$$dTC/dQ = -DO/Q^2 + H/2$$

Setting the derivative dTC/dQ = 0 and solving for Q, we get:

$$Q_{opt} = (2DO/H)^{1/2}$$

Substituting the figures for the case, this solution becomes:

$$Q_{opt} = (2 \times 4200 \times 52 \times 1500/1.35)^{1/2} = 22\,030 \text{ liters}$$

Thus, Garage ought to buy a little over 22 000 liters for each order. The observant reader might notice that such an order quantity is not possible, because the storage tank will hold only 15 000 liters, but we shall deal with that problem later.

For the moment let us accept the 22 000 liters and continue to compare order costs and holding costs as required:

$$\text{Order costs} = 218\,400/22\,030 \times 1500 = 14\,870$$

$$\text{Holding costs} = 22\,030/2 \times 1.35 = 14\,870$$

$$\text{Total costs} = 29\,740$$

We notice that order costs and holding costs are equal. This is actually always the case when you calculate an optimum order quantity in the way presented here. Therefore, the two items calculated separately will actually confirm that you found the correct solution.

However, in this particular case, the available storage tank will not hold as much as 22 000 liters. It will take only 15 000 liters and that will change the order costs and the holding costs. Since the real tank holds a smaller quantity that the optimal one, there will be a larger number of smaller orders than we originally calculated. Therefore, we may assume that order costs will rise and that holding costs will diminish. But the total of the two items should be larger when we deviate from the theoretical optimum.

Accepting that orders may not exceed 15 000 liters, we get the following order costs and holding costs:

$$\text{Order costs} = 218\,400/15\,000 \times 1500 = 21\,840$$

$$\text{Holding costs} = 15\,000/2 \times 1.35 = 10\,125$$

$$\text{Total costs} = 31\,965$$

From this calculation we can see that the total cost of managing inventories has increased by somewhat over SEK 2000 per year. Furthermore, order costs have increased and holding costs have decreased. But the decrease in holding costs was, as expected, not big enough to compensate for the increase in order costs.

■ 2. Expanding the storage tank

The assignment does not tell us by how much to expand the storage tank, but a very obvious possibility, I think, would be to expand it to such a size that the outcome of the EOQ formula can be directly applied to the situation.

As we have already seen, total yearly costs will fall from SEK 31 965 to SEK 29 700. The difference is roughly SEK 2265 per year.

Now, find the value of a cash stream amounting to SEK 2265 per year forever:

$$PV \text{ (15 percent, forever)} = 2265/0.15 = 15\ 100$$

The reader will remember from the section on corporate investment that the accumulated present value of a payment that lasts forever can easily be found simply by dividing the number by the appropriate interest rate, in this case 15 percent.

Thus the upper price limit of expanding the tank with the restrictions given will be just around SEK 15 000. To build a storage tank at such a low cost is probably not possible. On the other hand, if we were to accept a somewhat lower interest rate, say, 10 percent instead of 15 percent, the outcome will be:

$$PV \text{ (10 percent, forever)} = 2265/0.10 = 22\ 650$$

This amount might still not be enough. In such a case, there might not be any obvious solution available, and we will have to refer the problem back to the Garage owner and ask him to think it over.

(Although, knowing him quite well, I fear that he might go fishing instead.)

■ 3. Turning to the low-price chain

If Garage turns to the low-price chain and accepts their conditions, we get the following yearly order and holding costs:

$$\text{Order costs} = 218\ 400/30\ 000 \times 1500 = 10\ 900$$
$$\text{Holding costs} = 30\ 000/2 \times 1.35 = 20\ 200$$
$$\text{Total costs} = 31\ 100$$

The new yearly total cost will be SEK 31 100. This is SEK 865 lower than in the original case, because with 15 000 liters per order the yearly cost was SEK 31 965. However, in addition Garage gets a discount on all purchases, amounting to SEK 0.2 for every liter bought. That will be a lot of money:

$$\text{Discount} = 218\ 400 \times 0.2 = 43\ 680 \text{ every year}$$

Consequently, the total yearly gain on switching to the low-price chain would be as follows:

$$\text{Yearly gain} = 43\ 680 + 865 = 44\ 545$$

Evaluating such a flow of funds over a large number of years, we get the following outcome:

$$PV \text{ (15 percent, forever)} = 44\ 545/0.15 = 296\ 967$$

That money could be used to build a new storage tank, and it might be good enough for such a project. We will conclude that it would probably be a profitable project if Garage were to switch to the low-price chain.

6.2 Beare Market

At the Beare Market in the northern countryside, companions Beare and Deere sell a number of basic supplies to nearby farmers, forest owners and hunters. They have two lines of products:

- animal feed
- farming equipment.

This case deals with animal feed only.

Since hay is normally grown by the farmers on their own land, Beare Market mainly supplies additional nutritional feeds for cows, sheep, horses and pets on a daily basis.

They plan their inventories very carefully. They do not buy anything until it is absolutely necessary. But, luckily, they have a very dependable supplier, who always arrives on time and delivers the quantities that are needed. For pet food, we have the following information:

$$\text{Demand} = 6000 \text{ kg per month}$$
$$\text{Order costs} = \$120 \text{ per delivery}$$
$$\text{Holding costs} = \$0.5/\text{kg per year}$$

Traditionally, they used to by these things according to the economic order quantity (EOQ) formula. But last year Mr Beare's daughter, Lillie, came home after her first year at university and said she had studied business management very carefully. Lillie said that she had understood that there might be other ways of treating inventories rather than just optimizing the traditional formula. At the outset, she could see two possibilities:

1 They could plan for shortages in dealing with inventories. After all, most of the customers had supplies of their own and might not be hurt very much if they had to wait for a while before they could get the goods they were asking for. Therefore, Lillie said, Beare Market ought to delay the next order until they were out of supplies. Then, when they received supplies again, they could notify their customers to pick up the goods as soon as possible. In that way, she explained, the average level of inventories would fall and so would the holding costs. Even the order cost might fall if they could buy larger quantities every time.

2 They could rebuild their warehouse to make it possible for the Bully Feeds Co. to deliver all the animal feed they need without any orders at all. If they comply with the conditions of Bully Feed, they will be included in the weekly route of the large Bully delivery van and all feeds will be replenished to such an extent that there are virtually no more shortages. Furthermore, there will not be any ordering costs provided they never buy these goods from anybody else.

Mr Beare was very enthusiastic about Lillie's suggestions, but also puzzled. The first suggestion, he felt, would entail adopting the same system as before, only buying everything too late and losing the goodwill of the local customers. Of course, cows and horses could wait a couple of days for nutritious feed but still, if customers do not get supplies when they want them, they might decide to travel to the city instead of waiting. Mr Deere felt this might end up losing them customers.

'But you see,' said Lillie, 'you include the bad will in the formula and just recalculate the order quantity accordingly. It is not very difficult!'

Moreover, Mr Deere felt the second suggestion could be quite expensive. Rebuilding the warehouse to allow the van from Bully Feeds to pass through every week appeared to be quite costly. And what about the traditional independence of the Beare Market, which they had always enjoyed? But Lillie Beare was quite insistent, so he decided to allow her to make a thorough study before making any decisions.

Solution: Beare Market

■ The traditional formula

First, let us see how the managers of Beare Market would treat a product like the one described in this case if they were to apply the traditional formula in the regular way. The EOQ would be calculated as follows:

$$Q_{opt} = (2 \times 6000 \times 12 \times 120/0.5)^{1/2} = 5\,880 \text{ kg}$$

In other words, for practical purposes, they would buy supplies for 1 month at a time.

When performing the calculation we have to remember that we need to adjust the numbers to the same period of time. Since holding costs were given per year we had to multiply the monthly demand by 12 to make it yearly too.

For simplicity, let us work with 6000 units per order. Now the yearly order cost will be:

$$(6000 \times 12/6000) \times 120 = \$1440$$

The yearly holding cost will be:

$$6000/2 \times 0.5 = \$1500$$

Because they are ordering 6000 kg each time, instead of 5880 kg, the holding costs will actually be somewhat higher than order costs. Adding holding costs and order costs together, we get the total costs in the following way:

$$1440 + 1500 = \$2940$$

■ Allowing shortages

Now, if we follow Lillie's advice to allow shortages, there is actually another formula we can use. To apply that formula we should assume that customers, occasionally finding that Beare is out of stock, will accept the wait until the next load of supplies is received and will then pick up all their things at once. By doing so, they will help Beare to keep average stocks lower and the holding costs should fall. On the other hand, they will not like it and therefore Beare will lose some goodwill, which might

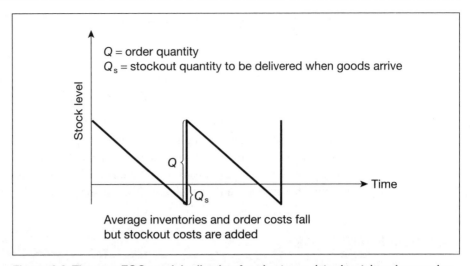

Figure 6.2 The new EOQ model, allowing for shortages (stockouts) and assuming customers can be persuaded to go along with the new arrangements
Source: The EOQ model was developed by F.W. Harris in 1913 ('How Many Parts To Make At Once' *Factory, The Magazine of Management*, 10(2), 135–136, 152 (1913)), and further developed by R.H. Wilson ('A Scientific Routine for Stock Control' *Harvard Business Review*, 13, 116–128 (1934)).

be compensated by a discount for those customers that are affected. If we assume that discounts are proportional to the length of the delay for an individual customer, the new formula becomes quite easy (see Figure 6.2).

Deducing a new formula for the EOQ is a little bit more complicated than before, but this is how it turns out:

$$Q_{opt} = (2 \times D(1 + C_h/C_s) \times C_o/C_h)^{1/2}$$

In the formula C_o is the order cost and C_h is the holding cost. C_s is the cost of shortages, which was not included in the original EOQ calculation. From the formula you will find that the EOQ is now be bigger than before. The increase in Q_{opt} will be decided by the size of C_s. If C_s is very big, there is only a small change, but if C_s is small, the EOQ rises significantly. The assumptions regarding stockouts are explained in Figure 6.3.

- We assume that customers will allow themselves to be persuaded to go along with the new arrangements. They are assumed to be prepared to wait until the goods arrive, at which point they will buy immediately. Stockout costs only show their degree of irritation.

- If customers buy their goods somewhere else and never return to Beare, the consequences could be serious.

Figure 6.3 Our assumptions regarding stockouts

Although Beare will buy larger quantities every time, the net average stock will still be smaller than before. This is because we assume that some customers will pick up their goods immediately when Beare receives new supplies.

Now, if customers do not mind waiting for supplies, theoretically, we could delay buying new goods for sometime. Then Q_s will be almost as large as Q. But, in reality, customers will want new supplies when they want them and not at a much later date, which will therefore increase the costs of shortages considerably.

To get started on this case, let us assume that the cost of shortages is five times the holding cost. Thus $C_s = \$2.5/kg$ per year. In this case we get:

$$Q_{opt} = [2 \times 6000 \times 12 \times (1 + 0.5/2.5) \times 120/0.5]^{1/2} = 6440 \text{ kg}$$

The optimum order quantity, Q, will now be 6440 kg instead of 6000 kg. In the new situation the shortages to be picked up by customers will be:

$$Q_s = Q \times C_h/(C_h + C_s) = 6440 \times 0.5/(0.5 + 2.5) = 1073 \text{ kg}$$

Calculating holding costs will also be harder than before. Now, average stocks are smaller and Beare will have stocks on hand only part of the time. Here is how it comes out:

$$\text{Holding costs} = C_h \times (Q - Q_s)^2/2Q$$

In this particular case we find:

$$\text{Holding costs} = 0.5 \times (6440 - 1073)^2/(2 \times 6440) = \$1118$$

Our cost of shortages will be:

$$C_s \times Q_s^2/2Q = 2.5 \times 1073^2/(2 \times 6440) = \$223$$

Ordering larger quantities each time, the new order cost will be:

$$6000 \times 12/6440 \times 120 = \$1342$$

Adding all costs together, we get the following totals:

$$\text{Holding costs} = 1118$$
$$\text{Costs of shortages} = \ \ 223$$
$$\text{Order costs} = \underline{1342}$$
$$\text{Total costs} = 2683$$

Comparing these numbers to the original case, we find that we have not saved very much:

$$\text{Savings} = \$2940 - \$2683 = \$257$$

But to save that money there will have to be shortages every month. We will have to trust that some customers will accept those delays at a fairly small discount. We calculated the cost of shortages to be $2.5/kg per year. If an average customer buys 50 kg at a time and the average delay is 5 days, the normal discount will be:

$$\text{Normal discount} = 50 \times 5/365 \times 2.5 = \$1.71$$

That is perhaps too little to persuade customers to accept delays. Still, Beare will gain only $257, which is less than 10 percent of the total costs! Maybe working with planned shortages is not a very good idea after all.

Let us try Lillie's other idea.

■ Rebuilding the warehouse

If we rebuild the warehouse to allow weekly deliveries without any orders, then all animal food will be delivered by Bully Feeds every week. There will never be any important shortages again and average holdings will be smaller than before. Compared with the original case we will save all order costs and quite a big part of the holding costs. But to find the new holding costs we have to make some assumptions.

We know that if Beare signs a contract with Bully Feeds, their van will pass through the premises once a week. Each time they will fill up Beare's supplies to make sure that sales can go on undisturbed until they arrive again the following week. The optimum weekly quantity will depend on the variation in weekly sales and, since it might be different for different feeds, it might not be possible to find a reliable number. But to get going, let us assume that they replenish Beare's supplies to such an extent that there are 2 weeks' supplies in stock every time they leave.

In the new situation Beare will have supplies for 2 weeks when the Bully Feed van has just passed through. When they arrive the following week, there would, on average, still be supplies left for another week. Therefore, the average supplies will be 1.5 weeks. Since the monthly needs are 6000 kg, we shall assume that supplies for 1 week are 6000/4 and we can calculate the yearly holding costs in the following way:

$$\text{Holding costs} = 6000/4 \times 1.5 \times 0.5 = \$1125$$

This is somewhat smaller than the original amount. The difference will be:

$$1500 - 1125 = \$375$$

In addition, we save order costs amounting to $1440 per year, bringing the total savings on pet feed to:

$$\text{Savings on pet feed} = 375 + 1440 = \$1775$$

Would that amount justify rebuilding the storage space? A good guess is that it would not.

But actually, it might not need to be enough. After all there are around five to 10 kinds of animal feed in stock. Therefore, signing a contract with Bully Feeds might save Beare just as much on several other feeds. To start, let us assume that there are 10 kinds of feed of a similar caliber. In that case the yearly savings might be 10 times as big:

$$\text{Yearly savings} = 10 \times 1775 = \$17\ 750$$

If those savings can be made for 10 years to come, and assuming 10 percent cost of capital, we get the cash flow in Figure 6.4.

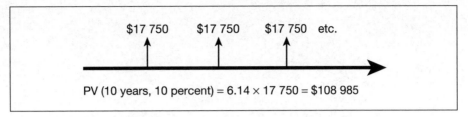

Figure 6.4 Yearly savings assuming Beare has 10 types of feed

Taxes? No, we did not include any tax consequences. Including taxes might lower the value of savings somewhat, but then taxes would also lower the cost of rebuilding the warehouse. We just do not have enough information to know how taxes might influence the whole situation. Nevertheless, we have got an indication. If Beare could rebuild their premises at less than, say, $50 000, the project appears to be on the safe side. If the project is more expensive than $110 000, then it will probably be too expensive. If the costs appear to stay between those limits, we would have to study the project more carefully.

Chapter 7

Profit measurement

7.1 Northern Trucks, Inc.

Northern Trucks, Inc. produces heavy trucks and buses for markets all over the world. All trucks produced belong to the heavy segment (> 16 tons), which means that they are designed mainly for long-distance travel with heavy loads.

In the market, Northern Trucks enjoy a very good reputation for long-lasting quality. Both new and used trucks trade at a premium compared with most other available brands. The market share in Europe is quite large. In certain countries, Northern is the market leader.

For the sake of efficient production, Northern has decided not to compete in the US and Canada. Truckers in those countries prefer to create their own trucks, by selecting the body from one company, the engine from another and perhaps the driver's cabin from a third. Since such a mentality does not fit well with Northern's understanding of overall quality, the company has decided to stay away from the market. In Latin America, however, Northern is one of the major producers of heavy trucks with a completely separate organization. In this case we are going to disregard the Latin American part of the company.

Northern Trucks has several truck-building plants and several sales subsidiaries. In each of the sales subsidiaries, there are a large number of sales companies, some of which are wholly owned.

■ Financial difficulties

During the financial downturn at the beginning of the new century, the truck market underwent a downturn in several countries. The financial results were not very bad, but neither were they as good as expected. Journalists attacked the CEO, saying he had cheated the public when bragging about the future of the company. Board members complained that the shares they owned or represented were not maturing as well as they would have wished. The CEO explained that the poor financial outcome was due to the financial crisis and promised rapid improvements.

After a period of time, the CEO decided to raise the required return of all subsidiaries. Instead of earning a 12 percent return on equity after tax, all subsidiaries were now expected to earn an 18 percent return on equity after tax.

At Northern Trucks, return on equity (RE) was calculated after tax according to the following formula:

$$RE = (GP - IP - Tax) / Equity,$$

where GP is gross profit before interest is paid, IP is interest paid, and tax is 25 percent of profit before tax. Because of group adjustments, subsidiaries did not always pay exactly 25 percent tax on profit before tax, but everybody was used to the formula and everybody felt it could be well understood.

■ Local reactions to the change

Mr Peter Smith, managing director of one of the sales subsidiaries, found the new required return outrageously high. He called a meeting with all sales managers within his area, his finance director and a consultant in finance.

At the meeting Mr Smith told the sales managers about the new required return and went on to explain that he was not in a position to influence the actual percentage. However, because of the very high required return on equity, he had decided to pay back half of the subsidiary's equity capital to headquarters. By so doing, he could lower the sales company's equity ratio from 46 to 23 percent. After all, he said, borrowing from the local bank was now much cheaper than using group equity capital.

In spite of this financial change, he said, he had to follow the rules of the game, raising the required return for all sales companies to the new level. For practical reasons, internal calculations were made before tax, which meant that required returns now would amount to:

$$18/0.75 = 24 \text{ percent}$$

where 0.75 shows what remains after the sales company has paid regular 25 percent tax on profits before tax.

'This means,' Mr Smith said, 'that from now on, you will have to make 24 percent profit before tax in order to receive a bonus. But, since geographical reasons make some sales companies more profitable than others we are going to make certain adjustments in our calculations.'

At this point, Mr Smith asked his director of finance to step forward.

■ The finance director

The finance director, Mr Sundin, explained that he had discussed the matter with a consultant in finance. The consultant had written a report on profit measurement, and concluded that return on equity would not be a good ratio for local management control.

After investigating the matter, Sundin decided to suggest a change from RE to one of the more modern ratios. Together with the consultant, he had studied the possible consequences of using each of the following indicators:

ROI – return on investment on total capital

ROCE – return on capital employed

RI – residual income

EVA – economic value added.

Together, Mr Sundin and the consultant decided to introduce residual income for local sales offices in the sales company.

'From now on,' Mr Sundin said, 'we are going to compute residual income for each sales office.' Normally this is done according to the following formula:

$$\text{RI (in theory)} = \text{gross profit} - (\text{total capital}) \times \text{COC}$$

In this formula, COC, cost of capital, is the weighted cost of all capital, considering borrowed capital and equity capital. However, he said, to come closer to their external accounts they had decided to compute residual income in their own way, according to the following formula:

$$\text{RI (in our company)} = \text{gross profit} - (\text{interest paid}) - 0.24 \times \text{equity}$$

'In addition,' he said, 'we are going to use three different indicators at the same time. We start with the number of trucks sold, then we calculate capital turnover and finally we calculate RI. Bonuses are calculated as a function of all three measurements. But to receive a bonus at all, most sales offices need to show residual income above zero. However, for offices in large cities, RI has to be above an individually set amount, and in the rural area, minor losses will be allowed as long as sales are reasonably good.'

■ The discussion

One participant in the meeting said that it would be difficult to explain the calculation of residual income to employees at home. However, he added, return on equity was equally difficult, so perhaps it would not make much of a difference.

Another participant said that you could never make 24 percent return on equity in most regions. Therefore, it would not matter what formula you followed. It would not work whatever you do.

The consultant was very unhappy. He felt that the whole idea behind residual income was being distorted in the formula suggested by the director of finance. He had suggested calculating the true cost of capital instead of enhancing equity. He suspected that they had not quite understood this. He decided to shut up and to stay quiet.

Since measuring profitability is a universal problem in large companies, let us have a discussion mainly around the following issues, highlighted in the case:

1 the CEO's decision to raise the required return of all subsidiaries;

2 the decision of the management group of the sales company to pay back equity capital;

3 the decision of the finance director to introduce residual income in his own way.

Comments: Northern Trucks

■ 1. The CEO's decision to raise required returns

The CEO had been forced into a corner. Profits were not developing as well as everybody had expected. To some extent that was due to the company changing models, but the worldwide economic crisis was also to blame. Truckers just did not change trucks as often as they did in more normal times. Of course, he could not take responsibility for the crisis as such but he still felt he had to do something.

Many steps were taken to try to improve the situation. Only one of them was described in this case. Of course, raising the required return of subsidiaries will not automatically improve company profits, but on the margin it might help because managers of subsidiaries will look for all possible ways to increase local profits in order to keep their bonuses as high as possible.

Another effect is mainly to improve the appearance of things. When business is very poor and there is a danger of laying off workers, it does not look very good if certain managers get high bonuses. The CEO's decisions were probably due to a combination of those effects.

■ 2. Paying back capital

This is quite an unusual decision. When the CEO suddenly raises the required return on equity, one can easily understand why managers of subsidiaries might wish they did not have so much equity. But, in fact, the amount of equity in a subsidiary should not be decided by the management of that subsidiary. Normally, the amount of equity in a company is decided by the board, and if the company is a subsidiary in a large group there would normally be board members representing the main owner, the parent company. They ought to be the ones to decide. Perhaps they did, although the case does not give us any information on this issue.

In this case we can see that the return on equity, RE, is actually not a very good way to measure the profitability of a subsidiary. The amount of equity can easily be changed by a board decision. Therefore subsidiaries could be told to pay back equity to the parent company, or they might receive additional equity from the parent company if needed for new investments that require a lot of capital.

In this case the management of the sales company decided to pay back equity to the parent company and to borrow a similar amount of money from a local bank. The true profitability of the subsidiary will not change as a result of this maneuver, but the reported RE will rise. On the other hand, the debt/equity (D/E) ratio of the subsidiary will rise. According to the theory of finance, that will mean that the required return of regular shareholders will rise because they will now be exposed to a riskier situation. After all, the shareholders will have to take the losses if the company is not able to meet its obligations in the financial markets.

But at the local subsidiary, that's not how they see it. In their minds, the required return on equity capital is set by the group CEO and is not influenced by their own decision to borrow money on the local market. Therefore it appears to them that increasing the D/E ratio makes it easier to meet the required returns and there are no costs. Seems like a free lunch!

But, in fact, there is no free lunch. The cost of increased leverage will just hit the parent company instead of the subsidiary. After all, when a subsidiary of the well-known Northern Trucks wants to borrow money from a local bank, they will easily be allowed to do so! Not because they are a very solid company (even if they are), but simply because they are a subsidiary of the Northern Trucks group and every banker knows that Northern Trucks never fails to fulfill its obligations. So, when trading on the equity, the manager of the sales company is actually trading on the equity of the parent company.

These things could be improved a great deal by two changes to the general control system:

1 Do not allow boards of subsidiaries to change their D/E ratios unless they adhere to the intentions of the group management when doing so.

2 Stop using RE to measure the performance of subsidiaries. Instead, subsidiary performance should be measured by some kind of measurement that is indifferent to the formal equity capital of the subsidiary. Since all the capital of a subsidiary belongs to the parent company anyway, applying RE will just open up possibilities for maneuverings such as what happened in the sales company! Instead we should apply one of the other measurements that will be discussed further in the following section.

■ 3. Profit measurement at the sales company

At the sales company they do need to change their approach to profit measurement. Measuring the profitability of individual sales companies by RE will just open up the field for similar maneuvering as described in the previous section. Instead they need to find a measurement that is indifferent to the sources of capital. All the measurements discussed by the finance director will meet those criteria and therefore they are all possible.

The original plain ROI will quickly reduce the room for maneuver and it will put focus on the operations of each company instead of its financing. ROI has been used for very many years to achieve this purpose. A few decades ago, ROI was supplemented, or even replaced, by another similar ratio, called return on capital employed (ROCE). Actually ROI and ROCE are very similar. The formulas are as follows:

$$ROI = profits\ before\ interest\ payment/total\ capital$$

$$ROCE = profits\ before\ interest\ payment/(total\ capital - free\ debts)$$

'Free debts' in the ROCE formula means those debts, like liabilities to suppliers or advances from customers, on which you do not pay any interest.

Clearly, clever managers will understand that there might be several ways to improve the ROI and ROCE ratios:

- You improve operations to increase the true return on your business.
- You avoid all new projects unless they give a higher yield than the average yield of your old projects.
- You stop new projects altogether. Considering traditional rules of profitability measurement, old projects (after depreciation) tend to show higher profitability than new ones!

In many cases the third solution might be an easier way out of a profitability problem than the others. But if you never start any new projects, your business will probably get smaller over time. And a very small business will not yield much profit even if the percentage is high.

Also, if you have two profitable projects to choose from and you discard one of them just to raise the average profitability, then you might actually forego company profits. If both projects are profitable, both of them should be carried out.

Now, residual income and economic value added were designed to eliminate such problems. Here you calculate the profit of a subsidiary before interest costs and then you subtract interest on all company capital. If you want to exclude free debts you can do so in these measures too.

By introducing residual income, the finance director is trying to focus on real operations of the sales companies. But unfortunately he felt very much restrained by the overall system of the company and has introduced a very peculiar variation of residual income.

If you do the mathematics carefully, you will find that residual income at the sales company is identical to the normal residual income measure. But it does not look that way. Here is what it looks like:

$$\text{RI (in our company)} = \text{gross profit} - (\text{interest paid}) - 0.24 \times \text{equity}$$

This new measure emphasizes the cost of equity very clearly, and makes everybody aware of its very high cost. That might restrict the will to invest in new projects, just like the possible effects of ROI or ROCE.

In fact, when you design a RI system, you should take care to avoid raising the cost of capital in the formula above the true cost of financing. If you do so, you are likely to make managers of subsidiaries restrict investment activities unnecessarily. They will avoid unprofitable projects, which is a good decision, but they will also avoid profitable projects that give a lower return that the one stipulated in the formula. Some of those overlooked projects might have been able to give a good return on shareholder money.

7.2 Shareholder value

■ An unhappy board

The CEO was thoughtfully peeling an orange at a resting place at the far end of a lovely cross-country skiing track. The sun was shining and we had completed the first leg of our trip around the beautiful little mountain. We had covered 7 km in the first hour and there were six more to go. The circumstances were perfect, but I could see that he was not happy.

In fact, I had already realized it during the first part of our journey because he did not speak to me as enthusiastically as usual and, above all, he did not try to leave me behind, not once. And I knew it was important for him to beat me at skiing every now and again.

'So Peter, what is the problem?' I asked, picking up a piece of the orange.

'You know, the chairman of the board called me last night and asked me what I plan to do to improve our share price at the stock exchange. At the last board meeting they were harassing me, saying that they want a higher share price and they want it soon. But I am just the CEO and I cannot influence the share price. That price is set by the actors in the stock market and I am not a major shareholder. You know very well that I don't have the money needed to influence the share price.'

'What do you mean? Do they want you to manipulate the price of the shares? I think that might be illegal!' I said.

'You see, they don't say, they just want the share price to be higher! Do you know something that we might do?'

So, that was the problem. We were not just on a regular winter conference with heads of the subsidiaries, but we were also supposed to manipulate the share price! And we were supposed to do it soon!

At the time I had been a consultant to Peter for several years, and I knew him quite well. We had organized conferences with all subsidiary heads several times before and we had created quite a good atmosphere in the group. I know that was what Peter wanted, so I had been happy to help him. But this one was different. Now, suddenly I was supposed to raise the price of company shares. I had never done anything like that before.

I said: 'If you ask Arthur [the CFO] to email me the latest quarterly report, I'll take the afternoon off from the conference and see if I can do something.'

'But you can't, you know. How could you?'

'Maybe not, but you can get me that report, can't you?'

And then he put his skis back on and kept working his way around the mountain. He did not say a word and after lunch he gave me the preliminary version of the annual report. You will find it in Table 7.1. All numbers are SEK millions and many items have been clumped together to facilitate reading it.

As can be seen, the company was not a very big one, but they still were quoted on the stock exchange, and they had some 10–15 subsidiaries in the consulting business. They had been doing reasonably well over the years. They made a profit every year and paid dividends to shareholders every year. According to the rules of the company, the yearly dividend was normally set equal to 50 percent of yearly profit per share rounded down to the nearest integer. With a yearly profit of SEK 54 million and five million shares, this comes out SEK 10.8 per share. The stock market expected a dividend this time of SEK 5 per share. The share price was hovering a little above SEK 100.

Table 7.1 Preliminary version of annual report

	SEK m
Balance sheet	
Fixed assets	375
Receivables	340
Cash	85
Total assets	800
Equity	375
Provisions	175
Debts	250
Equity and debts	800
D/E ratio	1.13
Income statement	
Sales	1 300
Operating costs	1 230
Operating profits	70
Net interest	5
Profit before taxes	75
Taxes (28%)	21
Net profit	54
Profit per share	10.8
Return on total assets	9.38
RE after tax	14.40

■ Possible actions

Now, looking at the report, you will find that there is quite a lot of cash on the asset side of the balance sheet. That cash is not really needed for the regular business, but is has been sitting there for quite a long time because of the managing of the dividends. Every year half the profits were set aside and saved to support future expansions. But perhaps not all of it was needed.

The stock market expects a dividend of SEK 5 per share. But let us investigate what happens if we distribute an additional dividend of SEK 10 per share, thus getting rid of most of the cash.

'A stupid idea,' said Peter. 'Anybody would understand that if the company gets poorer the stock price will fall. At least, there is no way it could rise!'

'But we could do an analysis, couldn't we?' I countered.

'I guess we could.'

Table 7.2 shows the analysis of what would happen if they were suddenly to announce that the dividend would rise from SEK 5 to 15 (once only) by distributing all the spare cash to the shareholders. In the table we can see what might happen in two possible cases:

■ In one column there are forecast numbers for next year if we pay the regular dividend this spring.

Table 7.2 Change to annual report with increased dividend

	Now SEK m	Next year 1 SEK m	Next year 2 SEK m
Starting balance			
Fixed assets	375	405	405
Receivables	340	365	365
Cash	85	70	20
Total assets	800	840	790
Equity	375	404	354
Provisions	175	185	185
Debts	250	251	251
Equity and debts	800	840	790
D/E ratio	1.13	1.08	1.23
Income statement			
Sales	1 300	1 400	1 400
Operating costs	1 230	1 325	1 325
Operating profits	70	75	75
Net interest	5	2	−1
Profit before taxes	75	77	74
Taxes (28%)	21	22	21
Net profit	54	55	53
Profit per share	10.8	11.09	10.66
Return on total assets	9.38	9.17	9.37
RE after tax	14.40	13.72	15.05
1) Dividend SEK 5 per share	25	25	25
2) Dividend SEK 15 per share	75		
Growth in equity		30	28
Growth in equity (%), g		7.53	7.99
Share price		108	119.7
Required return, k		12.16	12.16
$k - g$		4.63	4.18

- In the other column there are similar numbers that show the likely outcome if we were to suddenly raise the dividend this spring to SEK 15 and then go back to SEK 5 for the next year. That means SEK 10 additional dividend per share, costing the company SEK 50 million in addition to the regular SEK 25 million.

In both cases, the total business is supposed to grow by 7 percent. Therefore fixed assets and receivables both grow by that amount. But we do not plan for any new long-term loans. Therefore cash will actually decline in both cases, in case 1 by SEK 15 million and in case 2 by SEK 65 million. The difference will match the difference in dividends, SEK 50 million. All told, total assets will either grow to SEK 840 million or decline to SEK 790 million.

In the income statement, the consequences will be similar. Sales are expected to grow by 7 percent and so will operating costs. Operating profits grow to SEK 75 million. Net interest will decline in both cases and it will actually be negative in the second case. There is not much interest-bearing debt, but when most of the cash is gone, the net interest will be negative.

The remaining numbers follow from what has been said so far.

But the really interesting issues come after the regular part of the income statement. For this year we either pay SEK 25 or 75 million in dividends. For next year we will go back to paying only SEK 25 million in both cases. But that means that – for next year – growth in equity will be different in the two cases. The actual profit will be bigger in case 1, but the profitability (a percentage on equity) will get bigger once we have paid an additional dividend.

In the stock market there is a well known formula, called *Gordon's formula*. It states that the price of a stock can be calculated as the present yearly dividend divided by the required market rate of return, less the yearly growth in that dividend. This is how it looks:

$$P = D1/(k - g)$$

where P = expected stock price

$D1$ = starting dividend

k = market required return, and

g = growth in dividends.

The formula assumes that the ongoing growth will continue forever.

■ Deciding what to do

After performing the calculations we can now enter the values of our parameters into Gordon's formula. On the day of the analysis the share price was SEK 108 per share. Entering that number and next year's regular dividend (not this year's higher one), we get:

$$108 = 5/(k - 0.0753)$$

We find:

$$k = 0.1216$$

In other words, the required market rate of return of the company shares was 12.16 percent.

Now, knowing k, we can find out what would happen in the case of an additional dividend. After paying that dividend, when we are back to the regular dividend we get the following numbers:

$$P = 5/(0.1216 - 0.0799)$$

Solving for P, we find:

$$P = 119.7$$

This result means that if we were in the second situation for next year, today's long-term market price of the shares would be SEK 120. That price would include the regular traditional dividend to be paid fairly soon. But in addition to that, there is the additional dividend, SEK 10 per share. This means that the temporary share price before paying dividends will rise from 108 to 119.7 + 10 = SEK 129.3, which is roughly SEK 130 instead of today's trading price. That means that the share price will rise by over 20 percent if we declare an additional dividend corresponding to SEK 10 per share.

Peter looked at me as if he had seen a ghost. 'This time you are completely out of your mind!' he said.

'Well, I don't know these things, but I am quite good at elementary mathematics and I don't think I made a mistake,' I replied.

'But you couldn't know the likely market reaction to an additional dividend. How could you expect the share price to rise when you pay out a lot of money so as to diminish the true value of the company?'

'Well, they say that all stock market agents have Gordon's formula in their PCs. I don't know,' I said.

'I think you are crazy, but let's talk to CFO Arthur about it,' he said. 'After all, he is a good accountant!'

And so we did. Arthur also felt that the whole thing was crazy, but still, he did not have a better idea and after a while he accepted the plan. 'But we would need to have the full support of Kent [PR manager],' he said.

And so we asked Kent to come in. He started by telling us that we were crazy, but then he accepted the idea because he did not have a better plan. He designed a document to be published where we explained in detail that we were going to raise the dividend only once and then we would go back to the original formula.

Finally, when everything was prepared in detail, we presented it to the chairman of the board to have it included in the next board meeting, when the dividend would be decided anyway. The chairman was hesitant about the idea, saying: 'Maybe, but I don't promise! I'll allow you to present the plan to the next board meeting, but not until all other business has been covered and the stock exchange has closed!'

And so we did. I don't think that the board members actually understood the design. They did not ask any questions, however. I think they just trusted the chairman and Peter and this is why they voted for the scheme. They paid a lot of attention to Kent's information document, and they took care not to finish the meeting until the stock exchange had closed for the day.

Later in the afternoon Kent published a résumé of the board's decisions, including a complete description of the higher dividend scheme. He took great care to make it absolutely clear that there was no money for a systematic increase in dividends. The project was just a one-off event and as soon as the bigger dividend had been paid we would go straight back to our traditional rules. Also, the board decision was taken so late in the afternoon that that the stock exchange was closed and nobody could trade in the stock until the information was available for everybody.

The following morning the stock price went straight up to SEK 128. The next day the stock traded above SEK 130 all day and it stayed there during the remainder of the week. In fact, the price of the stock never fell back to the original level.

■ What did we do?

Some time after the board decision, there was a meeting with all heads of subsidiaries. I knew them all fairly well, because we had met at a series of conferences over the previous few years. In fact, most of them were present at the winter conference when the issue was initiated. We had always been on very friendly terms and I looked forward to seeing them again.

We met and I explained our reasoning. Some of them were concerned. One was angry: 'You took our money and gave it to the shareholders!', he said, practically shouting at me, and he stood up in a threatening way.

'What do you mean, your money? We took a part of the accumulated profits, and profits belong to the shareholders. They have every right to get that money since their investment has turned out to be quite profitable. You know very well that one of the big investors is using the money to support research and development in our own business area,' I said.

'But there is no more money when I want to expand my business by buying a small competitor or just adding a section with some new employees.'

I turned to Peter for support. He said to the man: 'Don't you worry Walter, when you have a good project you should just come to me and ask for support. If the project is good enough, there will also be enough money!'

Walter was quiet and sat down, but then there was another question that worried me more afterwards: 'Don't you feel that you are manipulating the stock price in an unfair way? After all, the real value of the shares must have fallen when we paid out all that money, and you made the price rise in spite of that.'

This was a tougher issue. It is a fact that the market price rose, but what happened to the real value of the shares?

First, is there a real value, which is different from the market price? Many people would say that there isn't. The real value is decided in the market and it is correct when everybody has full information, which was the case in this particular situation. If we believe in that thesis, then clearly the real value of the shares must have risen!

So why might the real value of the shares rise when we pay out a lot of money and weaken the financial position of the company? The explanation might be found in financial theory, which I do not know very well. But still, as has already been mentioned, the market is very concerned with growth, g in the formula, and when g rises the market price will also rise, all other things being equal.

But in this case all other things were not equal. We paid out SEK 50 million more than expected to the shareholders, and even after the payout the price of the shares remained higher than before the decision. Adding these gains together, the shareholders benefitted to the tune of around SEK 100 million. In one way that would run counter to financial theory. When the debt/equity ratio rises, as it did in this particular case, the required return, k in our formula, is supposed to rise. But when k rises, the price of the shares should fall. I did not include that danger in my presentation to the board and, luckily for me, it did not happen. How could that be?

To the best of my understanding, this might be because we sent new signals to the market about board behavior. Before our decision everybody knew that we had a fairly stable and dull company and that the yearly dividend would very likely rise at a fairly slow pace over time. We had been collecting surplus cash to such an extent that there was actually a positive net income from financial payments. Interest income was bigger than interest costs. But the market would not want a very stable company to just collect a big bag of cash and sit on it. Instead, they want the company to use its cash to grow and, if there are no good growth opportunities, to pay out cash that is not needed. The market felt that there was a growing awareness about financial issues and they rewarded us for that.

Perhaps Peter's comment to Walter, about there still being enough money to finance interesting expansions, actually proved the second point as well as calming Walter down somewhat.

For a while after the event, I was happy about the outcome, but I kept worrying about the question of whether my suggestion was unethical. Now, a few years later, I can see that the stock price is higher than ever and I feel that we did the right thing. We paid out an additional SEK 50 million to the shareholders and the market price of the shares rose. All shareholders gained in two ways, and I do not think that there were any losers. Not even Walter. The price of his personal shares increased and Peter found financing for him without difficulty when he was ready for that expansion he was worrying about.

Unethical behavior? No, not really. All the members of the management team, and the chairman of the board were insiders and could not trade in the shares before the board meeting without making it public. I was the only one who might have managed to trade and gain in an unethical way and I did not. Of course, I gained something from the project. I was paid my regular consulting fee for a day or two and I gained a reputation among the managers of the company that gave me many more assignments for several years to come.

And it was fun! I enjoyed it! Why don't you try?

Chapter 8

Control system cases

8.1 Broad-gauge Transport

In a European country, they decided to privatize the national railroad system and create a private company, called Broad-gauge Transport, to run the business. The private company was divided into three divisions:

- Personnel Transport
- Goods Transport
- Railroad Tracks.

The two transport divisions were given all the moving equipment, such as engines and railroad cars, for the two types of transport. All tracks and fixed equipment in connection with the tracks were given to the Tracks division. Each division was regarded as a full profit center and was expected to deliver good economic profits. The required return of all divisions was set to 12 percent. At the beginning of the case we are going to assume that there is no inflation and no taxes.

Railroad Tracks division

This division was instructed to develop and maintain the railroad tracks and to make them available for the other two divisions at prices corresponding to full costs.

Let us assume that a new part of the track cost €200 million. The track is assumed to be used for 20 years. After that it will be changed due to technical requirements to increase the speed of trains considerably. We are going to look into the capital costs and the maintenance costs for this part of the track. The maintenance cost is expected to amount to €5 million per year at first and is likely to rise over time in accordance with inflation.

The following analysis is required (solve 1–5 disregarding inflation):

1 Find the full cost of the tracks using:

– traditional depreciation and interest
– an annuity including full capital costs.

Compare the outcome of the two methods for each of the years 1, 11 and 20 in the life of the tracks. Do not calculate the cost for any other years.

2 For year 1, the group controller decided to set the internal transfer price for this part of the track to €39 million, to be shared between the two transport divisions according to their needs of capacity. Explain how the profitability of each division will change over time if the price remains unchanged for a long time. To support your reasoning, find the return on investment (ROI) of the tracks division for each of the years mentioned above.

3 Find the NPV and the internal rate of return (IRR) of the tracks project.

4 Explain why there will be criticism of the management control system selected.

5 Suggest how to design internal transfer pricing and cost accounting of the Tracks division to eliminate as much of the criticism as possible.

6 In reality, inflation in the euro area is expected to amount to roughly 2 percent per year. Assume that this inflation is constant and that prices of equipment and maintenance will develop in line with inflation. Discuss how to adapt the control system to inflation in order to give good correct information to all divisions.

Solution: Broad-gauge Transport

■ 1. The full cost of the tracks

Calculating depreciation over 20 years and including 12 percent interest in the traditional way, we get Table 8.1.

In each year interest costs are calculated on the starting capital at the beginning of the year. Depreciation is assumed to take place at the end of each year. In that way, the capital costs will be treated as if they were a loan that might have been taken in order to finance the project and which is paid back with a yearly amount, spread evenly over 20 years.

The yearly annuity is found by dividing the capital investment by the accumulated present value factor for 12 percent in 20 years (7.47):

$$\text{Annuity} = 200/7.47 = 26.8$$

Table 8.1 Traditional calculation of depreciation and interest

	Years		
	1	11	20
	€m	€m	€m
Starting capital	200	100	10
Depreciation	10	10	10
Interest on remaining capital	24	12	1.2
Total capital costs	34	22	11.2
Maintenance	5	5	5
Full cost	39	27	16.2

Including maintenance, the yearly cost will be €31.8 million. This nominal annuity will remain constant over all 20 years since there is supposed to be no inflation.

We can see that traditional accounting will give very high costs in the beginning and low costs at the end of the period. The nominal annuity will spread the costs evenly over time in a way that will follow the rules of capital costs very nicely.

▪ 2. Profitability of divisions

If the internal transfer price is €39 million, the tracks division will make zero profit in the first year. In later years, the profit will increase over time according to Table 8.2. As with calculations for question 1, depreciation is assumed to take place at the end of the year. Therefore, the starting capital is assumed to be valid throughout the year. The development appears extremely strange. The profitability of the tracks division measured as ROI through the normal routine will rise in every year even if the staff of the division does nothing at all to improve it.

Table 8.2 Profitability of the tracks division

	Years		
	1	11	20
	€m	€m	€m
Starting capital	200	100	10
Income	39	39	39
Depreciation	10	10	10
Maintenance	5	5	5
Profit before interest	24	24	24
Interest cost	24	12	1.2
Profit after interest	0	12	22.8
ROI before interest costs	12%	24%	240%

Since we are assuming that there is no inflation, the other divisions will see no change over time. They pay the same amount every year. Fluctuations in their profitability would be due entirely to other factors.

▪ 3. NPV and IRR

		€m
Present value of cash flow	[+ (39 − 5) × 7.47]	254
Investment		−200
Net present value of the project		54

To find the IRR, we first need to find the appropriate accumulated present value factor to make the net present value of the project equal to zero:

$$(39 - 5) \times X = 200$$

$$X = 5.88$$

Now, we look for 5.88 in the table of accumulated net present values. We find it between 15 and 20 percent and much closer to 15 percent. Careful calculations will take us to 16.1 percent.

Consequently, we can show that the tracks division has a positive net present value from a project which, in its entirety, is delivered to other divisions in the same group. But that was probably not the intention of the group controller when the project started. When it was decided to charge €39 million per year, that amount was equal to the full cost in the first year according to the nominal linear method of depreciation. To keep the profitability constant in an economy without inflation, the yearly transfer price would have had to be lowered over time.

The outcome of the calculation of the IRR actually confirms the above results. If the NPV is positive at a certain discount rate, then the IRR is higher than that same discount rate if we are concerned with a regular investment (outflow in the beginning and inflows over a number of years afterwards).

4. Discussion of consequences

It appears very strange that a division that is supposed to sell its services at full cost actually makes an average profit (16 percent) which is much higher than the required return of the other divisions.

This happens because the internal transfer price was set equal to the full cost of the first year and remains unchanged although the invested capital will depreciate over time. Profitability will rise as capital is depreciated without any action from divisional management.

Management of the other divisions might feel that they are paying far too much for access to the tracks and that the possibility of them making profits will be quite small.

5. Changing the internal pricing system

If internal prices are set according to the annuity method, charges to the other divisions would be constant over time. If the same method is applied to cost accounting, profitability of the tracks division will also be constant over time. We get the analysis in Table 8.3.

The starting capital of year 11 is equal to the net present value of the remaining capital costs:

$$\text{Starting capital} = 5.65 \times 26.8 = €151 \text{ million}$$

6. Introducing inflation

If 2 percent out of the 12 percent were general inflation, we can easily adjust the annuity to a real one by using 10 percent real interest:

$$\text{Real annuity} = 200/8.51 = 23.5$$

Adding €5 million of maintenance, the starting value will be €28.5 million.

Table 8.3 Profitability of the tracks division

	Years		
	1	11	20
	€m	€m	€m
Starting capital	200	151	23.9
Yearly income	31.8	31.8	31.8
Capital costs	26.8	26.8	26.8
Of which interest	24	18.1	2.9
Depreciation	2.8	8.7	23.9
Maintenance	5	5	5
Profit before interest	24	18.1	2.9
ROI before interest costs	12%	12%	12%

This number should increase by 2 percent every year, starting in year 1, which gives (€ million):

Year 1: $28.5 \times 1.02 = 29.1$

Year 11: $28.5 \times 1.24 = 35.4$

Year 20: $28.5 \times 1.49 = 42.4$

Since these numbers just follow inflation, the other divisions will not see any real change, although nominal internal prices are rising.

If you interpret the original 12 percent to be a real interest number, then we start from the same annuity, which was calculated at the beginning of the case, €26.8 million. We add €5 million of maintenance and get a starting cost of €31.5 million per year, which is then inflated in the same way as the numbers above.

8.2 Changing cars?

(This case is adapted from one used by Professor Paulsson Frenckner.)

William was driving an old car of a well-known brand and he felt it was about time to exchange it for a new one. There was nothing really wrong with the old one, but servicing and maintenance were becoming more expensive all the time. He also knew that modern cars of the same brand were less thirsty in terms of petrol consumption.

William tried to get the basic facts straight in light of a possible exchange. The following is what he found out. His car was 8 years old and he knew that he could trade it in for around €5000. But it was quickly losing its market appeal and he felt that in 5 years it would probably not bring in any money at all. Annual costs of fuel, servicing and maintenance were €3000 and he felt that these could be brought down to around €2000 with a new car of the same brand. On the other hand, the price of a similar new car would be around €21 000.

Let us assume that the old car is still good enough to drive around. Therefore there is no quality difference between the cars. If we were to decide on economic grounds, would it be a good idea for William to buy a new car right now? Or would it be a better idea to wait for another year?

In fact, most of us already know that you can almost never find economic reasons for changing cars, but let us solve the problem systematically to see if we can prove it.

Solution: Changing cars?

■ An intuitive approach

Let us start by finding the yearly costs of the old car and the possible new car. We need to deal with the following items:

- yearly loss of value (depreciation)
- yearly interest costs
- yearly operating costs.

The yearly loss of value is probably the most important item. The old car is worth €5000 now and in 5 years its value will be close to zero. To be on the safe side, let us assume it falls to zero. In such a case the value loss is €1000 per year. Let us assume that it is worth €4000 a year from now.

The new car costs €21 000. It can be used for a long time, but let us assume that it behaves as the old one. Thus, when it is 8 years old it will be worth €5000 (at today's prices). Thus, the yearly loss is:

$$\text{Yearly loss} = 16\ 000/8 = €2000$$

But then there are interest costs. William will either borrow the money for the new car or he might be lucky enough to have the cash in his bank account. But in both cases there will be interest costs. If he borrows he will have to pay interest on the loan and if he withdraws money from the bank, he will lose interest income. Now those two interest rates might not be identical, but they are equally real and the interest costs have to be included in our analysis.

Let us assume that a fair interest cost is 5 percent per year. We can therefore compute the following interest costs:

$$\text{Interest on the old car} = 5 \text{ percent} \times 5000 = €250$$

If we assume that William will keep the new car for 8 years, as he did the old one, we need to find the average value during those years:

$$\text{Average value of the new car} = (21\ 000 + 5000)/2 = €13\ 000$$

We can now calculate average yearly interest costs in the following way:

$$\text{Average interest on the new car} = 5 \text{ percent} \times 13\ 000 = €650$$

Finally, we need to deal with operating costs. When William investigated the operating costs of the new car, he probably found the costs in the first year. Those costs were €2000. They will very likely increase over time and, in year 8, they might be

Table 8.4 Comparison between the old car and a new car

| | Old car | New car |
	€	€
Value loss	1 000	2 000
Interest costs	250	650
Operating costs	3 000	2 500
Total yearly costs	4 250	5 150

as high as for the old car, i.e. €3000. Thus the average operating costs for the new car will be €2500 per year. The total comparison is in Table 8.4.

As might be expected, the comparison shows that the new car is more expensive than the old one.

But before we decide, let us scrutinize our assumptions. In fact, without making it very clear, we compared two quite different things. For the old car, we calculated the cost for year 9, assuming that value loss in that year would be equal to the average number during years 9–14. That is probably a fair assumption. We also assumed that operating costs, €3000, were valid for year 9. Thus we calculated the cost of keeping the old car for another year.

But in the case of the new car, we calculated value loss as the average over 8 years, assuming that the price of the new car will develop in the same way as the price of the old one. We then added the average interest cost for the first 8 years and the average operating costs for the first 8 years. That was because we felt that William would keep the new car for such a period.

Therefore, we have compared the yearly costs of two quite different things:

- one additional year with the old car
- the first 8 years with a new car.

But that is right, isn't it? After all William was considering whether to change cars now or a year from now. Therefore we need to know the yearly costs of the old car for just one more year. But if he buys the new car, we assumed that he would like to keep it for 8 years and calculated the average yearly cost for those years.

In fact, we assumed that William will buy a new car either now or next year and that when he has bought it he will keep it for 8 years. After he has bought the new one his yearly costs will average €5150 forever according to our table. But right now it appears that he might get away with only €4250 a year by keeping the old car. This decision would save him some money.

But what about inflation? We did not pay any attention to it. We accepted all prices as they are right now, which means that we calculated in real numbers. In fact, nobody knows the likely future price of cars and we do not really want to try to find out. Incidentally, that means we assumed that the 5 percent interest rate that was used in the solution was a real rate of interest too. But perhaps it wasn't. If not, we would have to deduct inflation from the interest rate and adjust our calculations accordingly. Whatever we do, it will not change our conclusion. The first year of the old car is almost always cheaper than the average costs of a new one.

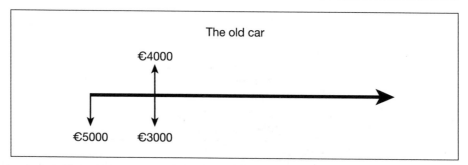

Figure 8.1 Applying a corporate investment model to the *Changing cars?* case – the old car

◼ A more formal solution

This case can be solved by corporate investment analysis even though, in this particular instance, it is a private individual who wants to change cars rather than a company planning to change machinery. Applying a corporate investment model we can illustrate the case as in Figure 8.1.

If William keeps the old car for another year, he will forgo a possible inflow of cash from selling it. On the other hand, he will receive €4000 at the end of the year and he will have to pay operating costs. The net present value of these payments at 5 percent interest will be:

$$\text{NPV (old car)} = -5000 + 1000 \times 0.95 = €-4050$$

Turning the NPV into a 1-year annuity we get:

$$\text{Annuity (old car)} = -4050/0.95 = €4263$$

This annuity could be compared to the yearly cost of the old car that we calculated in a more intuitive way in the previous section. It was €4250. We should notice that our intuitive calculation yielded almost precisely the same amount as this more exact annuity.

Let us now perform a similar calculation for the new car (Figure 8.2). Now we can calculate NPV of the new car in the following way:

$$\text{NPV (new car)} = -21\,000 - 2500 \times 6.46 + 5000 \times 0.677 = €-33\,765$$

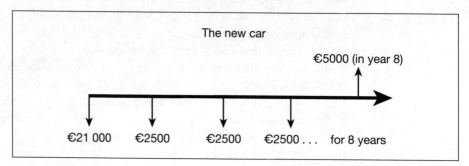

Figure 8.2 Applying a corporate investment model to the *Changing cars?* case – the new car

Turning this NPV into an 8-year annuity, we get:

$$\text{Annuity (new car)} = 33\ 765/6.46 = €5227$$

Again, we notice that the exact calculation differs from the intuitive one by a fairly small amount. Now the difference is a little bigger than before, which is due to cumulative interest. In the intuitive calculation we disregarded that kind of effect without noticing it.

In fact, what we have done shows that it is possible to find an intuitive solution to the problem of changing equipment. Normally, a change of equipment causes the following payments:

- a fairly big outlay in the beginning to buy the new equipment
- a change in operating costs
- a resale of the equipment at the end of the period.

To compare the two projects we normally try to compare the yearly costs of the first remaining year for the old equipment with the annuity of the new equipment calculated for the period of time that we plan to keep it.

Of course, there could be a problem finding the optimum time to keep the new equipment. Economically, the optimum time is often limited by rising operating costs towards the end of the life of the equipment. Sometimes these operating costs cannot be calculated very precisely because they do not occur regularly. But when there is major damage to the old equipment that causes disturbances to regular operations (such as the old car not starting when William needs to go to work) the losses will normally be too big to continue operations. The difficult thing is knowing in advance when this kind of damage is going to happen.

8.3 Southern Electronics, Inc.

In conjunction with a major building expansion program, Wilhelm Lindell, the financial manager of Southern Electronics realized that the investment appraisal would not be an easy task. The company had to choose between building from scratch or refurbishing an old property in order to establish the new factory, which they had planned to bring into service soon. Calculating the profitability of a large investment is always difficult. But in this particular case the profitability calculations for both courses of action were to be made even more difficult by the English parent company's instructions and measures of performance.

■ Background

Southern Electronics was founded in a provincial town called Ljungby by an entrepreneur with a good feeling about the impending development in the field of electronics. The production programs included measuring and control equipment for both industry and research purposes. The company succeeded in signing long-term contracts with the electronics industry throughout Sweden. It was profitable and grew rapidly. In the middle of the 1990s, it was bought by the English electronics group, Dayton Electronics. Shortly after this, the company moved to the larger town of Växjö, where they occupied more spacious premises. Business activities continued to expand.

Measures of performance in the group

Dayton Electronics gives the managers of its subsidiaries considerable freedom to act as they think fit in particular situations. However, each subsidiary and its managers are then judged based on the return on capital investment achieved, which is calculated as

$$ROI = (profit/total\ capital)$$

When using the ROI measurement, profit is calculated after tax but before interest costs. Total capital comprises both working capital and fixed assets. No attention is paid to financing activities and debt/equity ratio. Thus, the company's choice of financing – either within or outside the group – has no significance as regards the profitability calculation.

The minimum requirement is that ROI should amount to 10 percent. To the extent that ROI exceeds this figure, company management will receive commission on profit, which in certain cases can be quite considerable.

The new factory

After further expansion, Southern Electronics felt a need to acquire new factory premises at the main plant in Växjö. As project work had been going on for some time, management agreed upon the plant's technical requirements and a timetable for building and installation. A neighboring plot of land with nothing but an old warehouse on it was available. Detailed plans for a building, which would house the new production line, were drawn up according to the wishes of the company.

Wilhelm Lindell calculated upon the new plant enabling the company to achieve a major expansion. He anticipated that the annual contribution from these activities would be SEK 23.59 million in the first year and then would continue to increase by approximately 8 percent per year. Against this contribution, one would need to compare the increased costs.

Bearing in mind the company's previous experience with plants, he was of the opinion that the new plant would have a useful life of 30 years. However, after 15 years a suitable course of action would probably be to sell it.

Covering every alternative, he also decided to examine the refurbishment option and began looking into how the existing building could be used. In this case, the actual investment would be considerably lower, but the new plant would be less practical and the annual maintenance costs would be higher. With this scenario, he felt that the time for depreciation should be set at 15 years and that there would be little residual value after this period.

In order to examine the two alternatives fully, he collected the following information on costs. All numbers show increases compared to the old situation.

Alternative 1 – new plant

	SEK m
Annual increase in income	23.59 (+ 8% per year)

Initial costs

Ground rent before completion date	1.5
Construction equipment (an asset)	5.0
Building/plant (an asset)	71.5
Planning and design work and sundry costs	4.7

Annual costs

Leasehold, land	0.75 (increase after 10 years)
Regular production costs	4.15 (+ 6% per year)
Depreciation of construction equipment	1.0 (for five years)
Depreciation of building/plant	2.383 (for 30 years)

Alternative 2 – refurbishment

	SEK m
Annual increase in receipts	23.59 (+ 8% per year)

Initial costs

Ground rent before completion date	1.5
Construction equipment (an asset)	5.0
Planning and design work and sundry costs	4.7
Cost of refurbishment (an asset)	16.8

Annual costs

Leasehold, land	0.75 (increases after 10 years)
Regular production costs	4.95 (+ 6% per year)
Additional maintenance costs	5.35 (+ 4% per year)
Depreciation of construction equipment	1.0 (for 5 years)
Depreciation of plant	1.12 (for 15 years)

Current taxes will be applicable in both alternatives. Tax can be calculated on a standard basis of 25 percent, as the company will not be able to decrease taxes further.

In the event of purchasing the building, Dayton Electronics would be prepared to provide security for a loan payable in full at maturity in 15 years. The amount for the loan is calculated at SEK 67.5 million and has an interest rate of 11 percent. At the end of this period, Mr Lindell calculated that the building could be sold for approximately SEK 130 million. In this case, the company could anticipate having to pay approximately SEK 23 million in capital gains tax.

Mr Lindell saw that the net profit after tax appeared to be approximately the same in both cases. However, as the company's assets would increase if they decided to erect the new building, perhaps the ROI ratio would nevertheless be worse. At the same time, he had difficulty in understanding how refurbishment could be a better choice than building from scratch in a new and rational way.

Mr Lindell asked his financial team to create an investment calculation and suggest a solution.

Solution: Southern Electronics

To solve the case quickly, we have to eliminate all those payments, which are equal for the two main alternatives. Also, we need to find a discount rate, which is actually given in the ROI specification. There it is said that the parent company wants a return on investment of at least 10 percent after tax, but before interest payments. We can now easily compute the NPV of each alternative.

■ Alternative 1 – new plant

In this alternative, we first notice that the annual income is equal for both alternatives. Therefore when calculating the NPV, we can leave it out. Also, all the initial costs, except for the cost of the new building, coincide in the two cases. Therefore we can leave them out too.

Coming to annual payments, we find that the land lease and construction equipment coincide in both alternatives, and we can therefore leave them out. But yearly costs of operations and depreciation on the building will differ. We therefore include those items.

After those eliminations we can calculate the NPV in accordance with Figure 8.3.

When calculating the NPV we start with the original investment SEK 71.5 million. Then we add the positive tax effects from depreciation and discount them at 10 percent for 15 years. After that we observe that costs of operations rise by 6 percent per year. These rising payments counteract the discounting powers to a certain extent. We adjust the discount rate in the following way:

$$\text{Adjusted discount rate} = 10 - 6 = 4 \text{ percent}$$

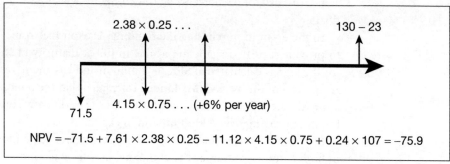

NPV = −71.5 + 7.61 × 2.38 × 0.25 − 11.12 × 4.15 × 0.75 + 0.24 × 107 = −75.9

Figure 8.3 Calculation of NPV for alternative 1 – new plant (figures in SEK million)

When doing this, we know that the adjustment is not absolutely correct. To make it exactly right we need to divide the discount factor by the yearly growth in the following way:

$$\text{Adjusted discount factor} = 1.10/1.06 = 1.0377$$

This number corresponds to a discount rate of 3.77 percent, which is the precise number. But we do not have any such numbers in our tables and therefore we are going to continue solving the case with a rounded discount rate, which is equal to 4 percent.

To discount the costs of operations, we find 11.12 as a discount factor for 4 percent and 15 years. Finally, we subtract the present value of the selling price 15 years from now, after subtracting SEK 23 million of capital gains taxes.

We can see that the NPV is negative, but that does not matter because we have disregarded the income flow. Let us just remember the NPV in order to compare it to the outcome of the next alternative.

■ Alternative 2 – refurbishment

After eliminating the same payments as in alternative 1 we can calculate NPV in accordance with Figure 8.4. We notice that the NPVs of both alternatives are negative, which is to be expected since we have eliminated their common income. But the yearly income stream is SEK 23.59 million in the beginning and grows very rapidly. Clearly, both alternatives are profitable and alternative 1 appears much better than alternative 2.

■ The value of the loan

The loan is a funny thing. It is only available if you select alternative 1 and therefore it will be interesting to find out if an external loan might be profitable to the company. (If not, group financing would always be available since the project is profitable.) The payments in connection with the loan are presented in Figure 8.5.

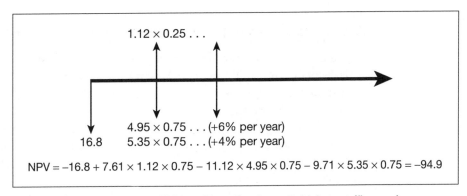

$$NPV = -16.8 + 7.61 \times 1.12 \times 0.75 - 11.12 \times 4.95 \times 0.75 - 9.71 \times 5.35 \times 0.75 = -94.9$$

Figure 8.4 Calculation of NPV for alternative 2 – refurbishment (figures in SEK million)

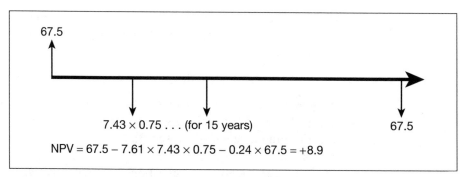

Figure 8.5 The value of the loan (figures in SEK million)

In the figure, the number 7.43 represents the yearly interest cost on the loan before taxes. But because of the taxes, the value will be reduced in accordance with the figure.

The value of the loan is positive. That will obviously happen because the interest rate of the loan is tax-deductible. After tax, interest will be only $0.75 \times 11 = 8.25$ percent, which is far below the group cost of capital. Thus, no further calculations are necessary.

◼ Evaluating alternatives

After finishing the NPV calculation, we can clearly see that alternative 1, building a new plant, has a higher NPV than alternative 2. The difference is reinforced by the conditions of the loan. Still alternative 2 will give higher ROI because the invested capital will be so much smaller. Therefore, alternative 2 will give higher income to the managers of Southern Electronics.

When presenting students with this situation, I have generally found them to be very certain about the answer. Most undergraduates have been told to select the highest possible NPV and they do so without hesitation. Students on master's programs are more hesitant and they often ask about the age and position of the CEO of Southern Electronics. In executive master's programs, participants choose the money and recommend alternative 2 without hesitation.

◼ Consequences of the management evaluation system

Managers will find that ROI will normally be higher for small investments than for large ones. Thus ROI might well contradict the outcome of NPV. Such a system will make managers prefer small investments, optimizing ROI, which might actually be to the disadvantage of the entire profit of the group.

On the other hand, group management will realize that such things happen. If they still stick to the suggested system, it probably means they are quite anxious to keep total investment low, possibly because they want to support a rapid expansion by reducing capital investments.

Most probably, such an outcome could also be produced by raising the required return to a number higher than 10 percent.

8.4 Water treatment plant

A large medical company had several divisions, and each of them was economically fully responsible for its business area. Some divisions were releasing large quantities of waste water into the local river. However, because of new regulations that are pending such releases would soon be illegal for most divisions.

To be able to continue production, the company decided to build its own water treatment plant. An agreement was made with the environmental control authority and permission was obtained to release treated water into the nearby river for a 10-year period.

The treatment plant was designed to treat 1.5 million cubic meters a year, although present volume would be no more than 1.2 million. Total building costs were expected to amount to SEK 65 million. Operating costs, including normal maintenance, were expected to be SEK 2.5 million a year, irrespective of the volume actually treated. Nothing was really known about the costs of continued operations after the initial 10 years, and there was no environmental agreement. When the investment was decided upon, yearly costs were estimated as an annuity of capital costs plus the cost of operations, and all divisions were informed of the outcome.

When the plant was ready for operation it turned out that total building costs were SEK 83.5 million, well in excess of the original budget. The plant was turned over to the central services department. The department head was instructed to sell treatment services at full cost in accordance with company internal pricing traditions. The central services department included the total investment in their accounts. They felt that yearly operating costs would stay in line with the original expectations.

After treatment had started, Mr Sjogren, head of the consumer division made it clear that his division did not want to buy the treatment services. This division had cleaner waste water than the others and could be admitted to the municipal sewerage system, paying only the municipal fee of SEK 10.78 per cubic meter. The consumer division produces around 0.2 million cubic meters a year.

In this case inflation and taxes are to be disregarded. Company cost of capital, 8 percent, is supposed to be useful for cost accounting as well as for capital budgeting purposes.

The company's accountants are asked to carry out the following analysis:

1 Find the full cost per cubic meter of waste water if total costs are calculated as an annuity of the investment plus yearly operating costs (as seen in the original project plan).

2 Find the full cost per cubic meter of waste water for the first year if total costs are calculated as regular capital costs (depreciation and interest on the actual investment) plus operating costs (as seen by the central services department).

3 Using your knowledge of activity-based costing (ABC) costing, calculate the ABC cost per cubic meter of waste water (in keeping with modern ABC theory).

4 Discuss the suggested method of internal transfer pricing and describe other possible pricing methods.

5 Disregarding company traditions, give a recommendation on how to deal with the consumer division and how this decision should influence the prices offered to the other divisions.

Solution: Water treatment plant

■ 1. Full cost per cubic meter (annuity)

The original investment was supposed to be SEK 65 million. Calculating an annuity, we get:

	SEK m
Annuity (8%, 10 years) (65/6.71)	9.69
Yearly operating costs	2.50
Total costs	12.19

Dividing by 1.2 million to find the full cost per cubic meter we get:

$$\text{Full cost} = 12.19/1.2 = \text{SEK } 10.16 \text{ per m}^3$$

■ 2. Full cost per cubic meter (regular depreciation and interest)

After finding out that the actual investment turned out to be SEK 83.5 million, we can calculate regular depreciation and interest in the following way:

	SEK m
Depreciation (83.5/10)	8.35
Interest in year 1 (83.5 × 8%)	6.68
Yearly operating costs	2.50
Total costs	17.54

Dividing by 1.2 million to find the full cost per cubic meter we get:

$$\text{Full cost} = 17.54/1.2 = \text{SEK } 14.62 \text{ per m}^3$$

As can be seen, the changes were quite considerable. First, in the original plan the investment was supposed to be SEK 65 million. Secondly, in the original plan, yearly costs were estimated as an annuity of that amount plus yearly operating costs. But in the real outcome, the actual investment costs were much higher than originally calculated and the annuity was replaced by a traditional calculation of nominal linear depreciation and interest. Both these changes made the actual costs much higher than was originally indicated.

■ 3. ABC cost per cubic meter

Either of the above costs should be allocated to 1.5 million cubic meters. In the first case we get:

$$\text{ABC cost (planned investment)} = 12.19/1.5 = \text{SEK } 8.13 \text{ per m}^3$$

In the second case we get:

$$\text{ABC cost (actual investment)} = 17.53/1.5 = \text{SEK } 11.69 \text{ per m}^3$$

Although it is not mentioned in the case briefing, there might be a third solution. We could apply ABC thinking to the annuity of the actual investment. Doing so, we get:

		SEK m
Annuity of actual investment	(83.5/6.71)	12.44
Yearly operating costs		2.50
Total costs		14.94

In this case, dividing by 1.5, we get:

$$\text{ABC cost (annuity of actual investment)} = 14.94/1.5 = \text{SEK } 9.96 \text{ per m}^3$$

Now, the case clearly states that we should disregard inflation and taxes. Still, if we do include inflation we might easily turn the nominal annuity into a real one. We first need to allow the nominal annuity (12.44) to grow by the yearly inflation rate. Then if we add on the operating costs at each particular time we would recover the investment in 10 years if the whole capacity were used. If only part of the capacity were used (as in year 1), somebody would have to pay for the unused capacity. Since we do not know who made the decision to invest in such a high capacity we cannot really determine what part of the organization should pay for it.

■ 4. Methods of transfer pricing

Ideal transfer prices should encompass direct costs plus the opportunity costs that occur because of the transaction. But in this case there is no real alternative for most parties. There is no indication that the capacity of the water treatment plant could be sold to outsiders, and there is only one division that could buy its treatment services from an outsider (the municipal network). But this price is a permanent market price and clearly an alternative to be included in our analysis.

In the other cases we will have to work out some kind of price indication based on costs or negotiations. Suggested prices are based on full costs. Although such prices are very common in reality, they are not seen as very good ones in theory. Full costs have several drawbacks that can be found in the literature. In particular, if full costs are calculated after the work is done, there will be virtually no incentives for the internal seller to keep costs low.

Marginal costs are much lower, but there is a long-term opportunity cost of building the treatment plant, and our best estimate for that opportunity cost corresponds to an annuity of the building costs (adjusted for inflation). In some cases, internal transfer prices could be based on market prices or negotiations or there could be double pricing, including a share of fixed costs plus actual variable costs. In this particular case, however, it appears that the only possible estimates are the market price of the municipal alternative for the consumer division and cost-based estimates for the other divisions.

■ 5. Dealing with the consumer division

In order to have an efficient volume, the company will need to keep the consumer division in the system. That means they have to meet the municipal price, SEK 10.78, at least for that division.

For the others, let us recall the third ABC solution from question 3:

	SEK m
Annuity of actual investment	12.44
Operating costs	2.50
Total costs	14.94

To find ABC of the annuity calculate $14.94/1.5 = 9.96$.

Thus it turns out that the ABC cost based on a real annuity is actually below the market price. On the other hand, the ABC cost is based on a volume that we cannot reach in the first year, and we know that the central services department will be expected to cover their full costs.

But let us see what happens if we were to let the consumer division pay the municipal price. In this case, charges to that division would be:

$$0.2 \times 10.78 = 2.16$$

If the remaining costs are shared between the other divisions we get:

$$(14.94 - 2.16)/1.0 = 12.78$$

This number is far below the price that was announced by the central services division, and although it is higher that the very first calculation it might be a viable compromise. After all, most divisions do not have any other choice but to buy the services of the water treatment plant!

Thus, charging the market price to the consumer division will not change prices to the others very much. Everybody will be reasonably happy and the central services department will make a profit as soon as they can find a buyer of the unused capacity. With such a solution all incentives will be correct.

8.5 The food ship

The letter below is an adapted version of a letter sent from a large Shipping Company to a major Food Company. It describes the basic facts of a shipping project designed to provide the Food Company with transport capacity on a time charter basis. Time charter means that the Shipping Company will build and operate the ship for a certain period of time and the Food Company will pay a daily rate for the exclusive rights to the services of the entire ship.

The Food Company is fairly well off and can afford the time charter agreement. But the controller and the CEO of the Food Company need to show to their owners that they paid a fair price for the services of the Shipping Company. Therefore a correct economic analysis of the situation is badly needed.

Letter from the Shipping Company to the Food Company

Dear Customer,

Coming back to our discussion last week concerning a new bulk food ship, I want to confirm the details of our discussion.

The price of the ship at delivery at the end of 1994 would be NOK 60 million, including all costs during the construction period, projecting costs and all necessary equipment.

Operating costs at 1994 prices were estimated to be NOK 7.91 million a year, including reservations for insurance and planned docking costs for recurring necessary repairs. Out of this amount personnel costs amount to NOK 4.66 million. According to our experience, personnel costs grow faster than other operating costs. During recent years our personnel costs have grown by 6–7 percent a year while other operating costs have grown by 4–5 percent.

Recommended rules for the depreciation of ships suggest a depreciation of 6 percent per year for 15 years and after that 2 percent per year for 5 years. This means that the ship would be fully depreciated in 20 years. Thus, the depreciation would be NOK 3.6 million per year for the first 10 years.

International interest rates range between 8.5 and 9 percent for fixed interest over 10 years for 80 percent of the total price, i.e. NOK 48 million. Local loans would be somewhat more expensive. I suggest that we stick to our original discussion, around 8.5–9 percent, which means that we can foresee a fixed interest cost of NOK 4.08 million in the first year.

The cost of equity capital, NOK 12 million, would be 15 percent, i.e. NOK 1.8 million. Administration of the ship, performed by the Shipping Company, would require NOK 0.6 million a year.

Considering all information so far, we can estimate income statements and cash flow statements as follows:

	Income statement NOK m	Cash flow NOK m
Operating costs	7.91	7.91
Administration	0.60	0.60
Depreciation and amortization	3.60	6.00
Interest	4.08	4.08
Cost of equity	1.80	1.80
Totals	17.99	20.39
Excluding amortizing equity		19.19

When calculating cash flow we assumed that the loan would be paid back in full during the first 10 years. Normally, our ships are not refinanced, because, in the shipping business, we need to keep total company debts fairly low.

After considering these numbers, and including a small profit for the Shipping Company, we found that the daily rate for the ship will be NOK 57 000 at 1994 prices, to be adjusted for inflation in later years. In fact, we expect the ship to be available for operations at the beginning of 1995. The price, of course, assumes that there is a time charter agreement between us. Such an agreement means that the Food Company will charter the ship on a permanent full-time basis (365 days a year) for 10 years unless both parties agree to change it or to sell the ship before the time is up.

Hoping to hear from you really soon.

Best regards

Supplier representative
Head of bulk transport division, Shipping Company

A firm of accountants is asked to conduct an economic analysis of the project on behalf of the Food Company, to be used as a starting point for discussions around the suggested time charter agreement.

(As always in the real world, some facts are given twice and certain important matters might have been omitted. Also, take into account that neither of the people involved had scientific training in management accounting. Do not hesitate to correct their mistakes. Please also notice that this assignment could be very cumbersome. Take care to make wise shortcuts.)

Solution: The food ship

The food ship case is based on a real letter from a major shipping company to a major food company. It was written several years ago, and, as mentioned, neither of the people negotiating had full training in management accounting.

To conduct an economic analysis of the case, we will perform the following steps:

1 Find the weighted cost of capital (WACC) of the Shipping Company in order to make a correct capital investment calculation.

2 Perform a real net present value (NPV) calculation to find the true cost of the project at today's prices.

3 Find a real annuity of the total costs of the project to be ready to adapt the costs to later inflation. There was quite high inflation in those years and most people expected it to continue.

4 Compare the real annuity with the suggested time charter price in order to find the true profitability of the project.

5 Perform a final review of the situation and give a recommendation to the controller of the Food Company.

■ 1. Finding WACC of the Shipping Company

Assuming that this is a normal project of the Shipping Company, the cost of equity will be 15 percent and the cost of loans will be 8.5 percent in accordance with the statement in the letter.

To find the average financing of ships let us assume that the Shipping Company builds one ship per year and keeps them all for 20 years until they are completely written off.

We were told that ships are seldom refinanced. Thus, when a ship is brand new, 80 percent of funds appear to come from loans, but those loans are paid back in the first 10 years, which is much faster than the depreciation rate of the ship.

For the remainder of the time there is only equity financing. But, on the other hand, the ship is now old and has a lower value. On average, ships are financed by somewhat less than 50 percent loans. To see the details of the financing analysis, please see the appendix at the end of this case (page 222).

We shall assume that the local tax rate was 28 percent.

Table 8.5 NPV analysis for 10 years of time charter agreement

Item	Years	Amount NOK m	Yearly growth NOK m	Factor	Present value NOK m	Comment
Buying ship	0	−60	0	1.00	−60.0	
Personnel	1–10	4.66 × 0.72	6%/year	7.72	−25.9	A
Other operating costs	1–10	3.25 × 0.72	4%/year	7.02	−16.4	B
Administration	1–10	0.60 × 0.72	6%/year	7.72	−3.3	C
Depreciation	1–10	3.6 × 0.28	0	5.65	+5.7	D
Remaining value	10	24 (real)	4%/year	0.51	+12.2	E
NPV total					−87.7	F

A. Assuming that personnel costs grow by 6 percent we apply 11 − 6 = 5 percent discount rate for 10 years to find the discount factor of 7.72.
B. For the remaining operating costs we apply 11 − 4 = 7 percent discount rate.
C. Administration is treated like personnel.
D. We include the tax shield of depreciation with a positive sign. The discount rate remains at 11 percent because there is no growth in depreciation.
E. Since we work with 10 years only, the ship will have a book value of NOK 24 million when the calculation ends. Accepting this as a real salvage value at year 10, we discount it by the real rate, 7 percent a year.
F. The remaining items of the original table of costs are left out because they do not belong in a NPV analysis. Cost of equity, amortization of equity and interest on the loan are taken care of by our discount rate.

Assuming 50 percent equity we get:

$$0.50 \times 15 + 0.50 \times 8.5 \times 0.72 = 10.84 \text{ percent}$$

This number is a nominal WACC. After rounding, let us assume 11 percent cost of capital after tax.

■ 2. Finding the NPV of the project

Table 8.5 shows an NPV analysis for the 10 years during which the time charter agreement is valid.

Note that the original letter includes NOK 6 million of depreciation and amortization in the cash flow column, meaning that the shipping company wants all their money back during the first 10 years. Since they assume that the ship can be used for 20 years, this means that they are overstating the cash flow.

Also notice that in the very last line of the cash flow analysis, they subtract 'amortization of equity', which confirms that they feel the customer should pay back equity funds during the first 10 years of the operations of the ship.

■ 3. Finding a real annuity

Since there is inflation, let us convert the NPV into a real annuity, changing to 7 percent real interest:

$$87.7/7.02 = \text{NOK } 12.49 \text{ million}$$

This amount is valid for the price level at the end of 1994. According to the letter, it will grow every year in accordance with inflation.

4. Comparing costs to prices

At NOK 57 000 a day, the suggested price of the time charter will bring:

$$57\ 000 \times 365 = \text{NOK } 20.8 \text{ million per year}$$

If this amount is calculated after tax, it will be $20.8 \times 0.72 = \text{NOK } 15.0$ million a year at 1994 prices. Since it is going to be adjusted for inflation it should be compared to the real annuity, which is NOK 12.49 million. Thus, the suggested price will bring a very large profit, in addition to the cost of equity, for the Shipping Company. After all, the full cost of equity is already included in the real annuity.

5. Further comments

It appears that when the people added a profit to the costs they forgot that a fair return on equity was already included in the costs. Actually, the suggested price of the time charter is some 20 percent higher than the costs on an annuity basis.

The true return on investment in this case can be found by setting the stream of payments equal to the NPV, which is already known. We get the following equation:

$$87.7 = X \times 15.0$$

$$X = 5.85$$

When looking for 5.85 in the 10-year row of the table of accumulated present values, we find that the real return of the project is close to 11 percent. The precise number, according to my calculator, is 11.17 percent. But the true required real cost of capital of the case is only 7 percent. Therefore calculations indicate that the Shipping Company would find the deal quite profitable.

Appendix: Financing the Shipping Company

If we assume that the Shipping Company buys one ship a year and keeps them all for 20 years, the financing situation right now will look like Table 8.6. In the first row you will find the ship that was just acquired. Its buying price was NOK 60 million, of which NOK 48 million was borrowed. In the second row you can see the ship that was bought a year ago. It has been depreciated by 6 percent, and 10 percent of the loan has been paid off. Therefore the starting value of the ship will be:

$$60 \times (1 - 0.06) = \text{NOK } 56.4 \text{ million}$$

The remaining loan will be:

$$48 \times (1 - 0.10) = \text{NOK } 43.2 \text{ million}$$

Going on all the way down, the table indicates that at any one point in time the Shipping Company will own 20 ships with a starting value of NOK 540 million, of which NOK 264 million is external financing.

Table 8.6 Financing the Shipping Company

Ship no.	Start value NOK m	End value NOK m	Financing NOK m
1	60	56.4	48
2	56.4	52.8	43.2
3	52.8	49.2	38.4
4	49.2	45.6	33.6
5	45.6	42	28.8
6	42	38.4	24
7	38.4	34.8	19.2
8	34.8	31.2	14.4
9	31.2	27.6	9.6
10	27.6	24	4.8
11	24	20.4	
12	20.4	16.8	
13	16.8	13.2	
14	13.2	9.6	
15	9.6	6	
16	6	4.8	
17	4.8	3.6	
18	3.6	2.4	
19	2.4	1.2	
20	1.2	0	
Totals	540	480	264

Thus the debt ratio will be:

$$264/540 = 49 \text{ percent}$$

Consequently, the equity ratio will be 51 percent, which is rounded to 50 percent in the discussion of the case.

8.6 Broadcasting Co.

In a Western European country, there used to be a national TV monopoly. The National Telecommunications Authority used to handle the broadcasting of national TV channels, with a network of high masts, cable connections and control equipment.

A few years ago, the country's telecommunications were privatized. New public and private TV channels were introduced and a private company – partly owned by the government – was formed to do the physical broadcasting of TV programs. The new company, Broadcasting Co., took over the high masts and quite a lot of ground-based monitoring and control equipment from the Telecommunications Authority in order to perform the necessary functions of ground-based broadcasting.

At the inception of the new company, only the two national TV channels were broadcast through the network of masts. The network covered around 95 percent of the area of the country and more than 99 percent of the inhabitants. Very soon a private TV channel was added to the network. This was fairly easy to do because most masts can support up to eight TV channels or a corresponding quantity of other business.

Originally, when the masts served only the two national channels, the costs of the system were shared equally between them. When the private network was added, rates were lowered for the two national channels, and a negotiation ended with each of them paying 37.5 percent and the private network paying 25 percent. The owners of the private network complained heavily, maintaining that they ought to pay only the additional costs of maintenance and service, which would be much lower. Because of the high costs of broadcasting, they said, the program quality would suffer, to the detriment of TV services.

There was competition working with satellites and cable networks. Satellites, however, can only reach the southern 60 percent of the country, which means that satellite-based networks can only access some 75 percent of the population. They are dependent on ground-based equipment to reach the northern parts of the country if they wish to do so.

When the new Broadcasting Co. was formed and privatized, it was decided that an expansion would be desirable to improve its profitability. Such an expansion could come from:

- adding new private TV channels to the existing network of masts;
- adding new growing services such as private telephone networks for large companies and superior-quality television;
- adding other new services that can utilize the national grid of masts and connections.

In order to facilitate such an expansion, a new organization was created, which is described in Figure 8.6. As can be seen, there are two customer-oriented units:

- Broadcasting, to take care of broadcasting customers.
- Other customers, to handle new products, such as national or private telephone networks.

There are also two production units:

- Systems Integration, to design the systems.
- Production to perform daily production services and regular maintenance on the physical equipment.

There is also a research unit, called Future Business, designed to develop possible services to be performed in the future by the existing network. Finally, there are three supporting units:

- controller and IT
- human resources
- market information.

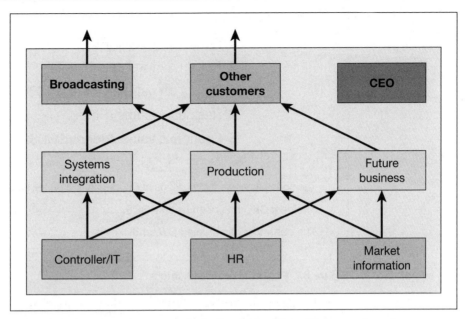

Figure 8.6 Creation of a new organization to facilitate the expansion of Broadcasting Co.

When the company was formed, there was a state requirement saying that monopoly business (mainly the two national TV channels) should be priced to give a return on equity equal to inflation plus 2 percent after taxes, and no more. On the other hand, the state would expect the profits from other business to equal at least inflation plus 5 percent after taxes. Currently, 'other business' is mainly one private TV channel and a few minor intra-company telephone networks.

When the company was formed a few years ago, inflation was around 5 percent a year. Today it is only around 2 percent.

A firm of accountants is called in to perform the following analysis:

1   Assume that TV channels will need 90 percent of the total capacity and that all TV channels are equal. Further, assume that total debt will be 150 percent of equity and that interest rates paid on loans will be inflation plus 3 percent before taxes. Calculate the return on total capital needed to meet the government's goals. The national tax rate is assumed to be 30 percent of earnings before tax.

2   The newly appointed managing director wants all units to contribute optimally to the success and growth of the company. Therefore he wants an overview of possible profit indicators and a recommendation as to which indicator is to be used for each unit. Some possible indicators are mentioned in Figure 8.7. Explain them all, and recommend which of them to introduce, giving clear reasons for your choice.

Some of the staff members feel that these profit indicators might be well suited for some of the units, but not for all of them. Try to explain these feelings

1 Return on equity (RE)

2 Return on total capital (RT)

3 Return on capital employed (ROCE)

4 Residual income (RI)

5 Economic value added (EVA)

- The state owner wants two kinds of RE, depending on the nature of competition.
- The new CEO has been using ROCE.
- The controller has studied EVA and likes it.

Figure 8.7 Potential profit indicators

and suggest alternative solutions for those units where the profit indicators mentioned might not be useful.

3 Will the comparison of profit indicators mean that internal pricing will have to be introduced? What kinds of prices are available? In view of your solution to question 2, suggest how to arrange a possible internal pricing system.

4 Since owning a nationwide grid of masts and ground-based connections means that the company is heavily capitalized, calculating costs to meet the government's goals might be a tricky and very important business. If a new mast costs €10 million and it can be used for 20 years, calculate the yearly cost:

– as an annuity using company cost of capital;

– as a yearly sum of depreciation and interest, showing a few illustrative years over the lifetime of the mast.

Both of these could be done in different ways. Can you give alternative solutions? Explain the differences to the company, owners and customers of using one method or the other.

Solution: Broadcasting Co.

■ 1. Required return on equity

After taxes

Since the government wants the company to provide government services at a lower return than they do private services, we could actually calculate two different numbers. One will be the required return for government business and the other will be the required return for private business. Here is what it would look like:

Government business: To cover inflation plus 2 percent for equity capital in government business plus borrowing costs as indicated (inflation plus 3 percent before taxes), we get:

$$RT_{(at)gov} = 0.4 \times 4 + 0.6 \times 5 \times 0.7 = 3.7 \text{ percent}$$

where 'at' refers to 'after taxes'.

Private business: For private business the owner wants inflation plus 5 percent on equity capital. Assuming that we have to pay the same borrowing costs in both cases we get:

$$RT_{(at)priv} = 0.4 \times 7 + 0.6 \times 5 \times 0.7 = 4.9 \text{ percent}$$

In fact, these calculations assume that the borrowing rate and the debt/equity ratio will be equal for both kinds of business. This is not absolutely certain, but there is not enough information in the case to identify differences in borrowing conditions between these two kinds of business.

Before taxes

Calculating the required return on total capital will be important for pricing decisions. But since most prices are set before taxes we would need to calculate the required returns before tax. These returns will be higher than the returns after taxes, but the difference is not very easy to determine.

If we apply the standard formula we get:

$$RT_{(bt)gov} = 3.7/0.7 = 5.29$$
$$RT_{(bt)priv} = 4.9/0.7 = 7.0$$

where 'bt' refers to 'before taxes'.

These numbers are probably too high because the company owns quite long-lasting equipment even though depreciation periods are quite short (see Case 4.8 on Regulating WACC). Therefore, deciding on returns equal to 5 and 6 percent, respectively, would normally be on the safe side.

Simplifying things

In many companies, management will not want to work with several different required returns. Most of the business is involved in production and normally things will be easier if there is only one required return on total capital.

In this particular case, 90 percent of the total business is TV broadcasting. There are three TV channels and they require equally large efforts. Therefore it would be reasonable to assume that 2/3 of 90 percent is for government business and the remaining 1/3 is for the private channel. In addition, the remaining 10 percent will be used for other business, which will most likely be private. In total, therefore, 60 percent of the capacity will be used for government business and 40 percent will be used for private business.

If we accept those shares of the business we could calculate a common required return in the following way:

$$RT_{(bt)total} = (0.6 \times 3.7 + 0.4 \times 4.9)/0.7 = 5.97$$

As was mentioned in the previous section, this number is probably too high because the efficient tax rate of this company will be below 30 percent. This happens because depreciation of the TV masts for tax purposes can be done over 5 years, even though they can be used for at least 20 years.

Still, management will probably feel uneasy about lowering the required return. Therefore, they will very likely decide to work with 6 percent as an average and to differentiate prices up or down depending on what is government business and what is private business.

■ 2. Profit indicators

These indicators were explained in case 7.1, Northern Trucks, Inc., on pages 188–93.

In this particular case, there are profit centers with very different characters. Some units, like Future Business and perhaps the administrative units at the bottom of Figure 8.6, have very little capital. They cannot very well be measured by traditional ratios like ROI or ROCE, because the denominators would be too close to zero. On the other hand, RI and EVA could probably be applied. Of these, EVA is difficult because it would contradict financial accounting. So a modernized RI could be a solution to be applied everywhere for a time. Over time, it could be developed further to get closer to a more complete EVA system.

When it is mentioned in the brief that some staff members feel that those ratios are not really applicable everywhere, they have an important point. In fact, do we really want the administrative units at the lower level of the organization chart to make a profit?

Personally, I think they are going too far in creating profit centers everywhere. I would prefer to have the administrative units breaking even. In this case it might be a good idea to make them charge a price for their services to the production units, and try to set that price at a level that allows them to break even if they work in an efficient way.

■ 3. Internal pricing

Yes, profit indicators for profit centers will require a system of internal transfer pricing. If not, profit center managers will be reluctant to help each other. A discussion of available types of prices can be found in case 3.1, Premium Motor Co., on pages 93–7.

The situation in the Broadcasting Co. is difficult, because in many of the relations between units there are no market prices available. Prices will have to be based on costs or negotiations. If there is an ABC costing system in the company, ABC costs would be a good choice. If not, we might have to accept some kind of full costing system as a starting point for negotiations between managers. But in that case it will be necessary to perform the negotiations before the work actually takes place in order to promote efficiency.

The administrative units should set their prices and charges to the production units at the beginning of the yearly budget process. After that, the research organization Future Business will negotiate prices to the production units, including due allowance for administrative costs.

■ 4. Yearly costs of masts

Annuities

A nominal annuity can be found by applying 6 percent interest to the original price of a mast. For 20 years, we get (€000):

$$\text{Nominal annuity} = 10\ 000/11.47 = 872$$

The nominal annuity will be constant over the life of the mast.

A real annuity can be found by applying 4 percent real interest to the original price of a mast. For 20 years, we get (€000):

$$\text{Real annuity} = 10\ 000/13.59 = 735.8$$

To be used for pricing, the real annuity will have to be adjusted for inflation. If inflation remains 2 percent over the life of the mast we get:

Year	Real value €000	Inflation factor	Nominal value €000
1	735.8	1.02	751
11	735.8	1.24	915
20	735.8	1.49	1 093

Thus the real annuity will rise over time in accordance with inflation. If inflation changes, we can easily adjust these numbers up or down to make sure that costs always develop in line with actual inflation.

Regular depreciation and interest

According to nominal principles, depreciation will be constant, €500 000 per year. Interest will be calculated on remaining value. We get the following:

Year	Depreciation €000	Interest €000	Total cost €000
1	500	600	1 100
11	500	300	800
20	500	30	530

According to real principles, depreciation will always equal 5 percent of the price of a new mast at the end of the year. Interest should be 4 percent of the remaining value at the start of the year. If the cost of a mast develops according to regular inflation, we get the following:

Year	Depreciation €000	Interest €000	Total cost €000
1	510	400	910
11	620	243	863
20	743	29	772

Differences to company, owners and customers

Regular nominal depreciation and interest will make the services very expensive in the beginning. Very likely, private customers will look around to find cheaper ways to transmit their TV programs. If they do so, the company will not be able to sell its services to the private sector. Profits will be insufficient and the owners will be unhappy.

The nominal annuity and the regular real depreciation and interest show more stable costs over time. In fact, if there are also operating costs that rise over time, either of these two methods might be quite useful. But still, even in this case, costs will probably appear highest in the beginning. Therefore, customers will look around for cheaper services. Because the traditional nominal depreciation dominates business in other newly established companies and there are virtually no old ones, they might not find them. Thus, these two techniques might work well in the market.

The real annuity will keep prices at a reasonable level at the beginning of the period and raise them over time in pace with inflation. Very likely, this kind of thinking will make it much easier to attract and keep customers at the beginning of the period. The company will find it easy to sell its services, customers will be happy to buy, and owners will be satisfied that the business is developing so well. But there will very likely be confusing differences between book depreciation, tax depreciation and annuity depreciation for pricing purposes.

8.7 Rail connections

The County Council of a large city was under strong pressure from commuters to improve the rail services in the greater metropolitan area. A much demanded improvement was the replacement of the single-track railway to a local suburb with a double-track railway. However, it was very difficult to find room for such a project in the capital budget of the County Administration, which was also busy replacing old trains and building a very important new university hospital.

Instead of building a double-track railroad, it was suggested to create an intermediate solution fairly soon and to postpone the main project by a number of years. This could be done through the immediate construction of a number of short double-track sections ('passing loops') where trains can run past each other. Such an investment would be much cheaper than a complete double-track railway, but would not provide as good a service. Also, most of the investment in passing loops would be wasted once the decision to build the complete double-track railway was finally made.

Let us assume that the investment in a double-track railway for part of the line is €50 million. Instead, two passing loops at €7.5 million each might take us through the first few difficult years.

According to financial statements, the County Council has virtually no equity capital. But they can borrow money at 4–5 percent nominal interest, depending on the time perspective. Inflation is currently between 1 and 2 percent per year and rising. However, borrowing is limited because future income statements might not be able to bear the increase in depreciation and interest that would follow from a rising debt burden. The County Council does not pay any taxes.

Accountants are asked to investigate the proposition and write a memo to the County Council explaining the economic consequences of installing passing loops instead of the double-track railway in the short run. Note that members of the County Council have no knowledge of WACC or other tools of advanced financing.

The accountants must also explain under what circumstances they would favor the building of passing loops in order to postpone the main investment in a double-track railway!

Solution: Rail connections

Basically, the choice stands between a big investment immediately or a combination of a small investment now and a big investment later. The choices are described in Figure 8.8. The NPV of the first alternative is always €50 million, whatever the life of the tracks and for all rates of interest. But to evaluate the second alternative we need to know the discount rate and the time between the two investments. Accepting the interest rates and inflation indicated in the case description, let us assume that we can apply a 3 percent real rate of interest.

If the passing loops could be expected to serve for 5 years, the second alternative will have the following NPV (€ million)

$$NPV = -15 - 0.86 \times 50 = -58$$

Since the NPV of the first alternative is only €–50 million, we conclude that the second alternative is not good enough.

Let us find out what is needed. To do so we need to find a scenario where the NPVs of the two alternatives are equal. Consequently,

$$-50 = -15 - X \times 50$$

The equation will be solved when:

$$X \times 50 = 35$$
$$X = 0.7$$

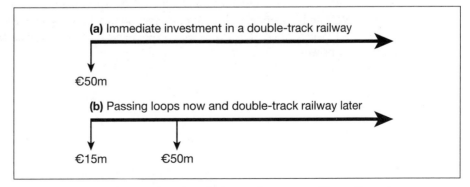

Figure 8.8 Investment choices in relation to the metropolitan rail services

In this situation, the passing loop alternative would be as good as the direct investment in the double-track railway. To make the passing loop alternative superior, the present value factor would have to be below 0.7. Consulting a table of present values, we find that the meeting points will need to be used for 19 years at 2 percent interest, for 10 years at 4 percent and for 7 years at 6 percent. To save money in a 5-year perspective, the real interest rate would have to be as high as 8 percent, where the present value factor is 0.68. Clearly, the higher the discount rate applied, the shorter will be the number of years required to make the passing loop alternative a favorable choice.

If we apply the discount rate suggested by the borrowing rate of the County Council, it turns out that we will need to postpone the double-track railway for a very long time to make the passing loop alternative economically meaningful. Since, in addition, the service level is lower in the passing loop case, these simple calculations create some considerable doubts as to the viability of the passing loop alternative. Still, we know that councillors in a metropolitan area are very likely to go for the passing loops plan because of a lack of funds in the short run!

But if there is a clear shortage of funds in the council, perhaps the discount rate given by the borrowing rate is not correct. Councillors always feel that there is a lack of funds! In reality, this means that there is capital rationing and that the correct discount rate should be higher than the borrowing rate.

In fact, if we accept that there is a clear limit to the amount of borrowing, we ought to find out the possible rates of return of alternative investment projects. If there are several projects around that are good enough to give real returns above 4 percent and the council still refuses to borrow more, that would bring the real cost of capital up to 5–8 percent in order to find an equilibrium in the internal capital situation. This could happen if there are several profitable capital-expenditure projects that are as important as the rail connections. Such a situation might provide the economic justification to build the passing loops.

Considering the situation as a whole, our main conclusion should not be a decision on the passing loops, but a strong recommendation to the County Council to appoint a financially competent group to reconsider the entire investment needs of the council. After considering all important investment projects, they should suggest a required return on investment capital. That solution should be of such a nature that the council will want to proceed with those projects that have a positive NPV and postpone or discard those that do not. In this way, NPV calculations could help the council in its decision-making instead of just creating confusion.

Appendix 1: Table of present values

	2%	4%	5%	6%	7%	8%	10%	12%	15%	20%	25%
1	0.9804	0.9615	0.9524	0.9434	0.9346	0.9259	0.9091	0.8929	0.8696	0.8333	0.8000
2	0.9612	0.9246	0.9070	0.8900	0.8734	0.8573	0.8264	0.7972	0.7561	0.6944	0.6400
3	0.9423	0.8890	0.8638	0.8396	0.8163	0.7938	0.7513	0.7118	0.6575	0.5787	0.5120
4	0.9238	0.8548	0.8227	0.7921	0.7629	0.7350	0.6830	0.6355	0.5718	0.4823	0.4096
5	0.9057	0.8219	0.7835	0.7473	0.7130	0.6806	0.6209	0.5674	0.4972	0.4019	0.3277
6	0.8880	0.7903	0.7462	0.7050	0.6663	0.6302	0.5645	0.5066	0.4323	0.3349	0.2621
7	0.8706	0.7599	0.7107	0.6651	0.6227	0.5835	0.5132	0.4523	0.3759	0.2791	0.2097
8	0.8535	0.7307	0.6768	0.6274	0.5820	0.5403	0.4665	0.4039	0.3269	0.2326	0.1678
9	0.8368	0.7026	0.6446	0.5919	0.5439	0.5002	0.4241	0.3606	0.2843	0.1938	0.1342
10	0.8203	0.6756	0.6139	0.5584	0.5083	0.4632	0.3855	0.3220	0.2472	0.1615	0.1074
11	0.8043	0.6496	0.5847	0.5268	0.4751	0.4289	0.3505	0.2875	0.2149	0.1346	0.0859
12	0.7885	0.6246	0.5568	0.4970	0.4440	0.3971	0.3186	0.2567	0.1869	0.1122	0.0687
13	0.7730	0.6006	0.5303	0.4688	0.4150	0.3677	0.2897	0.2292	0.1625	0.0935	0.0550
14	0.7579	0.5775	0.5051	0.4423	0.3878	0.3405	0.2633	0.2046	0.1413	0.0779	0.0440
15	0.7430	0.5553	0.4810	0.4173	0.3624	0.3152	0.2394	0.1827	0.1229	0.0649	0.0352
16	0.7284	0.5339	0.4581	0.3936	0.3387	0.2919	0.2176	0.1631	0.1069	0.0541	0.0281
17	0.7142	0.5134	0.4363	0.3714	0.3166	0.2703	0.1978	0.1456	0.0929	0.0451	0.0225
18	0.7002	0.4936	0.4155	0.3503	0.2959	0.2502	0.1799	0.1300	0.0808	0.0376	0.0180
19	0.6864	0.4746	0.3957	0.3305	0.2765	0.2317	0.1635	0.1161	0.0703	0.0313	0.0144
20	0.6730	0.4564	0.3769	0.3118	0.2584	0.2145	0.1486	0.1037	0.0611	0.0261	0.0115
21	0.6598	0.4388	0.3589	0.2942	0.2415	0.1987	0.1351	0.0926	0.0531	0.0217	0.0092
22	0.6468	0.4220	0.3418	0.2775	0.2257	0.1839	0.1228	0.0826	0.0462	0.0181	0.0074
23	0.6342	0.4057	0.3256	0.2618	0.2109	0.1703	0.1117	0.0738	0.0402	0.0151	0.0059
24	0.6217	0.3901	0.3101	0.2470	0.1971	0.1577	0.1015	0.0659	0.0349	0.0126	0.0047
25	0.6095	0.3751	0.2953	0.2330	0.1842	0.1460	0.0923	0.0588	0.0304	0.0105	0.0038
26	0.5976	0.3607	0.2812	0.2198	0.1722	0.1352	0.0839	0.0525	0.0264	0.0087	0.0030
27	0.5859	0.3468	0.2678	0.2074	0.1609	0.1252	0.0763	0.0469	0.0230	0.0073	0.0024
28	0.5744	0.3335	0.2551	0.1956	0.1504	0.1159	0.0693	0.0419	0.0200	0.0061	0.0019
29	0.5631	0.3207	0.2429	0.1846	0.1406	0.1073	0.0630	0.0374	0.0174	0.0051	0.0015
30	0.5521	0.3083	0.2314	0.1741	0.1314	0.0994	0.0573	0.0334	0.0151	0.0042	0.0012

	2%	4%	5%	6%	7%	8%	10%	12%	15%	20%	25%
1	0.9804	0.9615	0.9524	0.9434	0.9346	0.9259	0.9091	0.8929	0.8696	0.8333	0.8000
2	1.9416	1.8861	1.8594	1.8334	1.8080	1.7833	1.7355	1.6901	1.6257	1.5278	1.4400
3	2.8839	2.7751	2.7232	2.6730	2.6243	2.5771	2.4869	2.4018	2.2832	2.1065	1.9520
4	3.8077	3.6299	3.5460	3.4651	3.3872	3.3121	3.1699	3.0373	2.8550	2.5887	2.3616
5	4.7135	4.4518	4.3295	4.2124	4.1002	3.9927	3.7908	3.6048	3.3522	2.9906	2.6893
6	5.6014	5.2421	5.0757	4.9173	4.7665	4.6229	4.3553	4.1114	3.7845	3.3255	2.9514
7	6.4720	6.0021	5.7864	5.5824	5.3893	5.2064	4.8684	4.5638	4.1604	3.6046	3.1611
8	7.3255	6.7327	6.4632	6.2098	5.9713	5.7466	5.3349	4.9676	4.4873	3.8372	3.3289
9	8.1622	7.4353	7.1078	6.8017	6.5152	6.2469	5.7590	5.3282	4.7716	4.0310	3.4631
10	8.9826	8.1109	7.7217	7.3601	7.0236	6.7101	6.1446	5.6502	5.0188	4.1925	3.5705
11	9.7868	8.7605	8.3064	7.8869	7.4987	7.1390	6.4951	5.9377	5.2337	4.3271	3.6564
12	10.5753	9.3851	8.8633	8.3838	7.9427	7.5361	6.8137	6.1944	5.4206	4.4392	3.7251
13	11.3484	9.9856	9.3936	8.8527	8.3577	7.9038	7.1034	6.4235	5.5831	4.5327	3.7801
14	12.1062	10.5631	9.8986	9.2950	8.7455	8.2442	7.3667	6.6282	5.7245	4.6106	3.8241
15	12.8493	11.1184	10.3797	9.7122	9.1079	8.5595	7.6061	6.8109	5.8474	4.6755	3.8593
16	13.5777	11.6523	10.8378	10.1059	9.4466	8.8514	7.8237	6.9740	5.9542	4.7296	3.8874
17	14.2919	12.1657	11.2741	10.4773	9.7632	9.1216	8.0216	7.1196	6.0472	4.7746	3.9099
18	14.9920	12.6593	11.6896	10.8276	10.0591	9.3719	8.2014	7.2497	6.1280	4.8122	3.9279
19	15.6785	13.1339	12.0853	11.1581	10.3356	9.6036	8.3649	7.3658	6.1982	4.8435	3.9424
20	16.3514	13.5903	12.4622	11.4699	10.5940	9.8181	8.5136	7.4694	6.2593	4.8696	3.9539
21	17.0112	14.0292	12.8212	11.7641	10.8355	10.0168	8.6487	7.5620	6.3125	4.8913	3.9631
22	17.6580	14.4511	13.1630	12.0416	11.0612	10.2007	8.7715	7.6446	6.3587	4.9094	3.9705
23	18.2922	14.8568	13.4886	12.3034	11.2722	10.3711	8.8832	7.7184	6.3988	4.9245	3.9764
24	18.9139	15.2470	13.7986	12.5504	11.4693	10.5288	8.9847	7.7843	6.4338	4.9371	3.9811
25	19.5235	15.6221	14.0939	12.7834	11.6536	10.6748	9.0770	7.8431	6.4641	4.9476	3.9849
26	20.1210	15.9828	14.3752	13.0032	11.8258	10.8100	9.1609	7.8957	6.4906	4.9563	3.9879
27	20.7069	16.3296	14.6430	13.2105	11.9867	10.9352	9.2372	7.9426	6.5135	4.9636	3.9903
28	21.2813	16.6631	14.8981	13.4062	12.1371	11.0511	9.3066	7.9844	6.5335	4.9697	3.9923
29	21.8444	16.9837	15.1411	13.5907	12.2777	11.1584	9.3696	8.0218	6.5509	4.9747	3.9938
30	22.3965	17.2920	15.3725	13.7648	12.4090	11.2578	9.4269	8.0552	6.5660	4.9789	3.9950

Index